# CONFESSIONS OF A
# MICROFINANCE HERETIC

# CONFESSIONS OF A MICROFINANCE HERETIC

## How Microlending Lost Its Way And Betrayed the Poor

HUGH SINCLAIR

Berrett–Koehler Publishers, Inc.
San Francisco
a BK Currents book

**Berrett-Koehler Publishers, Inc.**
235 Montgomery Street, Suite 650
San Francisco, CA 94104-2916
Tel: (415) 288-0260   Fax: (415) 362-2512
**www.bkconnection.com**

### Ordering Information

**Quantity sales.** Special discounts are available on quantity purchases by corporations, associations, and others. For details, contact the "Special Sales Department" at the Berrett-Koehler address above.
**Individual sales.** Berrett-Koehler publications are available through most bookstores. They can also be ordered directly from Berrett-Koehler: Tel: (800) 929-2929; Fax: (802) 864-7626; www.bkconnection.com.
**Orders for college textbook/course adoption use.** Please contact Berrett-Koehler: Tel: (800) 929-2929; Fax: (802) 864-7626.
Orders by U.S. trade bookstores and wholesalers. Please contact Ingram Publisher Services, Tel: (800) 509-4887; Fax: (800) 838-1149; E-mail: customer.service@ingram publishersevices.com; or visit www.ingrampublisherservices.com/Ordering for details about electronic ordering.

Berrett-Koehler and the BK logo are registered trademarks of
Berrett-Koehler Publishers, Inc.

Printed in the United States of America

Berrett-Koehler books are printed on long-lasting acid-free paper. When it is available, we choose paper that has been manufactured by environmentally responsible processes. These may include using trees grown in sustainable forests, incorporating recycled paper, minimizing chlorine in bleaching, or recycling the energy produced at the paper mill.

### Library of Congress Cataloging-in-Publication Data
Sinclair, Hugh.
Confessions of a microfinance heretic : how microlending lost its way and betrayed the poor / Hugh Sinclair. -- 1st ed.
    p. cm.
ISBN 978-1-60994-518-3 (hardcover)
1. Microfinance. 2. Poor. 3. Finance--Developing countries. I. Title.
HG178.3.S56 2012
332--dc23
        2012009050

First Edition
18  17  16  15  14  13  12      10  9  8  7  6  5  4  3  2  1

Project management, design, and composition by Steven Hiatt / Hiatt & Dragon, San Francisco
Copyediting: Steven Hiatt   Proofreading: Tom Hassett   Cover Design: Kirk DouPonce, Dog Eared Design

This book is dedicated to the poor entrepreneurs struggling to create
a better world for themselves and their families, but in particular
to those paying interest rates of over 100 percent a year to line the
pockets of a few microfinance banks and their investors.

On a more personal note, I also dedicate this work of
financial critique to the man who first taught me finance:
my grandfather, William Clark.

# Contents

# Foreword

## By David Korten

*Confessions of a Microfinance Heretic* provides an insightful, well-documented, and devastating look into the tragic reality of how a good idea was derailed by the same mindless pursuit of financial gain that caused the global financial crash of 2008. It is essential reading for anyone involved in microcredit and for all who are committed to ending global poverty and injustice.

For some twenty years we have heard the story that microcredit is the cure for global poverty:

An amazing visionary economist in Bangladesh named Mohammed Yunus founded the Grameen Bank and demonstrated a simple, effective way to end world poverty. Small, low-cost loans to the poor unleash their entrepreneurial potential and allow them to start profitable businesses that bring prosperity to themselves, their children, and their communities.

It is a win–win solution that doesn't require charity, redistribution, rethinking economic policy, or restructuring existing economic institutions and relationships. Global investments of a few billion dollars can earn an attractive financial return for socially responsible investors and simultaneously banish the scourge of poverty.

That's the widely received story. The reality that Hugh Sinclair documents in this book presents a very different picture.

## Too Good to Be True

Microfinance is now a $70 billion industry and some investors and microfinance institutions enjoy eye-popping returns. The industry falls far short, however, of fulfilling its promise to end poverty. Indeed, as Hugh Sinclair spells out in detail, many microcredit programs are nothing more than predatory lending schemes rebranded as socially responsible investment opportunities.

There are effective microcredit programs. Sinclair describes one in Mongolia that truly serves the poor with low-cost loans used to fund successful microbusinesses. Tragically, these may be more the exception than the norm.

I lived and worked in Asia from 1978 to 1992 as part of the foreign aid establishment. During this time I regularly served as a consultant to several Bangladeshi nongovernmental organizations (NGOs) that were pioneering microfinance along with other innovative programs serving the poor. Two that I particularly admired at the time as world-class models of positive NGO leadership are now major players in the international microfinance industry.

Even back in the 1980s, I was concerned that microlending programs could draw energy away from efforts by these same NGOs to address the deeper structural causes of poverty. I also worried that such programs might leave the poor even more dependent on financial institutions over which they had no control.

The microfinance industry Sinclair documents has been corrupted far beyond my worst fears.

## Our Human Capacity for Self-Deception

Sinclair predicts that microfinance insiders will seek to discredit him and use vicious attacks to dismiss his conclusions. I urge those who may feel persuaded by these attacks to bear in mind what Nobel Prize winner Muhammad Yunus said in a 2011 *New York Times* op-ed. He noted that when he founded Grameen Bank in Bangladesh in 1983, "I never imagined that one day microcredit would give rise to its own breed of loan sharks. But it has."

Some of those responsible for the corruption of a noble idea may be true scoundrels. Several of the organizations Sinclair implicates in this volume, however, are led by individuals I have known personally as people of admirable ability, ethics, and intention.

Sinclair's insightful assessment of how even the industry's most honest and respected leaders become trapped by the imperatives and self-justifying stories of the institutions they head is an important contribution of *Confessions*.

I can relate to their experience. I worked in various capacities with and within the foreign aid system for some thirty years—rarely questioning its basic premise. It was little more than two months after leaving my post with USAID as Asia Regional Advisor on Development Management that a fresh insight hit me. Foreign aid, as practiced, is almost inherently destructive, because it increases the dependence of poor countries on the goods, technologies, markets, finance, and expertise of rich countries and leaves them exposed to classical colonial exploitation in a new guise.

It is hard to see the truth of a system on which your pay and prestige depend.

### Follow the Money

To my surprise and shock, I once heard a microlending advocate make the amazing claim that high interest rates are a rich people's concern. They don't matter to the poor. To benefit the poor, microcredit need only offer lower interest rates than local money lenders.

Those who work in microfinance commonly view the system from the perspective of the investor rather than that of the community and thereby lose sight of the bigger picture. Tara Thiagarajan, chairperson of Madura Micro Finance, a for-profit microcredit program in India, is an all-too-rare exception—as revealed in her insightful May 2, 2010, blog:

> The local moneylender ... may charge a higher interest rate, but being local will probably spend most of that income in the village supporting the overall village economy. So potentially, local lending at higher rates could be more beneficial to the village if the money is in turn spent in the village, compared to lower rates where the money leaves the village.

Suppose that a microloan extended by an outside agency actually supports an increase in village production. To cover the net outflow of rupees required to make loan payments, the village must sell to outsiders more of what it produces just to get rupees that immediately flow back out as loan payments. At the usurious interest rates often involved, this can result in a substantial net loss. When the loan does not contribute to an increase in productive output, which Sinclair notes is the most common case, the net rate of outflow of both real wealth and rupees is even greater. The same dynamic plays out at national and global levels.

Suppose that an investor in the United States invests in one of the microcredit programs in India described by Sinclair. The investor provides loan or equity financing in U.S. dollars and expects payment of interest and dividends in U.S. dollars. The transaction between microlender and borrower in India, however, is in Indian rupees. The invested dollars are exchanged for rupees in the foreign exchange market and become part of India's foreign exchange pool. The rich who need foreign exchange to buy things abroad get the dollars. The poor microloan borrowers get the rupees.

Interest on the rupee microloan flows quickly back out of the village in rupees to the national microfinance institution. A portion of that outflow is then converted to dollars that go to the U.S. investor abroad. This creates a negative drain on India's foreign exchange reserves that, given the rates of interest and profit Sinclair documents, may add up to several times the original investment dollar inflow. To pay this dollar obligation, India must produce goods and services for sale abroad. Or it may sell or mortgage assets to foreigners, creating additional future claims against its production and real assets.

In return for a short-term inflow of credit, the village and India as a country bind themselves to a long-term outflow of claims on their wealth—supporting a classic pattern of colonization and wealth concentration beneficial only to foreign interests and their local accomplices.

### Grameen Is a Bank

The key to fixing microfinance is to recognize the critical differences between the Grameen Bank and the vast majority of microcredit institutions that claim to be its replicas.

- Grameen is similar to what Sinclair calls a "regular" bank. Its lending is mostly self-funded by local deposits in Bangladesh's national currency, the taka.
- Grameen offers depository services with generous interest rates designed to help its members build a financial asset base.
- Grameen extends loans to its members at a maximum interest rate of just over 20 percent, a fraction of what many other microlenders charge.
- Owned by its member savers and borrowers, Grameen is rooted in and accountable to the community it serves. Profits and interest continuously recycle locally to support productive local exchange and build real community wealth.

Grameen has its flaws, as does every institution, but it is designed to be locally accountable and to build rather than expropriate community wealth.

Most of the microcredit programs that claim to replicate the Grameen model resemble it only in the fact that they make loans to poor people. They are not "real" banks with regular depository services. They are not owned by their borrowers. Some charge interest rates of more than 100 percent. Interest and profits are siphoned off by distant managers and foreign investors rather than recycling within the community. Whether on Wall Street or in the villages of India, control of money by distant financiers rewarded for seeking maximum personal financial gain is a path to outsized wealth and power for the few and debt slavery for the many.

Even member/owner accountable banks that lend at reasonable rates are not a magic-bullet solution to poverty. Grameen Bank, however, demonstrates that they can be one useful tool.

It is time to rethink and restructure the microfinance industry in ways that take the best of the Grameen model seriously. Instead of restructuring microfinance institutions into publicly traded for-profits that sell shares to foreign investors, the goal should be to restructure them as cooperative banks owned by their local borrowers and funded in their national currency.

This model will not generate profits for foreign investors. That, however, was never a proper purpose of microfinance.

# Preface

The microfinance community often resembles a religious cult. Criticism is considered heresy and is not tolerated. Impact on poverty is dogmatically claimed but demonstrated in only exceptional cases. Above all, the sector is highly profitable, and the origin of this profit is simple: the poor.

Criticizing microfinance thus antagonizes those who have power and money at stake—the owners of the microfinance institutions (MFIs) and those who control their funding. The goal of my heretical act in writing this book is to shed light on the actual practices of the microfinance sector and to prompt changes that will skew the odds slightly in favor of the poor.

I tried to influence microfinance from within, during a decade of work in the sector across three continents and in a number of institutions. I tried logic and reason first, but that strategy failed. I pointed out the immorality of exploiting the poor, but this argument was ignored. Good, honest, hard-working microfinance practitioners were gradually replaced with unscrupulous players with a simple motivation: profit. This was disguised as a beneficial development, with coordinated publicity and attendant hype. Naïve celebrities were employed for PR purposes, and large commercial banks soon realized that there was a whole new client group to profit from.

Unfortunately, only negative publicity seemed to actually shake people into corrective action, albeit begrudgingly. Slowly the popular press became aware of some of the atrocities and touted them as typifying the sector, which was not necessarily accurate; but such is the tendency of journalists seeking a scoop. Specialized academic texts questioning the validity of the claims of the microfinance sector do exist, but they are mostly technical, dry, and inaccessible to the average reader. The book you hold in your hands attempts to bridge this gap.

I have attempted to go beyond the dinner table description of microfinance and explain how the various players in the sector operate *in practice*, without venturing into excessive technicality. I use the decade in which I worked in microfinance as a backdrop. This decade coincided with the adolescence of microfinance, which before 2002 was a somewhat obscure niche of the financial sector. It is now a $70 billion business and is featured on *The Simpsons*.

I beg the reader to not throw out the baby with the bathwater. Some microfinance is extremely beneficial to the poor, but it is not the miracle cure that its publicists would have you believe. Microfinance has been hijacked by profiteers, and we need to reclaim it for the poor. The problem is not with a few rogue operators, alas, but with systemic flaws that permeate the sector. I offer no easy solutions to fix this problem, but the first step is to acknowledge it and identify its causes. In the concluding chapter I offer the reader some tangible suggestions as to how best maneuver within the microfinance sector.

We need to develop microfinance 2.0—a model that takes the lessons of the last decades and applies them cautiously and prudently to the benefit of the poor. Making modest profit from a well-run, competitive MFI is not unethical. Making millions of dollars for a few individuals by charging eye-watering interest rates to vulnerable poor women who cannot read the loan contracts they sign with a fingerprint is unethical. Expecting a client to repay a loan is reasonable. Hounding a delinquent client unable to repay her loan to the point of suicide is not. Claiming miraculous results with scant evidence is optimistic at best, and more likely deceptive. Rigorous research by independent, qualified academics and practitioners on the actual impact of microfinance on the poor is the only way we will gather the data to understand what is actually happening and how we can improve.

Microfinance 2.0 needs to be evidence-based and to balance fair returns with a focus on positive impact. There is no room for exploitative greed in such a model. Microfinance 2.0 will therefore require a culling of the less scrupulous players, who will not go without a fight. Were the substantial sums of capital currently deployed in the microfinance sector wisely applied, we could have a far greater impact on poverty. Instead, we have settled for a poor substitute that enriches a few while enslaving many with debts they can barely afford to service, let alone benefit from. We can do better.

The current state of the microfinance sector is simply unacceptable. The time for playing ball with those responsible for this deception has now ended, and I urge others who retain any faith in microfinance to do likewise. Microfinance 2.0 cannot be created by individuals, but must be reconstructed collectively. This book is therefore a call to action.

I have worked in microfinance for ten years. Since 2008 I have limited my work to ethical, genuine microfinance operators, and my client list is correspondingly short. Prior to this I was an insider, though one with ever increasing skepticism. I must therefore acknowledge my own role in the rise of microfinance. But to become a whistle-blower, or a heretic, one must first have been a member of the cult. Only by working in these institutions, with many of the people mentioned in this book, was I able to see what was actually taking place.

I remain convinced that well-designed, targeted microfinance to a subset of the poor can have a positive impact. Microfinance is not suitable for all poor people, and it needs to complement rather than replace other development strategies. Mohammed Yunus set out with a grand vision to eradicate poverty with fairly priced microfinance loans provided by institutions whose goal was to reduce poverty. But there was a problem with the implementation of his vision—most MFIs do not offer fairly priced loans and do not aim to achieve this goal. They have a myriad of excuses to justify this, but the outcome is the same.

This book is aimed at those with a general interest in microfinance; industry insiders; those who invest in microfinance via websites or dedicated microfinance funds; celebrities who may have supported the sector with less than a thorough understanding of what they were actually supporting; regulators who are charged with protecting the interests of the poor and those of the investors in microfinance; and the broader development community.

To respect the privacy of those individuals appearing in the book who are not public figures, I have changed the names of most persons named in these pages. The exceptions are senior figures and executives in the world of microfinance: the names of these individuals have an asterisk on their first appearance, signifying the use of their actual names.

Emails and documents referred to or quoted from will be available on the book's website with footnotes inserted in the text where appropriate. Links to websites will be relegated to footnotes and also placed on the book website. Where incriminating websites have been subsequently removed, the original screenshots will be uploaded. One audio recording is reproduced in full in the text and will be available to listen to on the website. A second audio recording is produced only partially in the text due to its length, but the full audio recording and transcript will be available on the website. Dialogue from a hearing of the U.S. Subcommittee on International Monetary Policy and Trade is transcribed directly from the video footage available online.

For all other conversations and dialogue where a recording is not available, I have reproduced these as accurately as possible, but these should *not* be considered as verbatim. I apologize for the abundance of endnotes, but given the magnitude of the claims and accounts of events that take place here, a rigorous approach to qualifying such comments is prudent. The interested (or astonished) reader can verify the sources at will. Most information is already publicly available, and the rest soon will be; see www.microfinancetransparency.com.

Those with nothing to hide have nothing to fear.

# 1

# Thou Shalt Not Criticize Microfinance

"I'm a dodgy moneylender, exploiting the poor with useless, overpriced loans, ideally obliging their children into forced labor in the process."

This did not go down well. I had been introduced to yet another gathering of bright-eyed microfinance experts at yet another microfinance conference, and I had incorrectly assumed that irony and sarcasm were within their grasp. They were not. I attempted to redeem myself.

"Guys, I'm joking ... it was a joke. I'm a microfinance consultant, we're all cool ... sorry."

I had broken the golden rule of microfinance, the unwritten code that bonds its practitioners together. I had criticized microfinance and, perhaps worse, I had implicitly challenged the developmental claims the sector proclaims so vehemently. This is unacceptable from an insider. But none of the experts offered a defense or rebuked my confession. Such comments cut a little too close to the nerve to warrant further conversation. It is usually better to discuss the weather or the palatial décor of the conference rooms instead.

Lack of tact had once again led me into an awkward situation, but it could have been worse. Twice I have narrowly avoided being punched in conferences for daring to suggest that microfinance was in fact falling a little short of miraculous.

There is actually surprisingly little evidence supporting microfinance as a practical tool of poverty reduction, but this rather critical detail is ignored within the microfinance sector for one simple reason. Microfinance does not apparently require evidence to prove it works—since, on the face of it, it seems to work. It works because the poor repay loans, and this is all the proof the sector requires. Some 200 million people now receive microfinance loans,[1] most of whom repay the loans. Therefore they miraculously became better off in the process. So the argument goes.

The majority of credit card holders in the U.S. and Europe pay their bills eventually, so therefore they too are becoming wealthier by the day thanks to Visa, MasterCard, and American Express. The argument is no more complex than this. The fact that a large proportion of these microloans are used for consumption, or to repay other loans, or to pay off the evil village moneylender, is irrelevant.

The fact that crippling poverty persists in countries like Bangladesh, India, Nicaragua, Nigeria, and Bolivia is seen as an irrelevant detail. The persistence of poverty means that we need *more* microfinance. When Indian women started poisoning themselves under the burden and shame of chronic overindebtedness, or when the citizens of an entire country refused to repay their microfinance loans claiming unfair treatment, those who provided the loans remained silent or claimed thathild it all had nothing to do with them.

Many people do rather well out of microfinance, and celebrities from Bono to the Clintons, President Fox of Mexico, and the Queen of Spain have jumped on the bandwagon. The sector is of course extremely proud of its Nobel Peace Prize–winning godfather, Muhammad Yunus.* Yunus had embarked on a courageous mission to rid the world of poverty using fairly priced microloans to entrepreneurs. Alas, those charged with achieving this globally had a slightly different vision. Even Yunus himself has criticized the microfinance sector for the extortionate interest rates some microfinance institutions (MFIs) charged, accusing such institutions of becoming precisely the loan sharks that microfinance had initially sought to replace. Yunus's flagship institution, Grameen Bank, with whom he shared the Nobel Peace Prize, charges interest rates of about 20 percent[2]—enough to make any mortgage-holder in the developed world weep, but actually very reasonable in the microfinance world. The fact that Grameen Foundation USA had inadvertently supported and invested in at least one bank that charged rates six or seven times higher has been largely ignored.[3]

Microfinance is a $70 billion industry, employing tens of thousands of people, predominantly managed by a closed group of funds based in the U.S. and Europe acting as gatekeepers of the private capital available, and increasingly some of the public funding as well. The industry is largely unregulated, opaque, and hard to investigate in practice. A tireless PR machine recruits spokespeople, advertises on television, and holds endless promotional events. An almost cultlike aura surrounds the sector. Insiders are expected to toe the party line. It's to all of our advantage to belong to such an epistemic community with a common set of broadly held beliefs.

The cracks started appearing when Compartamos, a Mexican MFI, did the first big stock market flotation of a supposedly "social" bank, netting a tidy $410 million for a handful of lucky investors, financed in large part by ridiculously high interest rates that the poor seemed bizarrely happy to pay. A few maverick academics had been trying to sound the alarm for some years, and some insiders began to question the fundamentals of pumping credit into mostly ineffective "businesses" at suspiciously high prices. But as with all nascent bubbles, promoters perpetuated the hype. Compartamos had woken people up to the fact that it was not merely a fringe of the poor who would reliably pay interest rates of 100 percent or more for a loan of $200, but hundreds of millions of them—the profit potential was massive. Forget sub-prime—sub-sub-sub-prime was way better, and what's more, there were few pesky regulators to keep an eye on such inconveniences as consumer protection. A new gold rush began.

The Department for International Development (DFID, the UK equivalent of USAID), a traditional supporter and investor in microfinance, funded a major study of the research surrounding microfinance and concluded that the entire exercise had been mostly ineffective:

[I]t might have been more beneficial to explore alternative interventions that could have better benefitted poor people and/or empowered women. Microfinance activities and finance have absorbed a significant proportion of development resources, both in terms of finances and people. Microfinance activities are highly attractive, not only to the development industry but also to mainstream financial and business interests with little interest in poverty reduction or empowerment of women.... There are many other candidate sectors for development activity which may have been relatively disadvantaged by ill-founded enthusiasm for microfinance.

However, it remains unclear under what circumstances, and for whom, microfinance has been and could be of real, rather than imagined, benefit to poor people... Indeed there may be something to be said for the idea that this current enthusiasm is built on similar foundations of sand to those on which we suggest the microfinance phenomenon has been based.[4]

While I do not refute the findings of this important report, I equally cannot refute the evidence I have seen with my own eyes: that *some* microfinance is very beneficial to the poor. I hope to explain how this dichotomy of opinions arises within the microfinance sector.

I stumbled into the microfinance sector in 2002. Initially I shared the naïve belief that microfinance was "the next big thing" and could genuinely assist the poor. The initial signs looked promising to an untrained eye, and I joined the club in promoting the panacea of microfinance.

The underlying concept of microfinance sounds so seductive. Ask a microfinance expert what microfinance is and they will recount a heartwarming tale of a woman living in a hut in some poor country who gets a minuscule loan to buy a productive asset, often a sewing machine or a goat,[5] and by working hard she builds up a small business that receives successively larger loans until she is eventually catapulted out of poverty. Depending on the creative flair of the storyteller, the loans may also lead to amazing benefits to her children and community, and phrases like "female empowerment," "human dignity," and "harnessing entrepreneurial flair" will be slipped in periodically.

This concept appeals to people in the "developed" world, many of whom are increasingly skeptical of simply handing money to traditional charities after apparently so few results of decades of this practice. Helping people to help themselves appears more compatible with the ethos of developed countries: hard work and ambition, competition, and developing new markets. The heroes of the NASDAQ are the pioneers who take a simple idea and propel it to become a huge multinational business—why not in developing countries also, on a smaller scale?

Microfinance touches on the core values of entrepreneurial vision, of teaching a man how to fish rather than handing him a fish on a plate. It appears to be such an excellent idea. Capital is loaned, invested wisely, recycled to the next wave of poor people, investors in Geneva and Washington make a reasonable return in the process, and soon poverty vanishes altogether. It appeals to the positive aspects of capitalism and economic development, and it leverages the positive desire to work hard and provide for one's family. Everyone's a winner. So how dare anyone ever criticize it?

The problems with these crass descriptions of microfinance blurted out at dinner parties by zealous microfinance experts are numerous. Insiders are conditioned to reel them off automatically, but many privately agree they are mostly fantasies. But the fantasy is more palatable than to admit to having negligible impact while charging high interest rates to the poor. We promote an end to poverty if only the poor would take out a never-ending series of overpriced loans.

To cite a selection of the flaws of the romanticized image of the female microfinance client living in the hut with the sewing machine:

1. Such cases are surprisingly hard to find in practice. Men often send their wives to get loans because they know they are more likely to be approved.

2. Loans are almost invariably not spent on the productive sewing machine or goat, but on a TV, repaying another loan to a very similar bank, paying other bills, or general consumption. The benefits of the loan quickly disappear, but the debt remains, accumulating interest at an alarming rate, often encouraging the client to obtain another loan elsewhere to meet the repayments, often from the very moneylenders the microfinance community claims to replace.

3. Interest rates on loans, when all the various hidden charges are considered, are substantially higher than those stated. Interest rates under 30 percent a year are disappointingly rare, and rates of 100

percent or higher are common. One celebrated MFI in Mexico charges up to 195 percent per year.[6]

4. The small business is rarely able to generate sufficiently massive returns over prolonged periods to cover these interest payments. And even if the loan does result in some genuine improvement to the life of the individual entrepreneur, it is quite possible that this is at the expense of other people in the marketplace. When Walmart opens in a town in America, many smaller shops are driven out of business. According to the microfinance sector this phenomenon does not occur in developing countries. We ignore the businesses that fail.

5. The number of people catapulted out of poverty is minimal, and no widespread measurable reduction in overall poverty has been detected. At best, a few individuals see their situations improve, and these lucky few provide the examples for MFI marketing materials. The real debate about actual poverty reduction fluctuates between it being marginal or negative. Serious belief in Muhammad Yunus's suggestion that poverty will be eradicated from the planet and become a historical curiosity in "poverty museums" within a generation or two is hard to find in practice.

6. It is assumed that every poor person is a budding Bill Gates. A quick glance at the overwhelming majority of businesses that receive microloans hardly suggests cutting-edge innovation—most market traders sell precisely the same products as everyone else in the marketplace. Not everyone in Europe or the USA is a budding entrepreneur, so why would we expect anything different in developing countries?

7. The use of child labor is a carefully avoided question. The reality is that many families involved in labor-intensive micro-enterprises employ their own children, and no one knows the impact of such labor in the long term. As universal education becomes a reality in more and more countries each year, particularly in Latin America, it is likely that some of these children are stacking shelves or selling cellphone cards at the expense of getting an education. Conveniently, few microfinance banks and only one microfinance fund have policies on child labor.[7] The self-regulatory watchdogs

carefully avoid discussion of child labor in their "Client Protection Principles."

8. Most microfinance clients are not part of the "extreme poor." In fact, quite a few are perhaps best described as lower middle class, and while it is a pity that commercial banks will not lend them money on reasonable terms, it does not follow that an MFI offering them a loan at 60 percent interest per year to buy a TV is necessarily contributing to development.

9. The clients of most MFIs are not generally covered by the regulatory protection afforded to people in more developed countries.

10. When joining groups of borrowers who guarantee one another, one rather unpleasant downside is overlooked for the defaulting client—not only do they incur the wrath of the MFI, which can be quite oppressive, but they also lose their friends, who are obliged to step in and meet the shortfall.

This list of valid questions to challenge the stereotypical microfinance loan is far from exhaustive. In response, the sector is slowly acknowledging that it overhyped microfinance, and that expectations of the imminent eradication of poverty were perhaps optimistic. But the machine has been set in motion. Large commercial banks have entered the sector, lured by the whiff of profit and the appearance of social responsibility. Universities now offer courses in microfinance. There are microfinance MBAs. There are even microfinance T-shirts. (See the appendix, "Microfinance Economics 101," for a quick review, and a critique, of the fundamentals of microfinance theory.)

My concerns about microfinance took a decade to develop and involved extensive travel across the globe, working with many of the key players and seeing microfinance in action (for better or worse) from a variety of perspectives. I drifted into the sector after prematurely finding myself unemployed two weeks after joining the ill-fated Enron. Disillusioned with mainstream finance, microfinance seemed to be an interesting, and perhaps more constructive, way to deploy a finance background. I thus packed my bags and headed to Mexico full of optimism. As cracks began to appear in the overall microfinance model, I initially assumed that they were exceptions, teething problems, or temporary blips. But the cracks did not vanish, and as the sector matured (if that is the right word), the propaganda machine worked overtime to disguise rather than repair them.

There do exist cases where microfinance is genuinely benefitting the poor, but in my experience these are few and far between. Accepted wisdom has come to believe that access to microfinance is a necessary step in the direction of development. We have managed to create a buzz around the very word *microfinance* that attracts volunteers, the media, and celebrities. Muhammad Yunus goes as far as to suggest that access to microfinance is a human right.

According to the generally accepted belief, the recent financial crisis was caused by reckless bankers designing esoteric and complex financial products, and providing loans to people who perhaps should not have bought a $1 million home in the first place. Entire European nations racked up debts of astronomical proportions. People began defaulting on their loans, governments could no longer service their debts, and the house of cards began to collapse, necessitating the mother of all bailouts that generations to come will have to repay. Meanwhile, MFIs across the developing countries continued to hand out ever more over-priced loans to the poor, and many of the investors in these MFIs managed to get a tax credit for such behavior since these were considered *ethical* investments.

A few hiccups along the way were covered up, but dissenting voices began to raise concerns. Some simply quit the sector entirely. A few funds closed the doors to further microfinance investments. The first country to spectacularly and publicly collapse was Nicaragua (previous collapses had been less public, such as Bolivia in 1999/2000). This raised some concerns, and cost the microfinance funds in Europe and the USA some painful losses. Never mind—it wasn't their money in the first place, and the collapse was blamed largely on "the populist government." Critical documentaries and books began to emerge, and then scandals involving the darling of the sector, Grameen Bank, finally hit the mainstream press.

With the benefit of hindsight most calamities can be avoided, but to understand the crisis in microfinance, we must look beyond the propaganda. Histories of the microfinance sector do exist, and they are generally pretty dry texts. The public impression that microfinance was invented by Muhammad Yunus in some Bangladeshi village in the 1970s is probably the industry's foundational myth.

During the colonization of Indonesia in the early nineteenth century the Dutch developed a system of financial services across the sprawling colony that bore a striking resemblance to the current microfinance sector. Bank Rakyat Indonesia (BRI) was formally founded in 1895, and to this day BRI is one of the world's largest, if not the largest, microfinance banks.[8]

Wilhelm Raiffeisen founded a credit union in 1864 specifically to provide affordable credit to farmers who otherwise relied on exploitative moneylenders for credit. In Quebec, Alphonse and Dorimène Desjardins founded a credit union in 1900, a forerunner to the North American credit unions, again in response to high interest rates. Desjardins Group remains active in microfinance to this day. Although many current microfinance operators have limited pedigree, Accion was founded in 1961 and began microfinance operations in Brazil in 1973. ShoreBank International was launched in 1988. It largely depends on how we define microfinance, but it is likely that some form of small lending activities predated even the Raiffeisen model.

Yunus was certainly a pivotal pioneer in the sector. He provided the sector with an iconic figurehead from a poor and downtrodden country. By the end of the twentieth century, microfinance was sandwiched awkwardly between the traditional development sector and the formal financial sector. It was the unwanted child of each. Many development specialists were skeptical of a practice so overtly commercial and capitalistic in nature. Bankers were skeptical of a practice that focused exclusively on poor people without collateral.

Early applications of microfinance beginning in the 1970s had yielded some positive results, and practitioners began to dream of it becoming a key tool in the eradication of poverty. There was certainly some profit to be made from microfinance for those who provided the original capital if the banks could reach a sufficient scale. It would require public acceptance to propel microfinance from the fringes of development and finance to the forefront of the battle against poverty. The microfinance strategy also fit well with a general disillusionment with traditional aid sectors. Unleashing entrepreneurial flair was a more attractive proposal than handing out free food. Bono summarized this succinctly: "Give a man a fish, he'll eat for a day. Give a woman microcredit, she, her husband, her children and her extended family will eat for a lifetime."[9] The general public was ready for a new approach to development.

Thus after extensive campaigning, the UN declared 2005 as the year of microcredit, and the following year it gained its ambassador. Muhammad Yunus received the Nobel Peace Prize, and microfinance stepped onto the main stage. It was now firmly acknowledged as a principal tool for development. Accelerated growth began, hugely profitable stock market flotations were launched, and microfinance became a household name. Presidents and rock stars opened conferences; specialist investment funds began sprouting up like mushrooms; universities began offering courses in microfinance; and the television messages of the "new cure for poverty" were beamed into living rooms across the planet. But by 2011 Muhammad Yunus had been unfairly fired from Grameen Bank under political pressure, the sector was facing widespread criticism in the media, microfinance clients in India were committing suicide by the dozen under the pressure of massive accumulated debt, and the sector was attempting to reinvent itself.

Was Muhammad Yunus's original dream flawed, or had the sector morphed into an entirely different beast that now faced a serious challenge? When did the crisis start?

I realized the magnitude of the crisis permeating the sector in 2009 when I received a call from the managing director of Deutsche Bank asking me to cease my criticisms of microfinance. I had been raising some awkward questions about a particularly questionable microfinance bank in Africa that appeared to be making incredible profits by exploiting the poor with extremely high interest rates. It had attracted some of the largest investors in the entire sector, including Deutsche Bank, many of whom claimed to be ignorant of the MFI's underlying activities.

Senior people in the sector had invested in the African MFI in question, and they were now appealing to me to keep quiet. I had visited this bank extensively, and I had seen the poor women struggling to repay loans costing them over 100 percent per year. It angered me and saddened me that the sector had morphed into little more than yet another means for the rich to exploit the poor. I declined the offer to back down.

Some months later the incident landed on the front page of the *New York Times,* explicitly naming Deutsche Bank, Calvert Foundation, and the darling of the public face of microfinance—Kiva. The article caused a major stir in the sector, yet another blow to the ludicrous hype that had been perpetuated for a decade about the miracle cure for poverty. I played a significant role in getting this article into the *New York Times,* and I knew that in fact this example was only the tip of the iceberg.

A subtle shift had occurred in the microfinance sector that Mohammad Yunus himself pinpointed perfectly: "I never imagined that one day microcredit would give rise to its own breed of loan sharks."

A key problem in the sector is the distance, not simply physical, between the poor recipients of microloans and those sitting in air-conditioned offices in Europe and the USA running the sector. The words *loans* and *clients* are used interchangeably. Most of those directing the capital that drives the microfinance sector have spent limited time actually *with* the poor. Photos and stories are meager substitutes for meeting and knowing the poor. In our case, and wife and I have spent eight of the last ten years living in developing countries. The staff and clients of MFIs were not mere curiosities to visit on a two-day trip to assess a potential investment in an MFI—they were our neighbors and friends. We attended their weddings, and they ours. We bought stuff from their shops and ate with them. We found that their situations are complex and challenging and not easily resolved with a $100 loan.

I enjoy visiting their small businesses and chatting with them about how their markets operate, the competition they face, their future plans. But I often leave wondering if credit is what they actually need. Some modest training, some advice on managing inventory, or strategic help on how to turn their plans into reality—these may be far more helpful than a $100 loan at 60 percent interest a year, but this kind of assistance is generally not available. Some MFIs offer such support, which I applaud. But I believe that in the sector's quest for relentless growth we have lost sight of the human element at stake: the poor are *people.* They *may* deserve access to credit, but they *certainly* deserve respect and fair treatment.

During my decade in microfinance I worked with countless individual MFIs, the rating agencies, and other transparency initiatives and service

providers, including consulting boutiques and IT providers to the microfinance sector. I worked with microfinance funds and peer-to-peer lending platforms that channel money from investors to the MFIs. I worked
with large microfinance networks with global operations, spoke in various conferences, and had some modest interaction with public multilateral investors such as the Inter-American Development Bank. I was
fortunate to witness the rise and fall from grace of microfinance over this
period, from a variety of perspectives.

This period may be best described as the *commercialization* of microfinance sector, when big banks and political ideology infiltrated
microfinance to the highest levels. What began as a good idea was gradually hijacked by large investors and a new wave of dot-coms, muddled with
media hype. Poverty reduction has been marginal. Some clients have found
microfinance more a curse than a blessing, at times driving them to suicide. Most investment funds, acting as the principal intermediaries between those with capital and the MFIs pumping out the loans to the
poor, have little idea about microfinance in practice, and are motivated
by a perverse set of incentives that benefit neither their own investors
nor the poor.

Each time a scandal erupts the microfinance funds are placed in an
awkward position. If they admit they knew of the practices but did not
challenge them, they seem to have betrayed their very raison d'être. If
they claim they had no idea, they admit that their due diligence is sloppy.
They are damned either way. Best to avoid the question altogether.

The average person on the street has been spoon-fed a deliberately
naïve view of microfinance. Most individuals who have invested in
microfinance have little idea how their funds are deployed in reality, and
many would be disturbed to find out the truth. They cannot board a
flight to Burkina Faso to check whether their $25 investment is being
used wisely, so they entrust their money to a fund or a website that offers
assurances of incredible impact. They read the website and magazines
produced by their chosen intermediary and assume the claims to be true.
Little do they know that these institutions are largely unregulated in practice and have a rather different view of microfinance from that presented
in their magazines, stuffed full of photos of poor women in action poses,
bouncing out of poverty every second of the day thanks to $25 loans.

Meanwhile the poor largely remain poor, even as billions of dollars in interest payments are extracted from their pockets justified by a few isolated but celebrated cases of successful tomato vendors splashed across the promotional materials of the companies leading the sector. An article in *Time World* summarized it succinctly: "On current evidence, the best estimate of the average impact of microcredit on the poverty of clients is zero."[10]

To highlight the unusual range of opinions, contrast this with the conclusion drawn by two-time Pulitzer-winning *New York Times* columnist Nicholas Kristof: "Microcredit is undoubtedly the most visible innovation in anti-poverty policy in the last half century."[11]

In my opinion the truth is likely closer to the former than the latter. While the poor are being deceived about the impact an over-priced loan will have on their actual situation, so are many of the well-meaning investors who believe their money is being put to good use. Microfinance can and does work if applied correctly. In practice it largely does not. This is a pity, and a missed opportunity. It was not always like this, and need not be like this. The sector morphed gradually over the last decade into its current state of crisis. I saw this happen from the inside, and this is my story.

# 2

# Baptism in Mexico

I stumbled into microfinance, partly out of curiosity, partly out of intrigue, partly for lack of anything else that excited me at the time. Some brief background is required to explain how this historical glitch occurred.

I was an investment banker for years, initially in Toronto, then in London. I'm an economist, and I worked for Barclays, which sponsored me to do a master's degree in finance. I had drifted into technical trading of derivatives, something now criticized with some justification for being destabilizing. I subsequently moved to the corporate finance department of ING Barings. I found the work dreary, but I needed to pay off some student loans and this job served that purpose for two years. At a loss at what to do next, I thought an MBA might be worthwhile, so I went to Barcelona for a couple of years for more studies.

During this period Nick, a friend from ING Barings, and I hatched an ambitious travel plan. We were determined to see more of the world beyond our air-conditioned offices, but backpacking no longer appealed. It had to be something "original," and we decided that the journey would have to be a Guinness World Record to qualify as sufficiently "original." We searched for a feasible journey and eventually settled on riding motorbikes from the north coast of Alaska to the southern tip of Argentina in record time.

We managed to get sponsorship from Honda, among others, which was incredible in hindsight: Nick had never even ridden a motorbike. Fortunately, being able to ride a motorbike was not actually a question in the interview. The publicity of obtaining a Guinness World Record was worth more to Honda than a couple of bikes and some spare parts, and we convinced them that we were sufficiently insane to embark on such a marathon expedition. Honda risked two bikes; we were risking our lives.

Toward the end of the MBA most of my thoughts were on the trip ahead, but potential employers were also circling like vultures at the business school, luring students into jobs upon graduation. Most companies had fixed start dates that clashed with the expedition, but Enron made me an attractive offer, including desperately needed sponsorship of the expedition, which they thought was awesome. The only additional condition was that I write up the expedition for the company's in-house magazine. Deal. I signed a contract and got back to the more pressing issue of expedition planning.

We successfully completed the expedition, driving almost continuously for weeks on end, and duly made our way into the Guinness Book of Records, a book read mostly by children in the few days after Christmas. Upon arriving in Ushuaia, the southernmost city in the world, I discovered that Enron had all but collapsed. I called to find out if there was much point returning to England, and the HR department warned me, extremely kindly, that if I didn't show up for work as agreed, the liquidators could consider this a failure to satisfy the terms of the employment contract and oblige me to repay the expedition sponsorship (all of which, of course, I had spent).

Then Argentina collapsed—the largest sovereign default in history.

I returned to England assured of unemployment. The next few months were uneventful. Jobs in finance were few and far between. I was technically ex-Enron (I did in fact spend two weeks in the London office). Having not worked for two years during the MBA did not strengthen my case. I spent a lot of time exploring Norway, reading, doing some small consulting projects, and sending off endless job applications. One assignment involved visiting an NGO called StreetCred, run by the Quakers. It was a small microfinance institution that lent money to Bangladeshi women in East London. It was intriguing: it seemed to work, was a novel idea, the women seemed grateful for the loans (none of them spoke English so I judged this by the smiles on their faces), and I remembered studying microfinance for development economics at university. Maybe this is what I should do? Combine a background in finance with helping the poor? This sounded fascinating.

Not speaking Bengali ruled me out of this particular MFI, but a quick browse on the Internet suggested a similar outfit in San Cristóbal de las Casas in Mexico. I knew and loved San Cristóbal, and I applied for a consulting position.

I received a prompt reply suggesting that they would love to have me. It was a three-month voluntary position, but if it went well I could perhaps convert it to a formal job. Either way, it would be cheaper and more productive than being unemployed in London. I discovered dirt-cheap flights from London to Mexico on the one-year anniversary of 9/11 and arrived at Grameen Trust Chiapas (GTC), a small MFI supposedly serving the rural poor women of the highlands of Chiapas. San Cristóbal is a wonderful city, and I found a lovely house, got a bicycle, swam every morning, did some climbing, got fit, and learned a new business.

The bank itself had a murky history that I didn't quite understand at the time. It was started with the vague "support" and seed capital from Grameen Bank in Bangladesh, arranged by a Harvard economist named Beatriz Armendáriz,* who is a well-known microfinance academic and author of the standard textbook on the economics of microfinance. After some "disagreement," the company had split in two. The archrival, Al Sol, retained good relationships with Grameen Foundation USA, while Grameen Trust Chiapas continued as part of the broad Grameen Bank franchise. They didn't want to change the name, since *Grameen* was helpful for attracting attention and funding. The company was run by the powerful Armendáriz family, and the CEO was none other than Beatriz's brother, Ruben,* who seemed like a pleasant guy.

At no point did I observe Ruben demonstrate much interest in the poor. I never saw him visit the field, or even speak to a client in the office downstairs. In fact, he appeared uninterested in microfinance in general. Most of the management team seemed to be old friends of his. Efficiency was low, and Mario, the operations guy, managed all field operations with Post-it notes, apparently on the basis that computers were of limited use. He would tour the office daily with a stack of little yellow papers and distribute them like a postman in a country suffering a severe paper shortage, with the various tasks for the day scribbled neatly. The company was losing money and clients, had few internal controls, had little chance of growth, and needed to get investors in order to grow. My task was to help improve all this, beginning with systematizing the loan repayments and savings.

In 2002 microfinance was still a relative unknown, including among most of GTC's staff, so having absolutely no microfinance experience didn't count against me. How different could it be from regular banking, just on a smaller scale? I was essentially working in a turnaround, and the best place to start was to understand the basic business model.

The first big lesson is that an MFI is nothing like a regular bank. The differences are not subtle tweaks, but fundamental divergences in the business models. Banks typically borrow money from clients (savings) and lend them to other clients (borrowers, with collateral). Most MFIs do not capture savings (certainly in 2002; this is changing now), and they lend to people without collateral, so the model is presumably simpler.

The MFI may have some capital of its own, but basically it operates as an agent. Investors, multilateral organizations such as the International Finance Corporation (IFC), or lenders such as microfinance funds, provide the MFI with large chunks of cash for long periods at reasonable interest rates. The MFI then lends to the poor at higher interest rates for shorter terms in bite-sized chunks. The profit it makes on the additional interest charged to clients over and above its cost of borrowing from the fund has to cover non-repaying clients, operating costs, salaries, etc. Anything that is left over is profit for the MFI.

The premise is that the poor have incredible investment opportunities that they are unable to realize because of lack of access to capital. They cannot go to regular banks, because regular banks don't lend to poor people without collateral. They are thus forced to forgo these opportunities or borrow from friends, family, or moneylenders. MFIs plug this gap at reasonable rates, so the poor can get fair credit and grow their own businesses. Loans are claimed to be for some productive purpose, and all the clients are entrepreneurs. Or so goes the usual story.

Two immediate problems occurred to me: the interest rates seemed quite steep, and many of the clients weren't investing in anything, but were simply borrowing money to buy a TV, pay a bill, or repay another loan. The famous sewing machines or milk-dispensing cows or other such productive assets that would constitute an actual business seemed worryingly scarce.

MFIs were generally NGOs or not-for-profits in 2002, and many have retained this structure. They have no shareholders, do not pay dividends, and pay reduced tax, and profit has to be reinvested in the MFI. By contrast, for-profit or private limited companies do make profit and pay tax. GTC was an NGO, or rather a trust (basically the same in practice), but the distinction between this and a for-profit seemed subtle. Ruben Armendáriz controlled the MFI, could veto any decision, and could pay himself and anyone he liked whatever salary he chose. GTC benefited from favorable tax treatment as an NGO. The added bonus was that an MFI could start as an NGO, enjoy this structure as long as it suited, and then convert into a for-profit company. It seemed like a no-brainer which structure was best. Any extraction of wealth from the MFI could be via salaries, so the inability to have shareholders or pay dividends seemed irrelevant.

An MFI then makes loans to the poor in two main ways: group lending or individual lending. Individual loans are self-explanatory, similar to those from most commercial banks. The interest rates were substantially higher than those charged by a commercial bank, and one had to wonder why anyone with access to a commercial bank would ever visit GTC, but some fairly well dressed clients occasionally took loans from GTC.

Group lending was far more interesting. This was the famous invention of Muhammad Yunus of Bangladesh, who would go on to win a Nobel Peace Prize for his insight. Groups of mainly women would obtain a loan collectively and would repay collectively each week. The interest and capital would be calculated as a single, equal repayment to be made weekly. This seemed less risky, since the members of the group would guarantee one another. From the perspective of the MFI, the group is one borrower. Whatever happens within that group is a black box of irrelevance. If one member missed a payment, the others would cover the shortfall. The group would also deposit a percentage of the overall loan into a collective kitty up front, conveniently kept at GTC, which

GTC could dip into if a loan remained unpaid at the end of the term. The overall risk was thus low, although these clients did not usually have much collateral and there was not a lot GTC could do in the event of an outright default other than never give the clients a loan again. Group lending was more expensive to manage for the MFIs, since they had to travel out to the villages to disburse and collect loans, although serving ten or twenty women in a single visit spread this cost.

The actual loans were quite expensive when translated into an annualized rate of the sort we are accustomed to in developed countries, but they were fairly simple: a loan term (usually six months or a year), a frequency of repayment (weekly, fortnightly, or monthly in some cases), an interest rate, and some penalties in case a payment was missed. That was it. The interest charged was in the region of 56 percent per year.

Loans would be managed by loan officers—junior staff who would actually go and find the clients, explain the rules, collect the payments, and hassle them if they didn't repay. They were essentially messengers and were treated as juniors in the head office, although from the clients' perspective they were the face of GTC.

Clients, with some prompting from the loan officers, would form a group of five to fifteen members and fill out some forms. This qualified as a due diligence. Information captured about the clients was fairly rudimentary, perhaps extending to a brief description of what they intended to do with the loan, but once the money left GTC there was little it could do if the funds were used for something else, and as long as the loan was repaid, no one really cared what the loan was for.

When clients failed to repay they would be hounded by the loan officers. After perhaps one warning the other members of the group would also be hounded, have the group's savings threatened, and be prevented from getting any subsequent loans unless full repayment was made. These measures would naturally oblige the other members to put pressure on the delinquent client, who would quickly become *persona non grata* within the group. In India some years later this would actually drive women to commit suicide. Mexican clients tended to take a more laid-back approach to non-repayment, most likely because less social stigma was associated with default in Mexico than in India.

The head office of GTC was actually an extension to the house of the CEO's sister, and GTC had to pay rent for the privilege. Downstairs housed the front office, where clients could directly come to apply for a loan or repay one. There were a couple of staff to deal with such cases, since the loan officers attended to their clients in the field, usually at the home of one of the group members. Mario, the COO, sat downstairs and would manage the loan officers, do some basic projections (on Post-it notes) to see how many loans he could do each week, and work out how much money would return to GTC as loan repayments. Another woman, called Liliana, had a job that was not well defined but had something to do with marketing. She had glorious nails, elaborate hair, lashings of makeup, and abundant jewelry, but no obvious function. She had initially held something of a director role at GTC, but was largely displaced when Ruben stepped in.

Upstairs sat the head of finance, who would manage the bank accounts and pay bills and salaries, and who worked quite hard. I was awarded a chair and desk in the corridor outside her office. And finally, the IT team would attempt to organize the endless disbursements and repayments and handle the cash, largely from Mario's Post-it notes and documents returned to the office by loan officers. This area was managed by two charming and well-educated young women who actually knew more about the operations of GTC than anyone else in the company.

This is essentially the basic structure of any MFI. It is not rocket science. I've worked at dozens of MFIs, and they all follow this broad pattern, whether in Latin America, Africa, Eastern Europe, or Asia. Flourishes can include supervisors of loan officers; sometimes loan officers are divided into those who find new clients, those who deal with clients once they have loans, and those who specialize in hassling delinquent clients. There is often an internal auditor who checks that things are working well and reports to the board (not at GTC). Large MFIs will have product development teams for working out innovative ways to lend to the poor and extract their savings, and to constantly monitor the market, particularly competitors, to try to keep one step ahead.

Loan products are generally quite simple, rarely even reaching the complexity of a current account with an overdraft facility. Some modest attempt to tailor loan products to the needs of clients is occasionally made, perhaps with a grace period for the first couple of months during which interest accumulates but the client doesn't have to make payments on the loan. Repayments may be linked to the harvest cycles for agricultural loans. Again, this is not Goldman Sachs.

Operating expenses can be high. Salaries are a major component, and while loan officers usually earn peanuts, senior managers usually earn decent salaries, particularly in NGOs where they get no dividends or stock grants. IT expenses can be significant, since it is complex to manage high volumes of small transactions. Vehicles are a classic expense. For some reason MFIs tend to love vehicles, particularly those that favored managers can use for personal use. Large SUVs with tinted glass and logos on the sides are favored.

Because of the relatively high fixed costs of offices, salaries, vehicles, and so forth an MFI needs to reach a certain number of clients in order to cover its costs. There is thus a drive to reach this break-even point as quickly as possible. Extending as many loans as possible, at the highest interest rates possible, is the most obvious way to reach this point quickly.

MFIs that capture savings from clients as collateral are not generally allowed to lend these to new clients, but must rather keep them in a separate bank account to be returned to the clients if repayments are made. Obviously, there is a temptation to lend this money to new clients and earn multiples more interest rather than merely depositing it in a current account at a bank, but the legality of doing so varies from country to country, and this option is often abused.

Products other than loans and savings can include foreign exchange services, remittances, or micro-insurance. A credit bureau can enable the MFI to check the credit history of a client, and is an added incentive to the client to repay a loan for fear of being branded a bad credit risk by the MFI at the bureau. However, these are only as good as the data provided to the bureau, and only relevant where a client has a previous history.

This, in a nutshell, is microfinance.

Returning to the antics at GTC, I gradually became aware that things were not quite as idyllic as had initially appeared. The problems began to emerge when the Inter-American Development Bank (IDB), a Latin American public multilateral development bank, came to visit. We needed to tidy up quite a few aspects of GTC in the hope of receiving funds.

The first problem was the accounting. GTC's external accountant fell short of adhering to Generally Accepted Accounting Principles. His balance sheets rarely balanced, he made constant mistakes, and his attempts at hiding expenses were unsophisticated. On one occasion I was forced to point out that IDB might find it strange that we had spent $8,000 on lubricants and maintenance for a single vehicle that was worth only $3,000. That the vendor of this overpriced lubricant shared the same surname, house, and presumably bed as one of our senior managers was simply a coincidence. The issue of the loans that were actually made to staff and friends of GTC interest-free was another tricky point, as were the sums owed to Ruben's father that were mysteriously omitted from the list of GTC's debts. Instead, in accounting terms, they were treated as a donation—albeit one that had to be repaid. The loan from Grameen Bangladesh had also vanished from the books.

The next problem was Ruben's business plan, which contained stereotypical optimism that surely the IDB would see through. Projections were made with little basis and without the assistance of actual calculations. Only half the actual problems GTC faced were discussed, and these vanished in the forecast. The document appeared little more than a marketing brochure.

When the IDB man arrived, we retired to Ruben's office, which was blessed with its own private bathroom (there was no way he would share a bathroom with the rest of us, or even the occasional poor client). Alas, the tap did not function well and water was dispensed under alarming pressure. The IDB representative spent a suspicious amount of time in the bathroom and eventually emerged with his trousers drenched, helpfully explaining that this was related to the tap and not to any other factor. He then turned to me and asked if I had been responsible for preparing the accounts.

"No, I had absolutely nothing to do with them whatsoever."

"Good. I did not expect someone from IESE Business School to prepare accounts of this quality."

I couldn't help but smile while Ruben squirmed. The accountant's flawed accounting would be visible to some canines. It had, unsurprisingly, been detected by Latin America's primary multilateral finance organization. He went on: "These are deeply flawed and need to be redone. There is no point analyzing them any further. We shall proceed to discuss the broader strategy." Without further ado, we all gathered around the main office and listened to the man from the IDB explain to us how to run an MFI. It was a somewhat dry lesson, but a poignant moment woke me from a stupor. He had written our mission and vision statements on the whiteboard:

> To help the women in the highlands of Chiapas to relieve their poverty via self-employment, providing microfinance and technical assistance, while respecting their culture and human condition.
>
> To be a self-sufficient microfinance institution with the principal objectives of poverty alleviation and the comprehensive development of the region.

Or some such optimistic claims.

"Microfinance loans are extremely useful for the poor people, but there comes a time when they require larger loans, and the current mission statement precludes such loans. Would it not be better to simply refer to loans *in general*, rather than microloans exclusively?"

Ruben thought this suggestion was ingenious and agreed immediately. The rest of us sat motionless.

"GTC focuses extensively on the highlands of Chiapas, but urban districts also are home to many poor people, and it seems unfair to discriminate against them. Would it be reasonable to alter this point so GTC can service *all* poor clients?"

I thought Ruben was about to start clapping. Yes, this was inspired. Scrap such constraints. Half of our clients weren't rural anyway, so it made little difference. We continued sitting and watching.

"Do you really want to lend only to poor people? What happens when they become slightly richer? Will you abandon them? Do you think slightly richer people don't occasionally have genuine needs for loans? People with slightly lower levels of poverty may be less risky to GTC. The focus is surely that you lend to *people in need*. Their poverty level is irrelevant. The rich will always prefer to go to commercial banks anyway."

"Bravo, yes, agreed. We will lend to people in need in general." Ruben was having a field day. Concerns about deviating from our mission began to worry me. Everyone else sat in stunned silence.

"And women, as we know, are particularly impoverished in many communities, but let us not forget the poor *men*." Bang went another cornerstone of GTC's original mission.

Even the man from the IDB didn't bother to discuss the issue of technical assistance, which we didn't do anyway, and presumably recognized that the issues of *human condition* and *culture* were pure window-dressing and not worth mentioning. That we would be active in the oft-claimed alleviation of poverty was implicit by our very existence—MFIs by definition alleviate poverty, that was obvious. It would be awkward to discuss the reference to self-employment explicitly. We all knew that many of the clients were not actually self-employed, so we skipped that one too.

There was a pause. I tentatively raised my hand.

"If I understand correctly, from our original mission statement, you are proposing removing the words *micro, poor, highlands,* and *women.* Do you think this somewhat deviates from the entire purpose of the institution?"

Ruben glared at me. This was not an appropriate comment. The rest looked at me in astonishment, and then back to the man from the IDB.

"No, I don't think it does."

And that was it. GTC became a general, overpriced credit provider to anyone who wanted a loan, for any purpose.

I left GTC shortly after this incident, since it was clear that the mission statement had been abandoned and the goal was simply to become a B-grade bank with no focus on alleviating poverty. I started working instead with an MFI called Conserva in Tuxtla Gutierrez that had a slightly more focused social mission. It was run by a longtime women's rights activist. It was also facing serious struggles, and it would eventually also increase its interest rates to the astronomical levels typically found in Mexico. However, in late 2003, when I worked with Conserva, it was a fairly well run, decent MFI that actually seemed to have some positive impact. It was also conveniently located near some of the best climbing areas in Mexico and I knew some of the staff there. My main assignment was to analyze the loan portfolio, install an IT system to manage the growing portfolio, and tidy up their accounts according to international accounting standards. This was a pleasant change from working at GTC.

Work at Conserva helped me learn the core business model in more detail. The main discovery over these months was made during the software installation, which did not go entirely smoothly. The young IT manager, a short Mexican by the name of José Manuel,* was a genius. He had relatively little knowledge of business, I had almost zero knowledge of software, and somehow we just about managed to struggle through installing the software. We became good friends in the process and worked together frequently over the following decade. Although José Manuel initially focused exclusively on software, over the years he learned the core microfinance model inside out and was colloquially referred to by many as *El Mexicano Mágico*.

I did meet a particularly inspirational group of entrepreneurs in the highlands of Chiapas who clearly demonstrated the transformational impact microfinance can have. They were called *Las Mujeres de Zinacantan*—the women of Zinacantan village. It was begun by a small group of weavers, led by Doña Tomasa. She was perhaps fifty years old, and either a spinster or widowed (I never found out which). Zinacantan is an indigenous, male-dominated society, and single women over the age of perhaps eighteen are rare as most marry early. Divorce is almost unheard of, and women's rights lag even other parts of Mexico. The group was originally formed with a loan from GTC, and three or four women diligently created wonderful, original tablecloths, wall hangings, and clothes of high quality that yielded decent margins.

Over the next few years other women had joined the group. Some had chosen not to marry. Others may have experienced domestic violence or wished to divorce, and little protection was afforded to such women until this group formed. *Las Mujeres de Zinacantan* thus gradually began to challenge the status quo of male dominance within the village—women now had a choice. They could work and live independently of men, which previously had been hard in practice. Their business was economically viable, growing, and had had a positive societal impact that went beyond the women directly involved. This thoroughly impressed me. The impact of microfinance in terms of female empowerment was often claimed, and here was an excellent example of it in practice.

Jessica (my girlfriend at the time, and now my wife) and I visited the group shortly before leaving Chiapas to buy a wall hanging. I asked about their loans and discovered that the group had ceased borrowing from any MFI. I asked them why and was told that the business was doing so well there was no need to obtain credit. This is the ultimate sign of success for an MFI—not to retain clients, but to lose them when they become self-sufficient. The birds leave the nest. Shouldn't MFIs boast not of their ever-expanding clients, but rather those that they lose because they are no longer poor?

It was clear that serious money could be made from microfinance, and that it *could* be an effective tool in poverty reduction. The repayment rates really were as good as advocates claimed, and the poor did seem willing and able, for whatever reason, to repay loans at interest rates that seemed exorbitant to me. However, the actual impact on poverty was not as visible as claimed. Perhaps this was because it took a long, long time to appear. Or perhaps I was not looking for signs of poverty reduction in the right places. Maybe more microfinance than we thought was being discreetly directed to consumption and couldn't be expected to have an impact on poverty anyway—buying a television at 60 percent interest a year is unlikely to lead to a net reduction in poverty. But maybe, just maybe, the reason for the scarcity of any evidence supporting the claims of poverty alleviation made by the MFI industry was simply that there was none.

# 3

# Bob Dylan and I in Mozambique

To suggest that our decision to move to Mozambique was an informed one would fall short of factual accuracy.

I had met World Relief staffers in New York some months before while attending a conference. They were particularly interested in my experiences with struggling MFIs. A few months later they contacted me to ask if I would be interested in assisting them in Rwanda, Burundi, Mongolia, or Mozambique. Neither Jessica nor I had ever been to Africa or knew much about the place: it had animals, wars, and poverty. I remember reading something about two of the countries being particularly brutal and ruled them out immediately.

This was a major decision, and I needed to consult Jessica. I shouted upstairs: "Those American guys have offered us work in Rwanda, Burundi, Mongolia, or Mozambique. Fancy any of those? I think Rwanda and Burundi have wars or something, might skip those."

Jessica shouted downstairs, "What language do they speak in Mozambique?"

I searched online. "Portuguese. But don't you reckon Mongolia would be awesome? We could go on that famous train."

"You go to Mongolia on your own, but Mozambique sounds cool. It'll be easy to learn Portuguese, let's go for that one. It'd be nice to see a new continent."

I drafted an email along the lines of "after careful consideration of the options available ...," and a few months and phone calls later it was confirmed: we were going to Mozambique.

Mexico had been great, but my work there was drawing to a natural close. Walmart had arrived in our remote village. They had finally managed to build a highway to pump yet more tourists into the Chiapanecan highlands. There was an air-conditioned multiscreen cinema and rumors of a coming McDonalds. We had been there two years, and while we loved Chiapas, it seemed better to leave on a high note. Eventually the wonderful ancient city of San Cristóbal de las Casas would be much like any other Mexican city, with crime, pedestrianized streets for tourists, rising house prices that would drive all but the elite locals from the center into peripheral suburbs, and locals offering drugs and homogenous tourist trinkets to the endless stream of budget travelers. We chose an opportune moment to leave.

I had managed to negotiate a delay of a few months on the grounds of "tying up some loose ends" (a holiday). I went on ahead to Mozambique to sort out a house, meet the team, and get the project started. The first few weeks are usually the most intense as one digs around, unaware of the politics, trying to piece together what is really happening. That was best done alone, and Jessica could relax in Europe a while. The first alarm bell rang at Heathrow Airport. I approached the check-in desk of South African Airways and in a thick South African accent the kind lady asked me where I was going.

"Maputo," I suggested.

"Where?"

"It's the capital of Mozambique, which I believe is your neighboring country?"

She looked at me bemused, tapped away at the computer, and replied, "You're going for *two months*?"

"Yes, and then I will have to go back again after Christmas, for at least another year or so."

"Wow. Well, have a good flight, and a nice time in ... Maputo," she concluded, checking once again the actual name of the city.

The next alarm bell was landing at Maputo International Airport. From above it appeared a complete mess. I had never seen an African city and thus had no point of reference. There were a few tall buildings, but mostly the city appeared to satisfy the stereotype of mud huts. I turned on some music for the descent, on the advice of a friend of mine—Bob Dylan's song about Mozambique. Already I was feeling rather gloomy—this city looked like a war-torn, dirty, chaotic dump from a few thousand feet up, and as we got closer it appeared more so. How was I going to explain this to Jessica? Dylan perked me up a little. There was certainly abundant blue sky. "It's very nice to stay a week or two," he suggested—I wondered what he would think of a two-year stint. I certainly ended up agreeing with him that two weeks is ample time in Mozambique. He also mentioned that it was a romantic place with pretty girls. Frankly, neither of these seemed particularly relevant now—we were coming in to land and the so-called runway appeared neither flat nor fully paved, and preservation of life seemed a more pressing concern. If Dylan's first impressions of Mozambique had been the blue sky and pretty girls, I could only assume he had not taken the flight I was currently on.

Within only a few minutes of arriving I was embroiled in some scam that involved my having to pay a few dollars here and there due to some anomaly of my passport, or visa, or shoes, or something that was neither fully explained nor justified the provision of a receipt. At this stage my Portuguese amounted to a few words, and I relied entirely on Spanish. My principal concern was getting out of the airport to somewhere safe, ideally avoiding robbery, murder, or kidnapping. World Relief assured me that the CEO would meet me at the airport, and I trusted entirely that they would comply. Otherwise, I knew no one, had large bags, and would have to rely on the Lonely Planet guidebook to save me from a tense situation.

As one of the only white people on a fairly empty flight I was easy to spot, and a large American bounded over to me beaming from ear to ear. "Hugh? Hugh Sinclair? How are you? Glad you made it."

I had spoken to this guy by phone, once, and here he was in person. He was about a decade younger than I had anticipated, but at least he offered some semblance of safety. We got in the car, and despite his efforts at polite conversation, my focus lay beyond the confines of the vehicle. There were burnt-out cars and tires along the road, if *road* was the correct term; the city was dirty, with open rubbish dumps and litter everywhere; the crowds of people seemed aggressive; and the pretty girls that Bob Dylan had sung so eloquently of had presumably departed with him in the late 1960s. The buildings were run down well beyond the standard of the slums of Mexico City, and, curiously, people seemed oblivious to cars and would wonder aimlessly into traffic. It was hot and smelled rotten. Maputo bore all the signs of second-rate communist architecture left abandoned for a few decades. Streets were named after Vladimir Lenin, Mao Tsetung, Karl Marx, and even Kim Il Sung. With the exception of some vestiges of Portuguese colonial splendor, the city consisted mainly of classic communist concrete block monstrosities that lacked even the care and maintenance of suburban Moscow. Children ran about everywhere, apparently doing chores rather than playing, and in actual fact everyone seemed rather young. I was barely thirty years old at that point, but felt immediately old. The effects of crime, poverty, civil war, and an array of diseases had largely wiped out an entire generation.

Nothing a few million $100 micro-loans couldn't sort out.

I was familiar with extreme poverty in Latin America. The people living in the rubbish dumps around Mexico City must be some of the least fortunate citizens of this planet. The slums of Peru are not to be taken lightly. Nomadic Mongolian herders have a tough life. But my first impression of African poverty was one of simple astonishment. The road quality alone suggested that bombs had ceased dropping only days before my arrival. Documentaries and sporadic TV news segments had not prepared me for the reality of what lay ahead.

We arrived at the World Relief guesthouse. It was disappointing. It required no fewer than ten keys to get through the various security doors and gates, which at least provided some protection between me and the outside world, but it was in a squalid, poorly lit area up a dubious-looking alley. The rooms did have sheets and air conditioning, which was a pleasant surprise. The kitchen was home to a number of cockroaches. In short, it was perhaps the worst accommodation I had ever had to live in for anything more than an emergency night in a bus terminal hotel on some long-distance South American journey. Above all, two disturbing thoughts occupied my mind from the outset:

How can I get out of this?

Jessica is not going to be at all happy.

Maybe I should have done a little more research before accepting this assignment. The place had presumably changed significantly since Bob Dylan's vacation here, and I made a mental note to avoid Dylan's travel suggestions henceforth.

Over the next week I had a series of meetings, read a series of reports, and began to get some idea of the assignment at hand at the MFI, which was called Fondo de Credito Comunitario (FCC). The mess was far worse than had been described to me by the World Relief head office in the USA. Local management appeared sluggish and unmotivated. I had read reports from two members of the U.S.-based World Relief team. One was written by David Park,* director of MFI development at World Relief head office. David had spent some time in Mozambique. He was aware of, and concerned about, some of the problems at FCC, and he was highly intelligent. Park was a rare example of a professional, well-qualified practitioner with a passion for poverty reduction and an understanding of the tension between poverty reduction and profitability. The reports were not up to date, but both pointed to similar problems:

1. Appalling productivity and inefficiency spanned the entire organization, not simply when compared to other regions, or other African MFIs, but even within Mozambique.
2. Senior management in the USA and Mozambique were aware of the problems but had failed to take corrective action.
3. The entire institution was running dangerously low on funds and would shortly face tough decisions regarding future operations. It was already closing a number of branches.
4. There were a number of references to client savings being used for other purposes. At the time I did not realize the magnitude of this, but one haunting comment in a presentation from 2003 did make me realize that this was a total restructuring of a bank whose future was by no means certain: "Until FCC is able to tap into additional funding sources, FCC will need to use cash from client savings to maintain the continued growth of its operations."[1]

This was a delicate point and stated explicitly in a report provided by World Relief head office. Not all MFIs are allowed to take savings from the general public—this is usually a regulated activity. Anyone can risk their own capital making loans to people, although this is somewhat regulated, particularly in terms of usury laws and unfair practices toward borrowers. But to actually take deposits from the general public is much more strictly regulated, and for good reason. If a rogue operator takes savings from the poor and fails to return them, not only is this theft from the poor, but it can also have consequences for the broader banking sector. The moment the public loses faith in the ability of financial institutions to return their savings, their natural tendency is to remove money as soon as possible, a so-called "run on the bank" that would instigate the collapse itself.

Governments rightly fear such panics and thus regulate who can take deposits from the general public. This is not a fear unique to poor African countries: consider the recent collapse of Northern Rock in England during the financial crisis, with queues of people withdrawing their funds from the bank, and the government doing everything it could to persuade the rest that their savings were safe. Or of Argentines queuing up for days outside banks in 2001.

I needed to find out if FCC was allowed to take savings, and what it was doing with these deposits.

Some MFIs are essentially full-fledged banks. They take savings from some customers and make loans to other customers, just like Deutsche Bank, Bank of America, or Barclays Bank in developed countries. This is so-called "financial intermediation." Such MFIs make money by charging interest to borrowers at greater rates than the interest they pay to savers. However, in exchange for this margin, the bank has to manage its reserves in such a way that it can return funds to the savers when required. Even if the bank's borrowers do not repay the funds to the bank, the bank is still legally obliged to return savings to the general public, and thus the bank must assume and manage this risk. And naturally, the banks have to cover their operating costs from this margin. This is a risky business and is regulated. All commercial retail banks across the planet operate on variants of this model: take money from A, lend to B, manage the risk and operating costs efficiently, and hope to make a profit in the meantime.

Most MFIs do not engage in such financial intermediation, since most are not allowed to take deposits. Their business model is fairly simple: get money from investors, usually incurring some interest charge, lend money to clients at a higher interest rate, cover all administration costs and costs of defaults of borrowers who do not repay. What is left over is profit for the MFI and its owners.

However, there is a third type of MFI that is somewhere between these two extremes, and here occurs much of the abuse: MFIs that make loans and take some savings, known as *forced guarantees*, or *forced savings*.

The MFIs argue that they require clients to provide some form of collateral by way of a forced savings deposit to secure loans. They argue that such forced savings serve two main purposes. First, they encourage a savings culture among the poor. Particularly in regions where the poor do not have reliable institutions for securely holding their savings, this is a genuine service to the poor. The second purpose, of far greater importance to the MFI, is that in the event of a client defaulting on a loan, the bank can dip into these savings to cover a portion of the loss. This reduces the risk to the MFI of lending to the poor, so by capturing such savings the bank is better able to offer reasonably priced loans to more poor people.

The problem surrounds what these MFIs do with these savings captured from their clients. In theory, the funds are deposited in a separate bank account, usually at a reliable commercial bank. The MFI merely acts as an agent, administering the collection of the forced savings while depositing them elsewhere. Since the savings do not actually belong to the MFI, it is reasonable that they be deposited in a separate bank. If the MFI collapses, the clients' savings remain intact.

There are two main ways MFIs use to manipulate this system. First, they can quietly use the client savings for other activities. This may involve lending the savings to other clients, who in turn are obliged to make forced deposits in an ever-growing pyramid. Or the MFI may simply use the savings to cover its own operating costs. Both strategies are usually prohibited for MFIs not licensed to engage in full financial intermediation, but local regulators are often not sophisticated enough to detect this or fail to enforce the rules.

The second way MFIs can manipulate this system to their advantage is by blurring the difference between forced savings and voluntary savings.

The MFI is able to justify capturing forced savings as a guarantee, but then may also discreetly capture voluntary savings, which are deposited into the same account. Capturing voluntary savings is often prohibited, while forced savings may be permitted, but regulators may not be able to distinguish between the two in practice. A dollar deposited voluntarily looks remarkably similar to a dollar deposited as a condition to obtain a loan.

An MFI needs capital to grow, and its capital often comes from foreign investors. Funding is laborious to obtain, competition for such funds is fierce, and they are not free—the MFI must pay handsomely for such capital. The funds provided by foreign investors may also be denominated in foreign currencies, so the MFI also assumes exchange rate risk as well.

Thus MFIs have a great incentive to capture funds locally, and client savings are an obvious choice. The MFI can pay paltry interest on these savings, avoid any foreign exchange risk, and avoid dealing with the *relative* sophistication of the microfinance funds. Far easier, and very tempting.

The final issue with forced savings is that they effectively increase the cost of the loan to the client, but in a hidden fashion that MFIs rarely publish and investors turn a blind eye to: forced savings are not simply advantageous to the MFI, but also to its investors. If the MFI can confiscate client savings in the event of a default, this cushion makes the MFI less risky, and thus more likely to repay the loans to the investors. Everyone is a winner ... except the poor client.

Voluntary savings are a different matter—the forgotten half of microfinance. The poor often have no means to guard their savings, and they often live in insecure environments where robbery is common. A means to save anonymously is also useful—a woman may not want her husband or extended family to know she has $500 under the mattress to save up for her child's education for fear of it being used less wisely. But equally, she should have access to these funds and assurance that they are protected by the institution, which appeared not to be the case in Mozambique. At group loan repayments a woman would occasionally rummage around in her bra and proudly whip out some small crumpled bills, usually not even a single dollar. How dare an institution use such funds inappropriately?

Almost from the outset, it appeared that something untoward might be occurring at FCC—with the knowledge of the parent company, World Relief.

*"Until FCC is able to tap into additional funding sources, FCC will need to use cash from client savings to maintain the continued growth of its operations."* The comment haunted me. An unproductive, inefficient MFI with a stagnating or shrinking portfolio of clients would naturally find it hard to attract external funds. Perhaps World Relief had limited additional funding to pump into FCC, and it was not an institution that large investors would consider an attractive investment opportunity. This could quickly become a spiral—more dipping into savings would further reduce the likelihood of anyone wishing to invest in FCC, requiring further dipping into savings. Client savings, however obtained, and whether forced or voluntary, could be used to meet such a shortfall, but whether this was legal or not was a valid question. And even if legal, it was no free lunch: the cash *may* be accessible for use in other areas, but the obligation of the MFI to return these funds to clients did not vanish.

In a sense such practices can be likened to Bernie Madoff's recent Ponzi scheme. For as long as new investors keep pouring money in, there are funds available to return to early investors, and no one need know quite how the underlying portfolio is doing for as long as the dance maintains its momentum. The more recent investors are locked in for some period before they can extract their profits, by which point more investors have been found. This is remarkably similar to a microfinance loan—clients cannot withdraw their savings until they have fully repaid their loans, by which point new clients have provided new savings to be available for such withdrawals. Everything is fine if the portfolio grows exponentially and the operating costs are manageable. But when it became clear that Madoff's underlying investments were not doing so well, or when an MFI has high operating costs and a declining, poor-quality portfolio, the problem rapidly becomes critical. The tide goes out, and those without bathing costumes are left standing in their full glory.

Thus the need for tight regulation of any institution that takes money from the general public, regulation that is often absent in developing countries. Even the SEC in America missed Bernie Madoff for some years. How much easier for a bank in a forgotten African nation recovering from a bloody civil war and years of communism? The recent financial crisis has led to endless reams of new regulations in countries already tightly regulated—how much more is this true in countries such as Mozambique?

It was strange that so many alarm bells were ringing so shortly after my arrival. I certainly should have done better due diligence on Mozambique before agreeing to help fix a bank there.

The quality of FCC's management was lacking, to say the least. The CEO had few of the required skills to run an MFI. He had been there about three years and had failed to learn Portuguese. He was paid handsomely, was saving up to do an MBA, and was embarking on the time-consuming graduate school application processes. His attendance in the office was limited, and he could only communicate with the few staff members who happened to speak English. Within a few months I was fluent in *portuñol*—a hybrid of Portuguese and Spanish understandable to speakers of both. The CEO had a fairly new Toyota Land Cruiser mainly for his personal use provided by FCC—a classic sign of poor allocation of assets in any institution. The rest of the bank had one or two vehicles with which to manage all their operations. Head office was stuffed with staff with little apparent function, another classic sign of poor management, although also a symptom of strict labor controls preventing the firing of staff.

Not surprisingly, FCC was losing clients monthly. With this CEO at the helm, FCC had lost just over half its clients. And a final slap in the face: its loans were not competitively priced, but instead were some of the most expensive in Mozambique.

FCC was legally part of World Relief Mozambique, which was run by a Zimbabwean called Sam Grottis.* Although World Relief USA, based in Baltimore, provided most of the capital and technical assistance to FCC, it had to implement changes through the legal owner, World Relief Mozambique, a fact that provided Mr. Grottis with disproportionate power. I met him a couple of times. He was apparently a former businessman and freedom fighter in Rhodesia who had experienced a Road to Damascus moment of enlightenment and had become a fundamentalist Christian—a prerequisite for senior managerial positions at World Relief. Eventually Grottis met a suitable westerner who evidenced mutual agreement regarding the imminent end of the world and promptly made him CEO of FCC. All meetings had to begin and end with prayers, and it transpired that there was a long list of additional rules that I had not been informed of when we discussed the job, some of which would haunt us over the next year.

After two months in Mozambique I had discovered an MFI in an utter mess. My conversations with the Baltimore office suggested that they agreed with this analysis and had tried to instigate change. The U.S. staff were surprisingly well qualified and competent people, but they were unable to do much from the other side of the planet. Their reports were accurate, professional, and terrifying, and yet entirely ignored locally as far as I could see. I was, in a sense, their "man in Maputo." I was hired by them to be permanently on-site to push through the urgent changes that were required in the absence of competent local management. But, as usual, politics interfered with this process.

I returned to Europe for Christmas, failing to take into account the temperature difference, and arrived at Heathrow Airport at 6 a.m. dressed in shorts, T-shirt, and flip-flops with temperatures hovering around 0 degrees Celsius, and armed with an oversized giraffe as a gift for my nieces, all of which did not add to my credibility as I took the Tube to central London.

I delicately explained to Jessica that Maputo was no paradise. As an anthropologist she was curious to go to Africa, and I had arranged a reasonable apartment in a safe area of town with a view over the ocean and near some relatively safe restaurants and a gym. There was no way to hide the rubbish that veneered the city or repair the runway for her arrival, but I was relying on the fact that a pleasant house would cover up many of these anomalies. We arrived, and she was shocked. The house was fine but had almost no furniture. Still, we settled in as best we could. Jessica began working for the parent company, World Relief Mozambique, initially as a volunteer and subsequently as a paid employee. I continued uncovering unpleasant truths about FCC.

A recurring problem that inefficient, badly managed MFIs suffer is a failing IT system. Microfinance is actually quite complex when one considers the sheer number of transactions combined with poor infrastructure and limited IT skills. An MFI with 5,000 clients may appear small, but if these clients are making savings, interest, and loan repayments weekly, this could amount to 15,000 transactions per week. Add loan disbursements and savings withdrawals and a few other transactions, and this could quickly approach 1 million transactions a year. FCC was mainly using paper-based systems to record them, particularly in the branches. Its processes were prone to error and time-consuming, and consolidation of data was slow and inaccurate and led senior management to have relatively little idea of what was going on in their branches, some of which were two days' drive away.

Dedicated software programs were readily available to manage this complexity, and I was asked to find one, install it across the branches, train all the staff, and write all the training manuals. All with a generous budget of $10,000. The absolute cheapest software I could find was called M2, a legend in the budget-microfinance software world that we had installed in Mexico. We could obtain this for perhaps $7,000. However, I had no idea how to do this on my own. I needed a techie to do the complex bits involving databases. Only one sprang to mind: someone who might be willing to come to such a country, work for free in horrible conditions, sleep in our apartment and eat cheap local food, and do so for the sheer excitement alone.

"José Manuel, would you like to do another M2 installation?"

"No, thank you, not the most fun. Maybe if I get paid a lot?"

"No, it will be unpaid, and you'll have to stay in our apartment. The food is not great, it's dangerous, but it's in Mozambique. That's in Africa. Ever fancied coming to Africa?"

At that point in his career the opportunity for a twenty-three-year-old Chiapanecan to go to Africa seemed like a winning national lottery ticket. José Manuel would realize that this was possibly a once-in-a-lifetime opportunity and extremely good for his CV. His experience was limited to a few small assignments at obscure MFIs in a relatively unheard-of region of Mexico, and only one foreign journey in his life.

"Yes, I'll come. No need to pay me, I'll sleep anywhere. I will do it, you tell me when."

"Listen, I just about have budget for your flights, but if you agree, you cannot let me down. Are you sure about this? It'll be hard work—this is not like Mexico, this is a poor part of Africa. It's poorer than anything you've ever seen. The electricity is bad, there is infrequent Internet, it's hot, there are diseases and thieves everywhere, it's not safe, and the food is not great. Are you sure you want to do this?"

"Yes, one question. Do they have this animal in Africa, it's big, I don't think it can fly, it has a big long nose and big ears?"

"Hmmmmm, I think you're referring to the elephant. Yes, they have them here. Yes, you will see them. And no, they don't fly. Any other questions?"

"No. I am coming, I always wanted to see this animal. Cool, I'll await your email with tickets and dates, and then I'll see you in Africa."

Over the next month I worked closely with the head of IT at FCC, a remarkably talented Mozambican called Loko. He had done the best job possible with the ancient software World Relief had provided him and had managed to obtain a reasonable degree of control of the data arriving from the field. Most of the data would arrive in endless reports that Loko would type into the computers manually to produce some semblance of order. He would travel quite extensively to the field, since he was single-handedly in charge of everything, all data, all accounting information, all training, and all reports. To help make ends meet he was also a chicken farmer and would occasionally arrive in the office with a bag full of chickens and discreetly distribute them to staff, who knew Loko's chickens were good quality and fairly priced. The fact that FCC doubled as a covert chicken outlet gave some indication of managerial control in the company.

Loko was delighted with the prospect of new, professional software that was designed for an MFI, and he did as much research as possible to prepare for José Manuel's arrival. Perhaps most exciting for him was the opportunity to learn more advanced computer and database skills from a professional microfinance IT expert. One thing beyond doubt was that many of the Mozambicans were so eager to learn new skills. They listened attentively, and, although starting from a low knowledge base, they absorbed information like sponges.

We were aware of the core configuration decisions we would need to make, so we gathered all the data required to start the actual installation process. This included technical details about loan products offered by FCC, interest calculation methods, lending policies, and the accounting structure. We decided that the Chokwe branch would be the ideal pilot.

Its portfolio was performing well, and its staff were competent and honest. There had been almost no fraud, the branch faced limited competition from other MFIs, and the accountant, who would be in charge of the IT once installed, was a reliable, honest, and friendly guy with whom to work. We didn't know at the time that he was also the village priest.

As ideal as it sounded as a site for the pilot project, there were some disadvantages with Chokwe.

It is a miserable village a few hundred miles from Maputo by bad roads, just out of reach to return to Maputo for weekends. It was inland and thus lacked the marginal benefit of being by the coast. Other FCC branches were located in areas with amazing beaches, world-class scuba-diving nearby, great seafood—and Chokwe was most certainly not one of them.

Chokwe is unbelievably hot. It is a farming community, thus full of animals and the bugs that accompany them, including endless malarial mosquitoes. It had one restaurant, with only two items on the menu—tough, chewy beef or third-rate chicken. The world-famous Limpopo Hotel, considered a one-star venue in any other country, was beyond our budget. Thus we would sleep in the office on bunk beds with mosquito nets but without air conditioning. Outside the office there was precisely nothing to do. We would work seven days a week, awaking each morning when it was simply too hot to sleep any longer. We had one bathroom, alas lacking running water, which we would share with the entire office and the occasional client. The electricity supply was sporadic, which made a computer-based system of organizing an entire branch all the more challenging, and needless to say there was no Internet. Cellphone coverage was relatively acceptable, so at least we could communicate with the outside world.

We decided to strip the branch to the walls and redesign every stage of the process of making and managing a loan from scratch. This way we could ensure that the process was well integrated with the new software and also reduce the reams of paper that were currently used. Badly managed MFIs tend to undergo endless patching, involving frustrating duplication of effort and wasted time and paper. In such cases it is usually easier to start over rather than attempt to repair something complex, inefficient, laborious, and above all, broken.

When José Manuel arrived, we drove down to Johannesburg airport to collect him, getting robbed only once on the way, and thus qualifying it as a relatively successful trip. Attempting to cross the Mozambican border at night with possibly the first Mexican ever to set foot on Mozambican soil inevitably required a few bribes. Crossing into Mozambique is always a strange experience, particularly at night. There are no streetlights, and only the faint glimmers of campfires used for cooking interrupt the darkness. As we approached Maputo, where there is sufficient light to just make out people and their houses, José Manuel was shocked.

"That's a house? People live in that?"

"Dude, this is the capital. You should see where we're going in a few days—you'll think of Maputo as Hollywood."

During the first few days we introduced José Manuel to the staff. The CEO appeared relatively uninterested in him, or in the work he was going to do, but managed to spare him half an hour, during which time he convinced José Manuel that there was absolutely no point in a second meeting. At least this lack of interest suggested that he would be unlikely to interfere with our work.

We loaded up the car with all the essentials for potentially a month in Chokwe. This included drinking water, food, batteries, sheets, books, in fact most of the essentials required to sustain life, as few were available locally. As we weaved our way through some of the poorest areas of Africa on the northern outskirts of Maputo, I am not sure who was more surprised, the Mozambicans catching sight of a small Mexican squeezed in between five-gallon bottles of water in the back of the car, or José Manuel witnessing some of the most brutal urban poverty on earth. We arrived in Chokwe a full day's driving later, unpacked our bags, and introduced José Manuel to the team. They greeted him with utter amazement. Everyone had heard of the Mexican, and the Chokwe office was honored that they had been selected to be the pilot branch. We celebrated by going to the restaurant. José Manuel ordered shrimp.

"Shrimp no have."

"I'll have the *samosas*."

"*Samosas* no have."

"OK, perhaps the fish."

"Fish no have."

"What do you have?" he asked, somewhat desperately.

"Meat, chicken."

I intervened in this exchange: "Get used to it, these are the only two things they have. Forget the menu, it's yet another waste of paper. I usually do chicken for lunch, then beef for dinner one day, and then swap the next, to get some variety in. The beer is good, though."

Chicken and beer it was. Welcome to Chokwe.

We began analyzing all the paperwork. It is a fairly standard process of working out what core information is actually required, discarding the rest, and identifying the data that enters the IT system. José Manuel focused on the technical side, installing the software, cleaning the computers, setting up security and other configurations, and getting ready for the laborious task of manual data entry. Mabasso, the accountant-priest, was extremely diligent. He was perhaps sixty years old, and over the next few weeks developed a taste for hardcore techno music, which José Manuel found essential for any IT installation. Mabasso compared the Mozambican music he was familiar with to this new genre: "With normal music there is a feeling that the song will eventually end, but with this music it sounds like it will go on forever."

We spent three miserable weeks in Chokwe. Although the staff were delightful, there was absolutely nothing to do outside of the branch. There was a hippopotamus a few miles away apparently, a mildly interesting trip, but upon arrival said animal failed to emerge that day. We would sleep for eight hours and work for sixteen hours. When the electricity was down, we would plan stages in Excel and within M2 on paper, and then be prepared to seize every minute of electricity when service returned.

I always visit clients when working in the field, and I accompanied the loan officers on a trip to a local market in a village called Lionde, perhaps fifteen hair-raising minutes away by motorbike. The market was not particularly crowded, and it appeared that most people present were selling rather than buying. It was here that I met Mozambique's only vendor of ski clothing, a gentleman who had obtained a microloan to buy some remarkably cheap and high-quality clothes in South Africa, without considering the likely demand for such items in sweltering, arid Mozambique.

A serious threat faces such regions. For as much as microfinance could potentially assist the supply side of a market, demand evaporates as clients migrate to the cities. If demand is falling, why increase supply? Obviously sub-Saharan ski clothing vendors will always face challenges, but so do most products in rural areas suffering the common phenomenon of urban migration.

Even when a client sells a fast-moving product, such as food, usually in a competitive market, one can rapidly calculate that the net benefit of a loan to the business will be marginal, when interest, costs, depletion, robbery, and other factors are all considered. It is not hard to quickly make some projections and estimate a client's capacity to repay a loan, but many MFIs don't bother with such complex and time-consuming activities. Often it may be more beneficial for the bank and the client to not extend a loan, to wish the client the best of luck, and walk away. But such an attitude is contrary to the selling practices of loan officers, whose salaries depend largely on the volume of loans they can disburse, and the MFI's need to grow as rapidly as possible.

Back in the office we began the tedious process of data entry from the paper-based system to the new, flashy computer-based system. The excitement in the office was electrifying. We would convert all the static data, such as names and addresses, first, and then, over the following days, the savings and loan data, which changed each day as interest was applied. It was a tough, time-consuming job and we needed all the help we could get:

"Mabasso, we are not going to be able to enter this data in two days, so can you help us? It will be late nights for all of us."

"Please, of course I will help, you have traveled a very long distance to help us, even from Mexico. I will do anything I can, and also I will learn as I do it, and we will listen to music together."

"OK, we are going to basically close the bank on Friday at lunch. Not many clients do transactions on Friday afternoon anyway, and those that do, we will process on Monday. This way we know nothing will change from Friday afternoon to Monday morning, but over this weekend, we have to enter in everything, so on Monday, when we open the branch, we will be operating the entire branch on M2. So we need you to work all Friday, maybe until late, and then also on Saturday, maybe until late."

There was no point asking Mabasso to help us on Sunday, since that would be against the rules of World Relief, and also, as the village priest, he would have other duties.

"Oh, I am so excited. Monday will be a great day. A historic day. I am proud to be part of this."

On Friday, Mabasso turned up bright and early, and we began manually entering in all the savings data, in an exercise of such tedium that watching paint dry becomes an attractive alternative. Over the entire weekend one person would dig up the information for a client, check that it was valid, and call it out to the data entry person. All we needed were the current balances, but if the paper-based records were incorrect, these had to be corrected first. Then everything had to be verified manually by a third person. Absolutely the most boring activity possible in microfinance, and yet requiring complete concentration. It is little surprise that so many of these exercises fail.

That Friday evening, after a brutal day, José Manuel had finally lost his patience in the restaurant. We were clearly the best clients in the entire town, and yet the range of options had not extended beyond two. José Manuel demanded a third option, and the owner had begrudgingly agreed. They would get some *rissois*, a prawn pastry thing, abundant across the country, absent in Chokwe, but representing a 50 percent increase in the length of the current menu. Saturday was spent calling out names, telephone numbers, addresses, dates of birth, and so on, and typing these into endless forms. Perhaps a tenth of all clients were born on January 1, which we found coincidental. However, checking the paper records confirmed this was in fact their date of birth. How could so many women synchronize the day upon which they give birth? We consulted Mabasso.

"No, it's not their actual birthday, but the government made everyone pick a birthday in order to have an ID number, and then you cannot change it, so they try to first think of the year. That is usually fairly accurate, then many pick January 1, because that makes them older."

Once we had completed the data migration over the weekend and the branch was effectively operating by computer, we had to train Mabasso in the core activities. As long as he could do a loan disbursement and repayment and a savings deposit and withdrawal, we were 95 percent there, since these transactions account for 95 percent of the activities of a branch. The more advanced transactions (such as changing a configuration, adjusting security settings, rescheduling a loan) were less urgent. We designed a PowerPoint to explain everything to Mabasso that we could use in the subsequent branches. We would also train a couple of other staff, so if Mabasso was ill they could at least perform the core transactions in his absence.

We ran the branch ourselves on Monday, checking that everything was working smoothly, and polishing the training course. Mabasso watched us closely, but the formal training started the following day. That evening we had been presented with the *rissois* at the restaurant. They were excellent, and we ordered a second portion. The novelty of a third option was akin to discovering water on Mars. We had a fun evening with the locals, stayed a while extra for an additional beer, and went to lengths to congratulate the chef.

The next day we wired up the projector and I began the training. Five minutes into the presentation, as I was explaining how to enter a phone number of a client, I felt a deeply unsettling rumble in my stomach. I suddenly announced, "José Manuel will now explain how to enter an address," and ran out of the office. Fortunately the bathroom was free, and thus ensued a particularly brutal few minutes that inevitably happen from time to time when eating seafood in inland villages in developing countries. The absence of running water, or any ventilation, combined with searing heat, left the bathroom in an unpleasant, pungent state. I hobbled outside, filled a bucket, and returned to flush the lavatory as best I could. Had there been an "out of order" sign available, I would have placed it firmly on the bathroom door for the protection of others. I returned to the training room, and José Manuel shouted, "Now Hugh will do the basic loan application form," and he promptly bolted from the training room. I heard the bathroom door slam shut.

I could feel a time bomb in my gut, and began counting the seconds until José Manuel would return. After ten minutes I was re-assessing my options. There was a secluded spot round the back of the office, which I thought might be my only alternative to dramatically disgracing myself here in the Chokwe office in front of the village priest. José Manuel limped in just as I was about to announce a premature coffee break, so

I bolted. By now the bathroom, hardly palatial at the best of times, appeared in a particularly sorry state, and the smell was now permeating the main office.

Thus José Manuel and I trained the Chokwe branch in ten minute relays until lunch, by which point the contents of our digestive systems were reduced to nothing and the entire branch smelled so badly that staff had left the office and were standing aimlessly on the front porch. We ate no lunch. The staff were charmingly polite and understanding and did not comment on the state of the bathroom, or the rather unorthodox teaching method, and seemed to absorb the information well. That evening, we reverted to chicken.

We sat with Mabasso over the next few days to make sure he had learned the basics and attended to some minor details relating to the paperwork and accounting. He seemed to have mastered the basics, and he had a decent training manual in case he had doubts. FCC's Chokwe branch was now running, in real time, on M2. We were ready to depart. A car from FCC Maputo would come and collect us.

"Mabasso, listen, we're leaving later today, so if you have any questions, if you're uncertain about anything, you must ask us now. Because when we leave, we are not coming back, and you will be 100 percent in charge of everything."

"Yes. For example, when we lend money to the client, I know how to do this. But sometimes the opposite happens, and then what do we do?"

"You mean savings?"

"Yes, that's the word. I think we need to do that as well in the computer, no?"

"Mabasso, you remember last weekend when you sat there reading out all those savings balances, and then we typed them all in one by one and then printed them all out and you checked each one? And in the training, we spent a whole day on withdrawals, deposits, and transfers, remember? Yes, of course it does savings."

"Ah yes, now I remember, yes, it does savings. But in the paper files, say we want to contact a client. We need to know where the client is, and maybe if the client has a telephone, but if we use the computer, we won't know this information, so what do we do?"

"What! Mabasso, we entered in every single address and telephone number. Don't you remember when we found all those clients who had neither and we had to search for them in the original files? And all that training on the client data entry, surely you remember that? It took a whole morning to teach you—have you forgotten that already?"

"Ah yes, you are right, now I remember. But what happens if a client does not pay one day? How does the computer know this is a naughty client?"

I was nervous. Three weeks of our lives wasted, eating dodgy chicken and chewy beef, being sick, bored, miserable, hot, the hippopotamus never appearing, countless mosquito bites, and it appeared our number one man had learned little. He was the best IT guy in all the branches, and I was not feeling too optimistic about the others.

"Yes, Mabasso, the computer does know about naughty clients. There is a whole report all about who has been naughty, when, by how much, who the loan officer is, remember? Look, we are leaving today. You have the training manual—read it. You are going to have to deal with this, but I can't handle any more silly questions. Yes, yes, yes, the computer does these things. It does everything that you used to do before. It does everything."

"OK, no worries, I understand. Please, you relax, everything is fine here."

Alas, this was far from accurate. The car arrived, and we were delighted to finally see the back of Chokwe. We discussed our plans for the evening ahead in Maputo—sushi, then catching some live music.

I had delivered a presentation at IESE Business School that Christmas about microfinance, and each year I would take a summer intern from the MBA to some exotic location. A few of my consulting clients would ask me for volunteers, and ambitious MBAs are a particularly good source of free or cheap labor, so I would usually mention a few opportunities on behalf of my clients, and interested candidates from IESE or a partner business school would contact the clients directly. However, I had described the "deep end" of microfinance, working with me in Mozambique, on the off-chance someone would apply.

A Slovakian named Petr applied. Unbeknownst to him, he was the only one to apply for the Mozambique posting, and was a classic hard-working overachiever. He was an ideal candidate for McKinsey, or some investment bank, but for some bizarre reason he had applied to join me. He sent me an impressive CV and a detailed cover letter, and "after careful consideration," he appeared "the most suitable candidate." The biggest problem we were facing was in the northernmost branch, Vilanculos. It was so far away that no one had ever been there except Loko, and he had no immediate desire to return. The anomaly about this region was that there was a direct flight from Johannesburg to Vilanculos, so we arranged for Petr to fly there.

Alas, as we were arranging the final details of his assignment, I was still in Chokwe without Internet, and for some reason cellphones were not working but SMS messages were. Thus the finer details of his internship were arranged by text message:

"Go direct Vilanculos. Pick up @ airport, take 2 office, fix office, bus 2 Maputo."

"How fix office? No MF experience. What need 2 do?"

"No idea, take laptop, try 2 fix, if not pos, close branch, u decide, call when arrive."

Vilanculos was debatably in the "north," and World Relief was wondering whether to close it altogether along with the rest of the northern operations. It was a small, inefficient, unproductive branch in a sparsely populated area a long way away. Petr was our last hope.

Shortly after the Chokwe team had returned to Maputo I received a call from Petr.

"Hi Hugh, Petr here, all well. I've arrived, one of the staff picked me up from the airport and gave me a SIM card. Anyway, I have some questions."

We chatted about the flight and how he was feeling, but Petr promptly got to the point.

"Listen, I don't speak much Portuguese, but I asked this guy about where the office is, and he points to this little hut, where I am calling from now, but I don't think this can be the office, it's just a hut. Then I ask him about my hotel, and he also points to this hut. I don't understand what he says, and this hut doesn't even have electricity. Can you speak to him? I'll pass you over."

I chatted with the guy, and asked him to pass the phone back to Petr.

"Petr, the hut *is* the office, and underneath the table is a mat, which is your bed. There might not be electricity, but he is going to show you where you can get some, to charge your laptop battery, it's only five minutes away, so maybe you can do some work there in the evenings and charge the battery, and during the day you just use your laptop when you need it. Frankly, most of the work is probably paper-based. Trying to work out what's going on, you won't need electricity for that, you just need to find out what the situation is, see if you can fix it. If you can, great, if not, work out what you need to do to close the branch, and close it. Then, when you've done one or the other, take a bus to Maputo and call me. It is about two days to get here."

"You're kidding. I've never worked in microfinance, I don't speak Portuguese, how can I fix this?"

"I don't know, but right now, you are the second-best-qualified person in the country available to do this, and if you can't do it, fine, close it. But I have five other branches down here to worry about, there is no way I can also do Vilanculos. Just do your best, and see what happens. I told you this was the *deep end of microfinance*. You're in it now, put those MBA skills to good use. And go to the market and get some candles, a flashlight, and some batteries. It'll be dark soon."

He had wanted something extreme, and we had certainly checked that box on his list.

Over the next few weeks we finalized the training programs for the other branches and José Manuel finished his work. We had a small amount left over from the budget for the software installation and used this to send him on a scuba-diving course. Despite the abundance of problems in Mozambique, the diving is absolutely world-class, with four-meter-wide manta rays and whale sharks in abundance. On his way to Johannesburg we took him through Kruger National Park to see the legendary elephant, with which he was thoroughly impressed. The journey had boosted his CV beyond recognition: his intercontinental professional experience was unparalleled among his peers. To install professional banking software in Mozambique, on such a limited budget, and fairly successfully, was itself an extraordinary accomplishment. We would work together on numerous projects over the following years, and this was certainly not his last trip to Africa.

Petr returned to Maputo, and, contrary to expectations, he had actually worked out what was going on in Vilanculos, had fixed the branch to the extent possible, and had prepared the way for Loko to go up there and install M2. This was another miraculous piece of work. For the remaining weeks of his internship I asked him to focus on looking at the overall financial viability of FCC and to prepare a presentation for senior management and World Relief Mozambique. Alas, the consequences of his findings would wreak havoc, as his direct presentation style touched a little close to the bone regarding what was actually going on at FCC and who was involved.

In the meantime, a member of staff had returned from Chokwe with data from the branch, and the CEO-apparent called me in distress.

"Hugh, you need to go to Chokwe now—it's collapsed! I've just seen the reports, the portfolio is collapsing. Get back there now and fix it."

It was just early enough in the day for me to make it to Chokwe before office closing, so I pointed the car north and called Jessica to explain I would be gone until at least tomorrow. Damn, Chokwe was our pilot. If it failed, I no longer had José Manuel to resolve technical issues, and the other branches would be at least as challenging, if not multiple times worse. What could possibly have gone wrong? I drove to Chokwe, parked the car, and approached the branch manager. "What's wrong? Apparently the branch has collapsed."

"Hello, Hugh. I thought you were in Maputo now? Er, no, the branch has not collapsed, nothing much has changed since you were here. Ask Mabasso, perhaps he knows more—I am going home now."

I went into Mabasso's office unannounced. He was reading with his feet on the desk, which he promptly removed when I appeared. "Hugh, how lovely to see you. I hope you are well? I thought you were not coming back to Chokwe?"

"Well, Mabasso, I am fine, and I hope you are, and yes, I was not planning on returning, particularly so soon. However, the CEO informs me the branch has collapsed, and sent me here. What is happening?"

"Well, I don't know what he is saying. Everything is fine here, just as usual. We still have those few naughty clients, but otherwise there is nothing new."

It was hard to know where to start. There was no point asking head office. I approached the computer. It was off. I turned it on and waited the customary ten minutes for it to load and open M2. Where to begin? There was a report called All Transactions, which might shed some light on the issue. I printed it out for the period since we had left. One piece of paper emerged from the printer. I waited.

"Mabasso, the printer is out of paper. Do you have some more?"

"No, printer has much paper. I filled it a couple of weeks ago and haven't used it since—have a look." He was right, there was ample paper. The All Transactions report could easily have been twenty pages, and yet only one had emerged. I examined it. The column headings of the report were clearly printed, but there were no transactions listed beneath them. I returned to the computer and viewed the report on the screen. There were no transactions—not a single one since we had left.

"Mabasso, you haven't entered a single transaction since we left, have you?"

"No."

"Why not?"

"Because just before you left you told me that the computer does everything."

It was true. I had uttered these words. This was my fault. There was no alternative. I slowly walked back to the main office and began gathering all the paper receipts of all the transactions done over the intervening weeks and began entering them in individually. The reports from Chokwe had correctly suggested to the Maputo office that the branch was suffering, since they had appeared to show that no loan payments had been made. One by one, I began. The staff left for the evening. I eventually went to the restaurant. Chicken and a beer. I would save the beef for tomorrow.

# 4

# Another Mozambican Civil War

I had suggested to Petr that he hold little back in his presentation, as long as he could support what he said. He thus delivered a devastatingly critical report, with full supporting evidence. It largely revolved around a lack of leadership, poor decision-making, inappropriate capturing and use of savings, unsophisticated window dressing of the accounts, and incompetence at head office. It complemented my previous meetings with management, which had spelled out some simple truths:

1. Using client savings to cover operating expenses was not only illegal, but pointless, since it merely postponed the inevitable meltdown.
2. The branches were actually covering their operating costs. The drain emerged from one source—the Maputo office. Solving the "Maputo problem" was relatively straightforward, but this would mean slashing headcount and the salaries of those involved in decision-making. Client savings were not being raided to support the field operations but just the head office.
3. World Relief Mozambique was urging FCC to apportion certain unnecessary expenses at head office to the branches in a purely accounting sense. This simply shifted expenses from head office to the branches, but World Relief Mozambique was keen to push ahead with this accounting game regardless.

Unwillingness to cut expenses in an MFI is a common phenomenon caused by a very simple fact: those responsible for cost-cutting decisions and most likely to be fired or have their salaries reduced are usually those who are best paid. They will happily slash the field staff salaries, and it is entirely normal for well-paid senior managers to earn twenty or thirty times the salaries of field staff. I was not immune from this criticism—I was probably getting paid fifteen times more than junior staff, but at least I was trying to improve things, and I was getting paid substantially less than the highest salaries.

Suggestions to actually solve the underlying problems were brushed aside. World Relief Baltimore's reports had consistently pointed out the excessive cost base of Maputo. The most basic accounting revealed the same. Maputo had the fewest clients but the most cars. Despite contributing relatively little and barely visiting the branches, the CEO was earning $5,000 per month excluding "extras," a sum sufficient to cover the salaries of perhaps half of all FCC's junior, local staff. He had announced his departure from FCC, and there was no obvious candidate to replace him. Sam Grottis had asked me why I had not applied for the job, and I politely explained that life was too short to waste much more time at FCC. By simply failing to replace the CEO, FCC would save a substantial sum each month and perhaps improve the organization. But another problem was brewing.

Jessica and I had recently been robbed again. The thieves had managed to sneak undetected past two security guards in the reception area of our building. This was an act of considerable stealth, since the reception was so small that three or four people could barely fit in it simultaneously. The thieves had not only evaded detection passing through this narrow opening, but had entered with heavy metal-cutting equipment, taken the elevator to the ninth floor, removed our door from the wall, robbed us fairly extensively, and then left the building with their booty and equipment, once again evading detection from our ever-vigilant security guards. Was this possibly an inside job?

It was pure luck that no one had been in the house. I had been traveling to the field, which quite possibly the thieves would have known, but Jessica would normally have been in the house at the time of the robbery. She had fortunately decided to visit a friend after work that day. Friends had warned us about robberies in Maputo. We would be safe for the first six months or so, but then the problems would start, once the thieves responsible for our block had learned our habits. One thief had showed off how much he knew of our habits only a few weeks before the robbery. He was attempting to sell me some useless tourist trinkets, for the hundredth time.

"Not now, I am busy. I have to go to work, but one of these days I will buy some *batiks* from you. Just stop hassling me now, or I'll buy them elsewhere," I explained.

"No worry. If easier, I come to your office at lunch. You buy then?"

"No, don't come to my office. There's no rush, just stop pestering me."

"Kenneth Kaunda 1174."

I stopped in my tracks. This was my office address. How could this guy, whose entire life seemed to revolve around selling useless junk in the immediate vicinity of our house, know my office address on the other side of Maputo?

"How do you know where I work?"

"MK21 HRT, number your car, no?"

That was easier to understand; he could easily have seen me driving in and out of our garage, even through the garage was secure and underground. But to recall such data so easily?

"Falenda, your maid, she arrive 8:30 a.m., leave 4:00 p.m. Avenida gym, where your girlfriend go, she called Jessica, she work World Relief, but in Summerschield office."

Damn, this was entirely accurate. Needless to say, I didn't buy any *batiks*, but I realized that these guys were not quite as inert as they appeared. They sat around all day outside our apartment block observing, learning, waiting.

Another landmark event took place shortly before I had a meeting with Sam Grottis, which although mildly amusing was in fact the epitome of all that was wrong with FCC. An extremely senior and qualified global microfinance expert from one of the large microfinance networks had accidentally hit "Reply to All" on a blanket email that included FCC, as well as others active in the Mozambican microfinance sector. The bulk of the email discussed her view of FCC:

FCC is one of our partners. Frankly, it has not been an easy relationship. We have experienced a number of challenges working with FCC— some of them are systemic, methodological, staff related, but the significant factor is a lack of strong leadership. They [World Relief] are not prepared to deal with the real problem. Staff will participate in the various trainings/workshops/ one [on] one coaching but we find there is little follow through and constant staff turnover. Currently they are experiencing a major problem with their portfolio in the north (I believe they are closing some of their offices etc.). Our project director in the field would be able to share many stories....

This mail was sent at 9:13 a.m. on May 25. At 2:59 p.m. the same day a follow-up email was sent: "Please disregard my earlier email that you may have received earlier today. It was sent out by mistake and should be disregarded."

Personally I thought her email was absolutely concise and immediately sent a private email congratulating her for succinctly hitting the nail on the head. However, three days later, the (now former) CEO sent an email to everyone on the email list:

Concerning the email sent by xxxx [name redacted] on May 25th, I want you all to know that FCC/World Relief considers this as a very serious matter. Though I will be unable to follow up this issue myself since Friday was my last day with FCC/World Relief, do know that this defamatory communication has been taken up by the FCC Board Chairman and that xxxx will be called to account for its assertions. All communications on this matter from this time forward should be referred to the FCC Board Chairman [Sam Grottis].

Romans 8:31

(I looked up the Biblical reference: "What, then, shall we say in response to these things? If God is for us, who can be against us?")

I wrote to Sam Grottis urging restraint, particularly in light of the comments made being entirely accurate, and he suggested we discuss it in person. FCC was the laughingstock of the Mozambican microfinance sector. On top of all the other issues related to FCC, I wanted to discuss security issues with him following the robbery, but he brought up yet another one. "I was very sorry to hear you and Jessica were robbed, and the most important thing is that no one was hurt. But it was drawn to my attention that you both live in the same apartment."

"Of course we do. The other lucky thing was that I had the computer, projector, and all my scuba-diving kit with me in Maxixe, so they didn't get the only items of real worth that we have in Mozambique."

"Yes, well, the problem is that you are not married."

"What are you talking about? Who cares if we are married? The issues at stake are the robbery and the gradual collapse of FCC. Where we live and our marital status has nothing to do with either."

"Well, we're a Christian organization. It is not possible for unmarried people to live together."

"Sam, are you aware that half the staff in FCC have endless kids with random people and almost none of them is married? And besides, this has nothing to do with you. Jessica and I have employment contracts with FCC and World Relief, and this is an irrelevant detail."

"I disagree. This is in direct contravention of the local rules and regulations of all staff in Mozambique...."

"Which we were never presented with, nor asked about, and the time to have discussed this would have been *before* we moved from Mexico to Mozambique, not a year later."

"We are meant to be setting an example to the local staff, and this is in direct contravention of Biblical teaching."

"Look, Sam, if you want to set a good example to the 'locals,' why don't we start by not ruining FCC and failing to address obvious problems with simple solutions that have been known about for years? Second, I am unaware of any Biblical passage that says that people can't live together before they are married. Third, let's face it—you guys pick and choose the bits of the Bible you wish to take literally and those you don't. The Bible specifically says women shouldn't speak in church, but that one's been relaxed. Besides the fact that I find the argument flawed, I would rather you did not poke your nose into our private affairs."

Not entirely surprisingly, this did not help my case at FCC. We had become gradually aware of the fundamentalist nature of the organization. In Baltimore, the staff seemed honest, kind, and competent, and religion rarely came up in conversation. Meanwhile the parking lot of their church in Mozambique was littered with the most expensive cars in the country, and the congregation was skewed toward foreigners convinced they were saving the world from poverty and on the fast track to heaven. FCC was certainly not contributing to saving the world from poverty.

This looked like an attempt to pressure me: I was unwilling to apply for the CEO position; I did not hesitate to point out flaws in the organization including to the head office in the USA; and my presence was fast becoming a liability to World Relief Mozambique.

The bottom line was that FCC branch operations were now automated and functioning relatively smoothly, and were even generating a small profit each month. They did suffer from high client desertion and charged the poor some of the highest interest rates in the country. Meanwhile, head office was hemorrhaging money each month while contributing little. We had pulled off one of the most amazing IT projects in microfinance history, under brutal conditions and with a minimal budget. FCC now actually had some potential, for the first time ever.

The poor were paying interest rates of approximately 100 percent per year when all costs were considered. Also, there was this slight anomaly about the client savings that kept cropping up. Clients were obliged to deposit 20 percent of their loan amount as savings. However, one did not need to be an accounting genius to observe in the 2004 accounts that a loan portfolio of $663,622 could not warrant total savings of $453,571 unless clients were making deposits in excess of 20 percent, voluntary savings that were prohibited by law.

There is actually no need to revert to confidential documents to examine the activities of FCC. There is a source of data used by the microfinance sector called MIX Market. It is self-reported and unverified and so should be treated with caution. However, to the extent that this is information published by the MFI, it can shed light on certain activities. FCC has even published its audited financial statements.[1] If we look simply at the 2003–2004 accounts available on the MIX Market website,[2] we can see the following (rounding to the nearest $1,000 or 1 percent):

1.  From 2003 to 2004 the average portfolio was approximately $681,000. Interest income was $614,000, which suggests that for

every $1 of outstanding loans, FCC earned $0.90 in interest, that is, its effective interest rate was 90 percent—debatably inconsistent with poverty reduction. The "portfolio yield" statistic supports this observation. Over the period 2003 to 2007, for which there is data available, it fluctuated between 90 percent and 101 percent.

2. The ratio of client deposits to client savings was 68 percent in 2004, rising to 81 percent by 2006, somewhat jeopardizing the suggestion that FCC only captured forced savings of 20 percent from its clients.

3. The MIX Market also reports the ratio of total operating expenses as a percentage of the loan portfolio, which provides a measure of how much it costs to lend a dollar. 2003 had been a particularly poor year, when this figure reached 188 percent. It had thus cost $1.88 in operating expenses for each $1 of loans outstanding. This improved marginally in 2005 to a mere $1.67. It would have been cheaper for World Relief to simply give the poor money rather than embarking on the entire lending façade.

4. Perhaps most damning of all is the farcical nature of the cost per borrower. In 2003 FCC spent, on average, $124 per client, while each client borrowed, on average, a mere $71. By 2005, the year I left FCC, the average loan size had doubled to $141, but costs had increased in proportion, to a stunning $204 per borrower.

5. The auditors BDO Binder & Co. had failed to pick up on the legality, or otherwise, of FCC's savings activities. Conclusion: Be careful even with audited financial accounts.

It was time to confront management. The situation at FCC was spiraling out of control. The extent to which FCC was dipping into the client savings was worsening, and this was entirely inconsistent with the stated mission of FCC to help the poor. FCC urgently needed a cash injection from World Relief Baltimore, if only to plug the gap of client savings. Even closing FCC would require a cash injection. And Baltimore seemed hesitant to do so.

David Park had used data from MIX Market to draw humiliating conclusions about the company.[3] On almost every count, compared to the peer group of other Mozambican MFIs, FCC was performing appallingly.

I updated this report with more recent data, showing demonstrably that the situation had deteriorated yet further. Everyone knew what was happening, but no one wanted to do anything, because their own vested interests were too aligned with the situation perpetuating itself. Even World Relief Baltimore had an incentive to prevent an embarrassing wave of bad publicity. Some excerpts from the report:

**Personnel expense ratio:** The average in Africa was 15 percent; FCC was 33 percent. "FCC spends nearly double that of its nearest peer group on salaries." One year later this had worsened to 42 percent.

**Administrative expense ratio:** The average in Africa was 16 percent; FCC was 26 percent. "FCC spends nearly 50 percent more than that of its nearest peer group on administrative expenses." One year later this had increased to 36 percent.

**Operating self-sufficiency** (an overall ratio of income to expenses): The average in Africa was 105 percent; FCC was 38 percent. "FCC's sustainability lags far behind that of MFIs in all comparable categories." The CEO had claimed in his business plan that FCC would be 100 percent operationally self-sufficient within two years. This was pure fantasy.

**Yield on gross portfolio** (a euphemistic way of saying interest rates): Africa average 40 percent; FCC 74 percent. "FCC leads its peers by a considerable margin in generating revenue on its portfolio." One year later this had increased to over 90 percent.

David Park had not considered FCC's write-off ratio. This is simply the proportion of the portfolio that is written off as uncollectable each year. This had worsened from 7 percent in 2004 to 9 percent in 2005—an astonishing level in a single country over just one year. To write off nearly a tenth of the portfolio in a single year suggests that something is chronically wrong. Over the same period the average within Mozambique actually improved, from 3 percent to 2 percent, which is still on the high side.

In short, FCC was an inefficient, ineffective MFI charging over the odds to the poor while paying handsome salaries to a few lucky individuals, funded by U.S. churchgoers, and with no evident willingness to reform. Any attempt to reform FCC met with resistance. What's more, this information was largely from World Relief head office or publicly available, so there was no way to deny knowledge of it.

I had been looking for a way to put these issues on the table, and in fact I needn't have looked far. Petr presented the results in a meeting that exposed all the main shortcomings at FCC in front of World Relief Baltimore and World Relief Mozambique, backed up with hard evidence, and I openly recorded the entire meeting.[4] Ken Graber,* one of the senior members of the parent company, attended the meeting by telephone. Petr's presentation was masterful and convincing. Sam Grottis was unable to attend but sent instead a mysterious substitute named Steve.

Steve's real purpose became all too clear after the meeting. When he received the minutes of the meeting in which Petr had presented his findings, taken by Jessica, Steve censored them almost beyond recognition. He at least had the integrity to comment, "Please note they were taken by Jessica and edited by me." This was now a formal cover-up. Now was time to launch my formal complaint:

Steve, Thanks for the sanitized minutes, which some of us received in full from Jessica a week ago. I found it interesting to see which parts had been "edited." Indeed, it almost defies the entire point of taking minutes at a meeting: what is the point of attending if the official record is simply your personal opinion of what ought to be stated? This annoys me, as I am sure you are aware, as I attended that meeting to contribute, and yet the end result is a watered-down, hygienic set of notes that not only ignore many valid points, dilute any sense of urgency, but were recorded by me on an MP3 player in front of you, and Ken Graber [World Relief Baltimore] was present on the conference call....

If we look at the points you edited, they have one remarkable thing in common: they are all the negative, or critical points. Thus meetings chaired by you seem to be open only to those who wish to pat one another on the back for good work.

The main sections "edited," (that is, that were censored/omitted) were: Comments about the remaining high overhead costs (principally salaries) at head office, and the use of client savings being an illegal practice with no one accepting clear responsibility. Regarding self-sustainability: [World Relief] Baltimore is ultimately picking up the bill for the poor performance/excessive overhead of FCC, and that the cost management has been achieved with some creative accounting that shifted costs around rather than cutting them. The issue of wide salary discrepancies unrelated to productivity was also "omitted." An entire paragraph from the original minutes was deleted, discussing the rather important issue of competition and fund raising....

I feel that our donors, largely [World Relief] Baltimore, have a right to hear of the reality of the company they have so diligently funded over the last decade.

The omitted items were neither offensive nor untrue, and your omissions are on record to all those who received both copies, and I suggest an explanation would put everyone's minds at rest. If, of course, you dispute the original minutes taken by Jessica we can revert to the original dialogue, which I can send electronically to everyone concerned.

I was, not surprisingly, fired by Sam Grottis a few days later. World Relief Baltimore was in an impossible position. They could hardly disagree with me, but neither could they openly approve of the activities of local World Relief Mozambique management. They were also in a corner. There was little point pursuing them through the legal system in Mozambique, which moves at glacial speeds. I visited an employment lawyer, who confirmed that their activities did appear to violate banking regulations and local employment law, but who suggested that a better approach might be to simply present the evidence to the Central Bank of Mozambique, which I did in an hour-long meeting. What action did the Central Bank take? Precisely none, but bank officials seemed vaguely curious to learn how an MFI worked—even though FCC was not the best example. Did World Relief Baltimore intervene? Dream on.

David Park and at least one other senior member of the team left World Relief in 2005. By 2007 Ken Graber had also left. In late 2007 FCC finally closed, to be replaced by a new MFI that arose from the ashes, the ironically named Africa Works. According to MIX Market 2010,[5] since opening, this new MFI's portfolio had stagnated, actually a marginally healthier trajectory than FCC. Return on assets was –4 percent, return on equity was –7 percent, the net profit margin was –11 percent, and the overall portfolio yield, that is, the average amount stumped up by the poor who borrowed from this MFI, was 72 percent, slightly above its peers. I have no idea if it operates legally or not. Its website barely functions. World Relief USA had presumably despaired of FCC and finally decided to sell it off. Guess who bought it? Sam Grottis.

So what could we learn from Mozambique?

First of all, it was incredibly easy for MFIs to cover up their actual operations. This has happened time and time again and led to many of the major scandals of recent years. The regulatory authorities in developing countries are ill equipped to monitor the microfinance sector. The large NGOs and microfinance funds vehemently resist any regulation, declaring that it is contrary to free market principles. MFIs can present a few photographs of poor people to their investors 10,000 miles away, and that is sufficient to ensure the stream of donor funding. Even when the parent companies that are U.S.-based and SEC-regulated discover such activities, there is little incentive to clean up operations. A few individuals can earn generous salaries for minimal work, living in lovely accommodations with local staff attending to their every need, and the actual impact on poverty is minimal.

Nowadays a case such as FCC would barely be considered a scandal. However, the most troubling question in the entire FCC episode was not about the operation of a lone, ineffective MFI. What concerned me most was that World Relief Baltimore seemed unable or unwilling to control this MFI, even while steadily taking funds from their own donors.

Microfinance has two faces. One is that presented to the outside world. In the case of FCC this largely consisted of U.S. church-goers. Here microfinance is presented as miraculous, empowering, dignified, a genuine alternative to traditional aid that taps the abundant entrepreneurial flair that every human being apparently possesses. The second is apparent when viewed close up. The reality is the polar opposite of the PR: client desertion; interest rates so high no reasonable entrepreneur could make any genuine profit and repay the loan; massive inefficiency; and zero evidence of any widespread impact on poverty. As long as the MFI sends out occasional newsletters with supporting photographs, the money flows back. If someone did ever actually come to visit the MFI, there were always some isolated cases of successful clients who could be paraded on a "site visit."

It was time for a change. I had tired of Mozambique. The scuba diving was great, but I was disappointed with the entire experience. Somehow I had assumed that a Christian organization such as World Relief would perform slightly better and be more ethical than other MFIs: I thought they would treat clients and staff more fairly and charge lower interest rates; and I was shocked to see how they used clients' savings, money that did not actually belong to them. When confronted with a genuine internal crisis, I believed that they would be a little more pro-active in addressing the issues. Indeed, I would have expected the focus on salaries and nice cars to be less intensive at a Christian institution, not more. Staff turnover was high, as was the client dropout rate—both of which I would have expected to be better in an apparently "ethical" MFI.

Their website clearly states: "World Relief pledges prayerful and efficient stewardship of every donation."[6] Perhaps most fundamentally, the concept of stewardship of resources is a Biblical concept. It even gets its own parable in the Bible, and I assumed that above all, World Relief would take this seriously and at least try to do the best possible with the resources entrusted to them.

On almost every count my assumptions were wrong.

World Relief had been an interesting error, but I would later learn it was not typical of all religious microcredit organizations. I worked for another large Christian microfinance network some years later and found the precise opposite—an effective, ethical group of institutions, charging reasonable interest rates, treating staff and clients with dignity, with good client retention and a clear mission.

The moral of the story: Don't judge a book by its cover. The problems I had discovered in Mozambique were unique to the institution, not the religion. But what next?

We had been in Latin America. Africa had been an eye-opener. How about returning to Europe?

Jobs in microfinance abounded everywhere. The sector was becoming cool, attracting media attention as a revolutionary new development tool. Celebrities were beginning to latch on to microfinance, and new funds were popping up weekly. A friend from Argentina who worked at Oxfam Novib in Holland introduced me to a new microfinance fund called Triple Jump, which promptly offered me a job. Perhaps if I worked for a fund I would be less exposed to these frauds and would actually be able to play a constructive role by helping the fund direct capital to effective, beneficial MFIs. It was apparent that the funds had a limited idea of what was happening in the field, and most of the people I had met who worked at funds had almost no microfinance experience, so I could surely contribute there.

We moved to Holland and I took the job. It was well paid and based in a country with limited crime and reliable electricity. I didn't need to speak Dutch, and I had recently proposed to Jessica, who is Dutch, and Holland would be a far easier country in which to arrange a wedding.

Thus we arrived in Amsterdam, optimistic that this would be the dawn of a new era of work in microfinance—one in which corruption would be minimal and the impact would be genuinely positive.

Oh, how naïve I was back then.

# 5

# The "Developed" World

We first flew to London and packed up our apartment, then moved to the Netherlands. I hadn't lived in England for years, many of my friends had left, and I felt oddly like a tourist in my city of birth.

Holland has an immigration bureaucracy that's complex even for EU residents—moving to Mozambique is a doddle in comparison. Most problems catch you in a circuitous, disorienting paradox: "You need X to get Y, and Y to get Z, but you can't get Z without X." In Mozambique you just paid $50 and X, Y, and Z mysteriously ceased to matter.

While this exercise in repetitive head-banging was in full swing, I began work at Triple Jump on September 1, 2006. It had a pleasant startup feel about it—no furniture in the office and only a few staff. My first projects involved buying sofas, plants, and office supplies. There were few other occupants in our building, and one of them had kindly installed a table-tennis table in one of the empty offices on our floor.

We rented an apartment just across from the offices of DOEN, one of the original founders of Triple Jump and a leading light in Dutch development finance. The group would eventually distance themselves from Triple Jump, but over the years we got to know them quite well. The Triple Jump office involved a fifteen-minute bicycle ride mostly through a park, and initially I had few international travel obligations. It was a pleasing start to a new chapter.

Triple Jump had been the brainchild of Mark van Doesburgh* and Eelco Mol.* They had both previously worked at Oxfam Novib managing a dedicated microfinance fund. ASN Bank had also established a fund with Oxfam Novib focused on larger investments in more mature institutions, and it was also managed by Mark and Eelco.

A third company, called NOTS (Not One The Same—whatever that means), also wanted to start yet another microfinance fund, and Mark and Eelco came up with the cunning plan of setting up a separate, for-profit, private limited company to manage all these funds under one roof. They would have the same capital under management but could reap the benefits of private shareholdings. It was essentially a privatization. Oxfam Novib's money came predominantly from the Dutch government, ASN Bank's funds from pensioners and savers, and NOTS' capital mainly from high-net-worth individuals. The funds were then channeled through a private company, Triple Jump.

DOEN is an investment fund that obtains its funding from the Dutch Postcode Lottery and has been active in some of the most original and cutting-edge investments in the broad field of development for decades. It was an early investor in microfinance, via the Triodos-DOEN fund—a fund managed by the genuinely decent bank and microfinance fund manager Triodos Bank.

DOEN also had invested in the ProCredit group, one of the pioneers of commercial microfinance, and had made reasonable returns on its investments. ProCredit was moving out of microfinance in favor of financing the tier of entrepreneurs larger than the typical standard micro-entrepreneurs.[1] DOEN had initially planned to be a shareholder in Triple Jump but had scaled back to funding only Triple Jump Advisory Services (TJAS). DOEN was also an early donor, lender, or investor in Kiva, MyC4, and Calvert Foundation, facts that will become relevant shortly.

Mark, the CEO of Triple Jump, is a nice enough guy when you meet him—a little shy, but amiable and open. His microfinance experience was minimal, since he had never actually worked in an MFI, but he tried to get good people who could plug this rather obvious gap. One such person was Eelco, who was nudged aside from the joint managing director's role by a new kid on the block, Steven Evers.* I had not met Steven before signing the formal employment contract, and we didn't see eye-to-eye from the outset.

Eelco had extensive microfinance experience, particularly in Latin America, and was extremely well connected with people in the sector. He had lived in Africa, had traveled extensively, spoke fluent Spanish, and above all was a pleasant, honest, hard-working guy who inspired the colleagues around him.

Many of the staff were taken from Oxfam Novib in the Hague. This was part of the deal—Oxfam Novib couldn't simply fire people when they handed their microfinance portfolio to a private company, and although some of these staff were not necessarily that interested in microfinance, they were offered little alternative other than to move to Triple Jump in Amsterdam. This influx was a mixed bag. Most of the original Oxfam Novib transfers eventually left Triple Jump.

My main colleague was Lukas Wellen.* He was originally director of TJAS, with me as "senior consultant," until he dared to irritate Steven Evers and got fired as director and rehired the following Monday as a senior consultant. We were thus without a director, something that suited Steven well, since he could then assume total control over our two-man department.

Lukas had excellent microfinance experience, in Russia and Vietnam, and with some of the best institutions in the sector, and he and I accounted for the bulk of actual microfinance field experience in Triple Jump at that point. Lukas is a tad eccentric. He fluctuates from being so vague and nebulous that one wonders if the topic of conversation has in fact shifted entirely; at other times he is as sharp as any mind in the sector and it's worth hanging on to his every word. He sat on the boards of some MFIs and was an expert in governance and internal control in particular, but he had very broad, field-based microfinance experience. His main weakness, and his undoing at Triple Jump, was that he was consistently honest. He would openly disagree with management, would dare to complain, and would point out obvious flaws. Lukas and I immediately became friends as well as colleagues.

Within a year or so, Lukas and I were already discussing ways to leave Triple Jump. I eventually managed nearly two years and Lukas squeezed in a third before setting up a very successful mobile-phone banking company in Kenya. The main problems we perceived were petty politics and incompetence at senior management level, which drove us up the wall. We would return from complex missions to MFIs to discover that management appeared more concerned with putting expenses in alphabetical order than with the health of their investment.

Lukas and I were the only staff of TJAS, which was meant to be a company independent of the main investment company, but in practice did little other than fix the dodgy investments that Triple Jump fund management had stumbled into. Although we had most of the actual field experience of microfinance in the company, we were not involved in the investment selection process, which would invariably result in some rookie bounding into a flawed investment based on minimal due diligence, and us then having to fix a problem that should have been detected at the outset. Our independence from the fund management arm of Triple Jump vanished entirely when Lukas was demoted and Steven Evers became the de facto boss of our department.[2]

At this point it's worth briefly reviewing how a microfinance fund actually works, since they collectively dominate much of the microfinance sector as gatekeepers of the capital and bear significant responsibility for the mess that has ensued.

The first stage in setting up a fund is to concoct a mission statement. Given that most funds invest in the same MFIs, there is not a huge amount of difference between them, but each fund makes subtly different claims. For example, here is Triple Jump's current mission statement:

Triple Jump's mission is to contribute to the **sustainable development** of emerging market economies by facilitating investment in **micro and small enterprises**. Triple Jump seeks to support the expansion of **viable** microfinance institutions in all three stages of their development (emerging, expanding and mature) by providing capital and advisory services. Our objective is to work towards effective **social impact** in emerging markets by harnessing **entrepreneurial spirit**. We focus on MFIs which are committed to: 1) **Reducing poverty** in their society 2) Reaching **low-income and vulnerable groups**, particularly **women** 3) Respecting society and the **environment** 4) Achieving maximum efficiency, financial **sustainability and outreach**.[3] (emphasis added)

This is fairly standard stuff. It hits all the key buzz terms that donors and investors love: *women, poverty reduction, sustainability, social impact, entrepreneurial spirit. Environment* was largely ignored until quite recently, when it too became a buzz word and was quietly added. This is what investors want to see. BlueOrchard, another large European fund, is a little more concise: "BlueOrchard's mission is to **empower** the poor world-wide and improve their quality of life by promoting **income-generating** activities through private investments in microfinance [emphasis added]."[4]

Most funds are explicit about how they reduce poverty by harnessing some form of innovation. Mentioning women is always beneficial, slipping in some comments about the environment will get the Greens on board, and words like *empowerment* are practically obligatory. For example: "Triple Jump reaches half a million micro entrepreneurs, of which over 75 per cent are women."[5] Who knows if this is true or not— no supporting evidence is provided, but given that much microfinance is directed entirely to consumption and not to any entrepreneurial activity whatsoever, this is a bold statement. Funds rarely (if ever) discuss how much of their portfolio is actually directed toward consumption—*every* client is apparently an entrepreneur.

Most funds focus predominantly on lending money to MFIs (that is, on *debt*), but some are venturing into *equity* nowadays, where higher returns are possible. Debt essentially involves raising a large chunk of money from private individuals, governments, other NGOs, philanthropists, and others who believe the mission statement, and then putting this money in a large pot. The staff of the fund then fly around the world visiting MFIs and attending conferences working out whom to lend this money to. There are often rules stipulating that a certain amount of the fund needs to be invested at any particular point, in order to qualify for favorable tax treatment, rules that vary from country to country. It is therefore a race, a competition, to lend.

The microfinance fund then makes loans to MFIs, for which it earns a management fee, typically in the region of 1 percent to 4 percent; 2 percent is probably typical. As a manager of other people's money, it disburses funds from this pot and all repayments and interest return to this same source. A fund of $100 million may sound large, but when one considers that the management company receives perhaps only $2 million in management fees (from which it has to fund all expenses, flights, staff, offices, conferences, due diligence expenses, and legal costs), it is actually quite a low-margin business. If the typical deal size were $1 million, the fund would have to do 100 investments, and with only $2 million in commission, this is a mere $20,000 per investment from which to meet all fixed overheads.

There are so many microfinance funds nowadays that the competition is fierce, and margins have come down to about 2 percent. The management funds cannot easily negotiate higher rates because there are plenty of other funds that will do the job for 2 percent. Because of high fixed costs, the trick is to reach the largest scale possible. In 2002, a $50 million fund was considered huge. Nowadays a $100 million fund is considered small. To generate profit a fund has to be as large as possible to cover the fixed costs. It therefore must attract investors in any way possible. Alas, it then has to actually do something with the funds raised. The divergence between what the fund tells its investors it will do with their money and what it actually does with their money is the source of most problems.

When a fund lends to MFIs, the upside potential is limited. If they agree to an interest rate of 10 percent, the fund earns only this 10 percent even if the MFI does extremely well and grows into a gigantic institution. This is one of the reasons why funds are increasingly trying to buy shares in MFIs rather than simply lending to them, because share ownership gives them the possibility of earning substantial returns.

The most (in)famous case is the Mexican bank Compartamos, which made over $400 million for its shareholders when it floated an initial public offering (IPO) on the Mexican Stock Exchange, an amazing sum for any microfinance fund. Finding the next Compartamos remains the holy grail of the investment sector. The fact that Compartamos was charging interest of 129 percent[6] per year to the poor is conveniently overlooked by the salivating funds that were presumably more impressed by the return on equity of 57 percent[7] without asking too many questions about the origin of this stellar performance. In fact, noted academic David Roodman recently calculated the total cost of a Compartamos loan to poor Mexican clients at a stunning 195.29 percent when all taxes, fees, and forced savings are considered.[8] This is the highest rate I have ever seen.

Accion, the main investor in Compartamos, saw a $1 million investment grow to $270 million.[9] Its own mission statement reads: "ACCION's mission is to give people the financial tools they need—microloans, business training and other financial services—to improve their lives."[10]

How laudable. And to pocket $269 million in the process must be gratifying. Some $800,000 of the initial $1 million investment was a donation to Accion from USAID,[11] so this was indeed a profitable investment. Most of the profit remained within Accion, which is an NGO, but the CEO of Accion at the time, Maria Otero,* received adequate remuneration for her services: a salary of $245,940, an additional $1,060,292 in 2008,[12] and a further $733,952 in 2009.[13] Just over $2 million in two years could be considered a little generous for someone working to alleviate poverty. Accion's catchphrase on its website is "Helping Millions Help Themselves." It seems that some individuals didn't do too badly either, and the source of this profitability has a fairly obvious origin. The poor pay eye-watering interest rates, and some lucky individuals earn astronomical salaries: is any other conclusion possible? Perhaps "Millions Helping Some of Us Make Millions" would be more appropriate. Since August 2009 Otero has served as U.S. undersecretary of state for democracy and global affairs.

Though an interest rate of 195 percent a year may seem a little steep, it is in fact a bargain according to the chairman of the board of Compartamos, Alvaro Rodríguez. When questioned about the interest rates Compartamos charges during a panel at the 2011 Skoll World Forum he replied, "Our interest rates are about 25 percent lower than the average in the market."[14]

Returning from this minor detour into equity investments to the work of more traditional microfinance funds that focus on debt, some lend in hard currency (usually dollars or euros), while others lend in local currency. Essentially this determines who assumes the foreign exchange risk. The MFI usually pays one way or the other, and this risk is eventually passed on to the poor via higher interest rates.

*Due diligence* is the term applied to the exploratory investigations a fund sometimes does when researching a new potential MFI to lend to.

Much of it is done from air-conditioned offices in Europe and the U.S., involving reading a rating report if one is available, perhaps requesting one if not, sitting on the Internet for a few hours, making a few phone calls, looking at the various sources of publicly available information, and speaking off the record to other funds that may have invested in the same MFI. The funds will sometimes physically visit the MFI, although amazingly this is not true in all cases. Funds are naturally hesitant to admit the proportion of their investments that they have never actually visited. They may well be taking money from pensioners in Europe and investing them in some small MFI in an unfamiliar African nation without ever actually visiting the MFI.

Even when they do make on-site visits, these are often for no more than forty-eight hours: a quick trip to some example clients (carefully selected by the MFI to demonstrate positive impact), taking a few photographs of poor people in microenterprise action shots to put on the website and send to investors, and dinners with the senior management, with perhaps a few cursory questions to key staff. It is easy for an MFI to hide things from funds on such brief visits, particularly when the representative of the fund is a twenty-five-year-old with negligible day-to-day field experience in microfinance. Given the volume of transactions these MFIs generate, finding fraud or any other sort of malfeasance is like the search for a needle in a barn-sized haystack.

The fund has to keep its own investors happy, and it does so in three main ways:

- Reassuring them of the (almost miraculous) social impact their capital is yielding, backed up with photographs and heartwarming stories
- Keeping operating costs to an absolute minimum so as to generate some profit at the end of the year
- Avoiding any defaults, where MFIs fail to repay loans to the fund

The funds know that their own investors are extremely unlikely to actually visit the MFIs, and that if they do it will be part of a lightning trip and the MFI will ensure that the investors see some "appropriate" clients. There exists a catastrophic asymmetry of information between the MFI's knowledge of its clients and the knowledge of fund investors of what is actually happening on the ground. They have to trust the fund, which apparently acts in their best interests.

To keep operating costs as low as possible, two key expenses have to be managed by the fund: travel and salaries. The main reason for travel, other than endless promotional conferences and staying in fancy hotels, is for due diligence trips. These are quick, and if possible, a single fund representative can combine visits to a number of MFIs in neighboring countries. Salaries are generally not that great, and staff are often young and idealistic. Kiva, for example, has about 30 salaried staff but 436 volunteers.[15] Volunteers are abundant in microfinance because it is currently "trendy" (although less so with each passing day).

The third key objective for a fund is to avoid defaults at all costs. Defaults are expensive for three reasons: They have a direct cost of simply losing money that should have been repaid (albeit belonging to the investors, not the fund manager); they are expensive in terms of the management time and expense needed to go to the MFI and try to fix the problem; and they irritate the investors in the fund, who could decide to switch to another fund manager. But with mediocre due diligence it is hard to avoid default risk, so the funding sector has developed some creative methods of doing so. This is where the real problems emerge. This is not an exhaustive list, but simply indicates some of the most pertinent dangers.

First, the more profitable the MFI, the more spare cash it has available for repaying loans to the funds. Profit from an MFI comes from one principal source—the interest rate it charges the poor. Thus, while a fund may claim that its mission is to facilitate "affordable loans to the entrepreneurial poor," it has a direct incentive pulling in the opposite direction: *less* affordable loans result in *more* profitable MFIs, which are *more* likely to repay the fund. The funds may turn a blind eye to, or fail to examine in detail, the actual interest rates charged by the MFIs.

As the mission statements endlessly repeat, loans are apparently directed to micro-enterprises. This is essentially a form of venture capital, and so it is risky. Startup and small businesses are risky by nature, and the goal of the MFI, combined with the desires of the fund, is to reduce risk as much as possible while maintaining decent margins and low operating costs—that is, profit. Analyzing a micro-enterprise is not easy, and it takes time. Analyzing a loan to a salaried person, or a consumption loan to buy a new TV where the bank retains title to the TV in the event of a default, is far easier, just as profitable, and probably less risky. What percentage of so-called microfinance is directed toward such activities, instead of the oft-quoted productive investments? No one really knows, since no one has an incentive to dig deeply into this murky area. Estimates for consumption loans range from 50 percent to 90 percent of all microfinance loans. This is one of the most taboo topics to bring up in microfinance circles, along with the magnitude of child labor working in the underlying micro-enterprises. Mention these issues publicly in a conference and you will not be invited back. The *Harvard Business Review* touched on this in 2007:

> Many heads of microfinance programs now privately acknowledge what John Hatch, the founder of FINCA International (one of the largest microfinance institutions), has said publicly: *90 percent of microloans are used to finance current consumption rather than to fuel enterprise.* Abhijit Banerjee and Esther Duflo, of MIT's Poverty Action Lab, recently evaluated dozens of rigorous studies on the economic lives of the poor, finding that regardless of country or continent, *very little of each additional dollar of disposable income is spent on any form of investment, or even on food and shelter.*[16] (Emphasis added)

John Hatch is one of the most respected members of the entire microfinance community, and he publicly states that perhaps nine out of ten microloans are for pure consumption. Is this how microfinance is presented to the general public? As a glorified credit card?

The second method the microfinance funds adopt to reduce their risk is to work together informally. A few key, safe, and profitable MFIs have investors crawling all over one another to lend to them, while most other MFIs struggle to get a meeting with a fund. Why?

One possible explanation is simply "safety in numbers." Few funds do any meaningful due diligence, and thus the fact that BlueOrchard and Deutsche Bank both invested in Acme microfinance institution signals other funds that Acme must be a decent investment. Besides, if

Acme does default on its loans, no one will blame the fund in question if BlueOrchard and Deutsche Bank were also investors. So the argument goes. BlueOrchard and Deutsche Bank are happy to be followed by other funds, as each new investor provides more fuel for the MFI, solidifying their investment.

There are other, lesser reasons that explain the herd instinct. Staff members rotate rapidly between funds, spreading contacts and investment tips across the investment community. The information of "who invested in which MFI" is mostly publicly available and is discussed in rating reports. And there may be direct collusion between funds. If a fund is about to invest $2 million in an MFI, it is rational for that fund to contact another fund that is considering investing $2 million in another MFI. They agree to each invest $1 million in both MFIs to spread their risk. They still invest $2 million in total, and each has to do only one due diligence visit.

A final explanation of the herd instinct is simply that there is too much capital chasing too few genuinely decent MFIs. The microfinance hype saw an exponential growth in the funds raised from the public, foundations, and governments to invest in microfinance, but there was no comparable explosion in the number of decent MFIs in which to invest. Parallels—such as the trajectory of the dot-com bubble—are almost too hard to resist.

The so-called peer-to-peer organizations (P2Ps) add yet more fuel to this fire, the archetype being Kiva. These organizations attempt to replace the middleman (the fund) and offer a means for capital to flow directly from Mr. Smith in California to Mrs. Ougalougadou in Burkina Faso. This niche sector is discussed later, but in some respects is simply yet another microfinance fund.

Some microfinance fund managers manage multiple funds, often raised from different investors and sometimes including a debt-only fund and an equity fund. This is apparently not subject to potential conflicts of interest—there is no danger of the fund manager making soft, low-priced loans from the debt fund in the hope that it can then acquire shares in the MFI with a separate equity fund. In regulated investment banking this is (supposedly) prevented by Chinese walls. In the microfinance sector there is no such pretense.

I've provided this short outline of a how a fund operates in order to explain the incentives that drive their behavior, since they are well hidden from the public but of critical importance to understanding the crisis in the sector as a whole.

The summary of this entire unregulated mess is this: one cannot assume, a priori, that a microfinance fund is acting in the best interests of either the poor or of those who ultimately provide the capital. They act in *their own* best interests, and these are best served by minimizing operating expenses, investing in the safest MFIs (often the most profitable, that is, those charging high interest rates to the poor), and reassuring their own investors with the occasional newsletter full of reassuring photographs. For as long as the investors keep providing funds, and the poor repay, no one really needs to ask too many more questions. And no one really does.

But when overindebted women in India started committing suicide under the burden of high debts and aggressive collection practices by MFIs, questions began to be asked. When something murky happened with the Norwegian government's investment in Grameen Bank, eyebrows were raised. When a grassroots movement in Nicaragua decided to collectively stop repaying extortionately priced loans to MFIs and brought about the collapse of the entire Nicaraguan microfinance sector, questions were asked. When leading academics and governmental institutions had the courage to stand up and ask for some shred of evidence that microfinance has a measurable impact on poverty reduction, some people did start to listen.

When the annual survey of the microfinance investment sector came out in 2011 (appropriately called *Banana Skins*,[17] and published by an honest, genuinely independent group of experts), summarizing the views and concerns of the entire investment community, it was no coincidence that the principal concern was not political risk or foreign exchange risk, the financial crisis or operational problems, but reputational risk. The report is surprisingly frank in explaining this result:

Until very recently, scarcely a voice was raised against microfinance. It was regarded by governments, by academics and, increasingly, by the wider public as an unalloyed public good ... a lot of people—well-meaning, thoughtful people, who are in or close to the microfinance industry—are now worried that microfinance has taken a wrong turn, that it has drifted away from its original mission, that it has been co-opted (or even corrupted) by the pursuit of size and profitability, that it has become a political plaything etc.[18]

In a previous report in 2009, reputation risk barely received a mention (seventeenth of twenty-four risks ranked), but within two years it had risen to second place. Even the fallout from the financial crisis was brushed aside compared to the risk of consistent criticism of the sector as a poverty reduction tool. Overindebtedness was discussed at length:

> Above all, credit risk is seen to reflect the fast-growing problem of over-indebtedness among millions of microfinance customers: poor people who have accumulated larger debts than they will ever be able to repay, often as a result of pressure from business hungry MFI.... MFIs have brought credit risk upon themselves through their aggressive lending and their desire for growth. This also accounts for the rise in the risk of mission drift (up from No. 19 to No. 9) because of the perception that MFIs are abandoning their commitment to poverty alleviation in favor of financial profit.[19]

Mission drift is the risk of an MFI forgetting its own mission and pursuing purely commercial ends to the detriment of the poor. It is serious and rampant.

Note that this is an industry publication. It succinctly summarized the entire crisis facing the sector, albeit without explaining how this came about. It even quoted one respondent in a particularly disturbing section: "In some cases, I could see that they [clients] reduced their food to save money to repay their debts, or in others, they forced their children to drop out from school to find jobs to earn more income to support the repaying of debts."[20]

This is a major criticism from insiders, and yet the sector largely brushed it aside. How could the funds provided by well-meaning investors have led to accusations of child labor and *increases* in poverty?

In economics, this problem is referred to as the *principal-agent problem*. The principals (pensioners, philanthropists, NGOs, individuals, for-profit investors) hire the agent—a specialized fund—to invest their funds on their behalf. The impoverished end-borrower wants to pay the least possible for a loan, and the ultimate investor in a microfinance debt fund usually makes a negligible return (covering inflation and perhaps 1 or 2 percent more, but that's it). Most of the profit from offering credit to the poor is split between the two intermediaries in the chain: the fund and the MFI. It is therefore ridiculous to ignore the fact that their interests are entirely unaligned with either those of the ultimate investors or the poor. Absent effective regulation of the MFIs and the funds, it is extremely hard for the principal to monitor the actual flow of money and information independently of the agent: the fund and the MFI.

This is not to say that an ethical microfinance fund is not possible. But it does suggest that we cannot assume that all funds are immune from these problems, particularly when such profitable opportunities are sitting on the table ready for the taking.

In "developed" countries such problems are handled by formal regulation (albeit inadequately in light of the recent crises plaguing the financial services sector), but the microfinance sector in both "developed" and "developing" countries remains largely immune from such regulations in practice.

Light is being shed on the dark side of microfinance, and quite possibly those with the most profound questions to answer are not the MFIs that have pumped out $70 billion in loans to the poor, but the funds that channeled the capital. Supporting evidence for this idea was about to emerge.

And so I found myself in Amsterdam, working in a microfinance fund. The work was routine, but I was about to stumble across a situation that involved all these elements: exploitative interest rates, deception of investors, and collusion with other funds. And this time I would take notes, record conversations, document everything, so there could be no doubt at all about what was really going on.

# 6

# Something Not Quite Right in Nigeria

It was another dark, wet evening in Amsterdam. My boss had asked me to visit a prospective client in the center of town who was passing through Amsterdam. Fortunately I had the required waterproof rain trousers to hand and cycled for twenty minutes to a hotel on a canal somewhere downtown. It was a large Nigerian MFI and Mark wanted to do something with them. I didn't know much more. I was to listen to their problems and offer some free "technical assistance" in the hope that on the back of this we could win a deal to lend the MFI some money. Our business model was fairly simple.

I met the CEO, a gentleman named Godwin Ehigiamusoe.* He moaned for a few minutes about his IT systems, which barely functioned. It's the standard moan of many MFIs, a catchall excuse for the entire world's problems—blame it on the computers. It sounded like quite a straightforward case, and I had the team required to fix such problems, so I agreed to put together a proposal. Given that the proposal would be entirely free, in an effort for Triple Jump to secure the opportunity to invest in an MFI its staff clearly knew very little about, the deal was low risk for him.

That was how I first encountered the infamous LAPO.

LAPO stands for Lift Above Poverty Organization, a somewhat ironic title for the MFI I was about to visit. It had been started by Godwin

83

himself, apparently inspired by the good work of Muhammad Yunus and the Grameen Bank in Bangladesh. He said that he wanted to give something back to the people of Nigeria by helping eradicate poverty, a justification I have heard so often that it blurs into one standard patter.

The next day my boss was delighted. It would apparently be a dream to provide money from ASN Bank pensioners and Oxfam Novib (whose main donor was the Dutch government) to this institution. The fact that it had no functioning IT system but nearly 100,000 clients suggested to me that an MFI in utter chaos was not where I would like my pension invested—but my job was to fix the problem and hopefully secure the opportunity for the boss to write them a check with someone else's money and earn a fee in the process. The poor get catapulted out of poverty, we make money, Oxfam Novib and ASN are happy, and everyone's a winner.

I banged out a quick proposal. The CEO had little idea what was wrong with the system, but I knew the IT system they were attempting to use. It was the same system we had used in Mexico and Mozambique, called M2. José Manuel was a master of all things M2, and I had some morbid curiosity to visit Nigeria, reportedly the most chaotic and corrupt country on earth and the polar opposite to the lethargy of Mozambique. The LAPO IT manager sent me some details about the problem, and it was potentially quite technical and would require some assistance from the software provider. The proposal was facilitated by the fact that we had excellent prior experience in fixing precisely this type of problem, and LAPO was a Grameen Foundation USA partner, who knew we were good at making such fixes.

We needed to get various visas and vaccinations, particularly for José Manuel, so I began the tedious process of putting a trip together. Duncan, a journalist I had met previously at a conference in London, had said that he wanted to see something unusual and technology-related in Africa, so I called him.

"Er, Nigeria. The delta region? That's where the kidnaps occur, no?"

It took a little persuading, but he had asked for the deep end of microfinance technology and I was offering precisely that. He could hardly refuse, and thus Duncan also began obtaining visas. I knew the CEO of the company that made M2, Weng Liew,* and it seemed wise to bring him along, since he could fix problems on-site rather than emailing endless queries and software patches back and forth.

"Weng, do you fancy a well-paid trip to visit a client?"

I knew Weng was hard up—sales were down and his usual array of off-site work was poorly paid, so the chance to get in a couple of weeks on-site at top dollar would surely appeal.

"Yes, sure, times are tough—I could do with some more work. Thanks. Who's the client?"

"It's LAPO, Weng, one of your biggest clients. Quick trip down to Nigeria. José Manuel is coming—it'll be fun."

At this point the conversation shifted rather abruptly.

"Oh no, no, I no go visit them. No, no LAPO, no Nigeria. I no like them. Very rude to me. Bad country. No, I go to other country, other client, but not this."

This was a serious problem. This was going to be a tough assignment. José Manuel and I could work out the operational parts of it, but we needed Weng on-site to fix the software in real time. Plus, my boss was positively excited about the entire trip and our opportunity to "solve" a problem for LAPO and be subsequently invited to invest in such a profitable MFI. Things had been going relatively well up to this point, but Weng's refusal could spoil all our plans. Desperate measures were required.

"Weng, I need you on this, and I've done you favors in the past. I got you some good clients, and you'll get well paid. If we pull this off, M2 will gain some attention—you got criticized in the rating report, it specifically mentioned M2, so this is a time to redeem your good name."

"I no care, they say what they want, I no go to Nigeria. Please, any other place, not there, is not good place, not safe, not good for me."

I would later discover why this reluctance to visit LAPO was so particularly strong with Weng, but for now I needed him and had to resort to other methods.

"Weng, I'm doing quite a bit of IT-related stuff now, and if you help me with this, I am sure all of us at Triple Jump will be really happy with your software, and we often meet MFIs looking for new software to buy, and we can always put in a good word for M2. But if this project fails, and we need you to make it succeed, then maybe we won't be able to recommend

M2 to our other clients. Plus you'd be doing me a big favor and will get paid well. Please, Weng, I need you on this one."

This was as close to blackmail and coercion as I cared to get. Weng was a good friend, and he could benefit from this, but there was little doubt LAPO was no friend of his. He was approaching sixty and his appetite for adventure was not at its peak. He would also have to come from the Philippines, involving a few days of economy-class travel, so I could understand his reluctance.

"OK, I do it, just this once, but just for favor, and you pay me good, short trip only."

Thus in early February 2007 we all met in Schiphol airport. José Manuel had arrived from Mexico having obtained his Nigerian visa with the assistance of a not-entirely-genuine yellow fever certificate. Weng had arrived from the Philippines, Duncan from England, and I had hopped on the train fifteen minutes earlier. Duncan had managed to secure the world's only guidebook to Nigeria and was recounting amusing anecdotes and descriptions of what lay in store. I suspected that Duncan was already deeply regretting having signed up for this trip. José Manuel was chatting away with Weng in a language that only IT experts know. Weng seemed calm, given that he was heading directly toward the lion's den. I was rather pleased with the team, everyone got on well, and we had an adventure ahead of us. In actual fact, none of us had any idea of what lay in store.

The first alarm bell upon arriving at Lagos airport was an absence of any bags on the luggage carousel. There must have been a couple of hundred people on the flight, and only twenty bags on the carousel, so we waited diligently. After twenty minutes I approached a member of the airport staff.

"Excuse me, do you know where the bags are? We just arrived from Amsterdam, and our bags are not here. Will they come soon?"

"Sorry, sir, problem with bags. They're not here."

A couple of bags gone astray may be acceptable if not tedious, but had KLM really lost 90 percent of the bags on a direct, nonstop flight? There were some Nigerians collecting bags from a small room adjacent to the main baggage hall, and my new friend saw me inspecting this hive of activity.

"Maybe I help you find your bags, perhaps they're not lost?"

This seemed like an excellent idea, since we needed all the help we could get. I agreed.

"But help you find bags is not my normal job. Normal job is to carry bags for customer. This is extra to my normal job."

My first bribe in Nigeria: $10 seemed to do the trick. I gave our names, and we walked over to the doorway. We waited outside as he vanished through the door, and after perhaps half a minute all of our bags had miraculously appeared. KLM had apparently not sent all the luggage off to Papua New Guinea after all.

We went through customs surprisingly painlessly. LAPO had arranged a driver to meet us and take us to the hotel that evening, and the following day he would drive us to Benin City. For security LAPO had sent me a picture of the driver to assist in identifying him, and I had printed out copies for all the gang. The picture looked ominously like a prison mug shot, but armed with printouts of what appeared to be an excerpt from the Benin City Most Wanted list we turned the corner and were confronted with one of those memorable African moments.

It appeared that most of Lagos had come to greet us. We stepped through the main doors of the airport into almost pitch darkness and faced thousands of jostling, energetic Nigerians screaming and shouting at us with offers of help. Change money. Hotel. Taxi. It appeared that nocturnal illumination had yet to arrive in the city. We stared at the photo in our hands, back at the pandemonium of bouncing heads, back at the photo. Images of searching for a needle in a violently shaking haystack at night filled my mind. It was 10 p.m., and the relative safety of the airport was behind us.

Fortunately Duncan spotted our man. We all double- and triple-checked. Yes, it did seem to be our man. He had a crumpled piece of paper, and as we cautiously approached him it did appear to say something related to LAPO. Utter relief prevailed.

"Hello, sir, I'm your driver. Welcome to Nigeria, we go to hotel. You have money or we change money?"

We needed to change money, so our kind friend escorted us to the unlit car park where we exchanged crisp $20 bills for a wedge of filthy scraps of paper at an unknown exchange rate. My sole focus at this point was upon not dying, so we beat a hasty retreat to the chauffer-driven clunker that would take us to our hotel.

To describe that hotel as the worst I had ever visited would be accurate, had I not already visited the Tziscao youth hostel on the Mexico–Guatemala border. Apparently the Sheraton was full. It was now 11 p.m., and I was in no mood to argue. Clearly our chauffeur had been given money to take us to the Sheraton and saw an opportunity to take us somewhere cheaper and pocket the difference. Never mind—at least no one had died.

At reception he broke yet more bad news to us.

"Sir, hotel very full, not enough beds. We have two rooms, but only two double beds."

He explained this relatively discreetly to me. Things were not going that smoothly. Duncan, a journalist, would surely write something about the entire incident, and Weng was already in a panic and looked miserable. I called over José Manuel, and in Spanish explained, "Dude, they're a bed short. I don't want Duncan or Weng to get nervous or see what a mess this is. Sorry about this, someone's got to share a bed, do you mind? You and I know each other the longest, it's just a few hours, is that okay?"

José Manuel agreed—it was an awkward situation and he was as relieved as any of us to still be alive.

I explained to our guide, "Er, no problem with the bed, he and I will share a bed, no worries," as I pointed to José Manuel.

"Sir, you no understand. Five people, two bed, all share—one bed have two, one bed have three."

There was no way I could keep this from the team. As the apparent mastermind behind this trip, I conceded that I would go in the middle, and we decided that the chauffeur and Duncan would join me, with Weng and José Manuel in the next room. Duncan's surprise was tempered only by his relief at not having yet been mugged; Weng was furious; the driver was delighted with the deal he had struck; José Manuel was laughing; and I was tired. To our two beds we all retired, the driver presumably substantially richer as a result of this unfortunate "mistake."

The next morning we departed as soon as possible, on account of the breakfast being neither edible nor identifiable. The sooner we got out of this hole, onto the road, and eventually to Benin City, the better. We weaved through a few million cars until open highway extended beyond us and Benin City beckoned.

The following five hours were terrifying. It appears that Nigerians have not yet collectively agreed on which side of the road they ought to drive. Burned-out vehicles littered the hard shoulder, some still smoldering. There was no open road, no panoramic view, no wildlife, and a perpetual stream of traffic and people. The highway was divided by concrete slabs in random segments, and our chauffeur would switch from side to side to find the path of least resistance. Articulated trucks would approach us head on, but he would swerve at the last minute to avoid them. The quality of driving was in fact astonishingly high, since we saw no one die during our five-hour journey, something I would have considered mathematically impossible. Conversation was limited. We spent most of the journey convinced we were about to witness a terrible accident, possibly our last. As we approached Benin City Duncan showed us a map. It was a three-road town in the middle of nowhere, according to the guidebook, famous for bronzes and apparently little else. The map was clearly half a century out of date—Benin City is today home to some 3 million people.

We arrived at our hotel—the Royal Randekhi—"paradise on earth" according to its owners. Since it offered separate beds, a pool, and a degree of cleanliness, I was inclined to agree.

This would be our new home for a fortnight. Poor José Manuel had an additional two weeks there after we left, but the security guards were armed to the teeth, barbed wire adorned the entire circumference, and we were at least safe. The food was some of the worst, and most expensive, any of us had experienced, but my biscuit supply could keep us going for only forty-eight hours. After that, porcupine smoothies and vegetarian fish soup would have to suffice.

The next morning we were taken to LAPO Plaza, a gated building off some squalid mud street next to a dangerous-looking market. The building was comparatively well-designed and clean. We were shown to our office, with a rather unusual triangular table to work from, and a bathroom overlooking a children's playground with the sign "please try to flush the toilet." We unpacked and got straight to work.

The IT manager was a gigantic Nigerian called Onyeka, with whom we would all eventually become friends. He looked more like an irritated boxer at first meeting. After the pleasantries Weng had a look through the databases and began: "How many branch you have, please?"

"Now LAPO has sixty-three branches."

Weng seemed puzzled. "Sixty-three branches? All using M2 software?"

"It is as you say."

"But you only bought twenty-eight licenses."

"Oh, sorry. LAPO has twenty-eight branches."

Weng had a sniff through the databases, and saw sixty-three separate files, one per branch as would be expected. This was mainly pirate software. Weng had perhaps sold only 200 or 300 licenses of his software ever, worldwide, and LAPO had apparently stolen 35 already, and according to their aggressive expansion plan were intending to steal one more license a fortnight.

Weng was clearly annoyed, but I pleaded with him to continue working on the condition that I would confront the CEOs of LAPO, Grameen Foundation USA, and Triple Jump to ensure that he would be fully reimbursed for all licenses (which did in fact happen some months later), and Weng reluctantly agreed to continue. This would be a lucrative trip for him, despite the suffering.

The fundamental problem at LAPO was that it was a complete mess. There was little that one could build on. I could not fathom how anyone had ever invested in this MFI. José Manuel and I had spent years cleaning up messes in banks, but LAPO established a new precedent. The extent and depth of problems astonished me. The IT system was completely corrupted, and they had built various additional programs that would directly manipulate and contaminate the data contained within the database, so the actual core data was incorrect. The bank had one main loan product, used the simplest possible lending methodology one could imagine, and yet had managed to destroy any semblance of order. How could an auditor ever sign off on the accounts? How could there be any governance at all? There was even some dispute as to exactly how many branches LAPO had: the sixty-three cited was actually plus or minus five, depending on the day, and eventually two new branches would be discovered that even LAPO itself had forgotten about.

Our job was to fix the IT system, a scope thankfully limited to only one of the gaping holes in the institution, and toward this goal we began the march. The first issue to consider was why the database contained so much nonsense data. The problems seemed to revolve around two issues, both related to interest rates. M2 was apparently calculating the interest on client savings accounts incorrectly. The communication between LAPO and Weng suggested a grave error in M2 that no other M2 client had detected. LAPO paid clients 6 percent per year on their savings balances, which is 0.5 percent per month. However, when LAPO configured M2 accordingly, a client with $100 in savings would end up with marginally more than $106 at the end of the year. This was wrong, according to LAPO.

After one month, a client with a balance of $100 would earn $0.50 in interest. The following month the client would earn slightly more, since the interest was then calculated on a balance of $100.50 rather than the initial $100. The effect of this over an entire year would accumulate, so that the final balance of the savings account would not be $106, but $106.17. This basic law of finance, called *compounding*, had evaded the entire institution.

LAPO's solution to this critical "flaw" in M2, apparently unique to it, was to ask Grameen Foundation USA to help. Weng was well versed in the basic laws of finance and accounting and had been unable to find any problem in M2—because there was no problem. Grameen Foundation sent a consultant over to Nigeria to fix the problem, which he had apparently done.

José Manuel discovered large batches of transactions executed in precisely the same second that "corrected" the savings balances. All such transactions had a mysterious user ID: *transactionkiller*. Users could select a username at will, but we thought this name was unusual. We asked the IT department about this unusual user. "Ah, that is special tool that Grameen Foundation made for us. It makes the problem go away." Grameen Foundation's tool made the problem go away by siphoning money that clients were rightfully owed from their savings accounts. The $106.17 in savings of these poor clients was reduced manually back to $106.

All the savings balances were false. Every single one. This tool was designed by Grameen Foundation USA, not some irresponsible local IT geek; LAPO management was aware of its use; the auditors had approved the accounts; and some of the largest microfinance funds on earth were investing in this institution. The tool had its own button on each desktop to automate the process.

The next problem was that LAPO claimed to be charging clients 3 percent interest per month in interest for 8-month loans, or 24 percent. The *actual* number of weeks was 31—which is not 8 months, but 7.15 months. The interest charged was 24 percent regardless of the fact that the client did not receive the loan for 8 months. Thus the rate was not 3 percent per month, but 3.35 percent per actual month, or 40.26 percent per year. Clients were simply paying more interest on their loans than they should, while receiving less interest than they should on their savings. If 31 weeks was 8 months, LAPO was implying that the year was only 46.5 weeks long, which appeared to be at odds with accepted wisdom.

In addition to this, endless fees and commissions were charged to clients, and they were forced to make a 20 percent cash deposit in order to obtain a loan: more forced savings.

Most institutions using this practice keep the forced savings in a separate account that the bank cannot touch—this money does not belong to the bank but to the clients. Not at LAPO. LAPO would take these savings and promptly lend them back to clients, earning a hefty interest rate in the process and paying the clients peanuts on their savings, not even covering Nigerian inflation. Thus the real value of the clients' savings, even with the token interest payment, would be eroded through time—the poor would get ever so slightly *poorer*.

So, a client requesting a $100 loan would have to deposit $20, which would then be topped up by an additional $80 and lent to the client, with interest calculated on the basis of the original $100.

With a regular mortgage some form of deposit may be asked, but with one critical difference to the LAPO offering. If a house costs $100,000 and the bank insists on a deposit of $20,000, the bank in effect offers a mortgage of $80,000, and the client pays interest on only $80,000. At LAPO the client would pay interest on the full $100,000.

A final blow to the poor clients was the calculation of interest. Anyone with a mortgage is familiar with how interest rates are calculated— interest is paid on the amount outstanding. If one repays a portion of the mortgage, the interest paid on the mortgage goes down accordingly. Not at LAPO. LAPO uses an interest rate calculation method that is fortunately banned in many countries, called a "flat interest rate."[1] The ingenious benefit of charging clients flat interest is that the interest rate is calculated on the original loan amount even while the loan is being repaid. LAPO loans are repaid in 31 equal installments over 31 weeks. Thus, after 15 weeks approximately half the loan has been repaid, but the interest is still calculated at 3 percent per month (which isn't actually a month) of the original loan amount (which they never actually received in the first place due to the forced savings and other fees and commissions deducted from the disbursed amount). In short, the clients were getting entirely fleeced in all ways possible.

Fortunately all of this was clearly explained in the loan contract clients were forced to sign, although most signed with a thumbprint because they couldn't read or write.

Some rating reports of LAPO published by a company called MicroRate had specifically discussed some of these points, including the illegal lending of client savings. MicroRate was surprisingly accurate in its analysis of LAPO, stretching back to 2006, and yet investors had somehow managed to overlook the criticisms raised in their reports.

It quickly became clear to all of us that the entire institution was a mess, and there was no way we could fix it on this trip. All we could hope for was to understand the nature of the problem and devise a plan for a complete overhaul of the entire back office of the bank.

We returned to the Royal Randekhi. As a novel security feature, all items that could possibly be removed from the hotel were clearly labeled in large black letters "STOLEN FROM RANDEKHI HOTEL," including the towels. The hotel was permeated with some foul but fortunately subtle smell of decay. Power cuts were frequent, the Internet didn't work, the restaurant was a disgrace, and the TVs broadcast gibberish at high volume. Every bill for every meal was always incorrect. Fictitious items would be added consistently, and the total price was in excess of the individual items. In 100 percent of cases such "mistakes" were in favor of the hotel.

Every morning I would buy a bottle of water for the day ahead, clearly labeled as ₦25.

"One bottle of water, please."

"That is ₦30."

"No, the sign says ₦25."

"Sorry, that is ₦25."

I would hand over a ₦50 bill, the smallest the moneychangers would give, and await my change.

"Er, my change should be ₦25, not ₦20."

"Sorry, here, correct change."

Every morning the same woman tried the same trick, with the same bottle, the same price dispute, the same disagreement over the change, and would always eventually agree to charge me the fair amount and give me the correct change. After a week I felt obliged to comment.

"Every day I buy a bottle of water from you, every day you try to charge me ₦30 when it is ₦25, every day I correct you, and then every day you try to give me the wrong change. I know the trick. Every time I spot it. You know that I know the trick. Why don't you stop trying to trick me and charge me the correct price and give me the correct change without this argument every morning?"

"You're right, sir, and every day you discover the trick. But if I do this every day for 100 days, one day you might forget, and then I get ₦5 extra."

One had to admire her honesty.

While struggling to make progress at LAPO, we discovered many fascinating things about Nigeria. The 419 Internet Café was close to the hotel and apparently was where many of the notorious Nigerian spam emails originate. The staff explained to us the background of these scams, so-called because they are technically in breach of penal code 419 of Nigerian law. Naming an Internet café after the law your clients intended to break seemed another act of transparency.

On most houses we passed in Benin City was written "House Not For Sale" in large letters painted extremely visibly across the front. I enquired further. I was told, "So when the owner leaves house in the morning he knows that his house will not be sold during the day to new person and then he comes home at night and finds a new family living in his house."

The most edible food we discovered was a huge fish dish in a local restaurant, consisting of precisely one giant fish, alas without cutlery or plates, but world class in terms of taste and suitably spicy. The beer was exceptional and cheap. I was bursting for a pee after one such meal, so excused myself and asked José Manuel to come and rescue me if I wasn't back in five minutes. As I passed the last table before the bathroom someone shouted at me.

"Hey, white boy, come here. I have question for you."

Avoiding the question from a disturbingly large, blinged-up Nigerian and then vanishing into the confined space of a bathroom seemed like a very unwise idea, so I approached him and asked how I could help.

"Where you from, white boy?"

This is always a dangerous question to answer. As he had correctly observed, I was not a local. I could claim Holland, as I did live there and it was unlikely he would speak any Dutch to catch me out. England is usually OK in Africa, but some people dislike us. I could claim South America on account of speaking Spanish most of the time when working with José Manuel. I opted for England.

"Good, that is OK. You not from Holland then?"

I stuck with England.

"Good, that's OK. I don't like Holland, Holland police racist against black man. You know what I do if I meet Holland boy?"

I shook my head. I doubted that it would involve a firm handshake and a chat about Ajax football club.

"I kill them." Roars of laughter swept the immediate vicinity—this was apparently an absolutely side-splittingly funny joke. I feigned a laugh and suggested that I would keep my eyes peeled for Dutch people.

The bathroom experience was terrifying. I had to get back to the relative safety of our group. I left as soon as possible and passed the table of my new Nigerian friend, where the laughter had subsided. As discreetly as the only blond-haired white person within 100 miles can be in the Niger Delta, I attempted to sneak past his table without attracting attention.

"Hey, white boy, I make mistake. You come here."

Maybe it was a joke, or he meant a different country? I had no idea that the Dutch police were racist. I reluctantly approached the table again.

"I say I kill Dutch man if I see him. That's not true. You know what I do with Dutch man if I find him?"

I had no idea, nor little desire to find out. Still unlikely to be the Ajax football club chat.

I shook my head.

"I kidnap him, take him into Delta, and get much money from his company."

"Yes, well, like I said, I'll keep my eyes peeled. If I find one I'll be sure to point out your table. Have a good night." This was no joke—the guy appeared completely serious this time. No one was laughing. Kidnapping expat oil workers in the Niger Delta is a well-established revenue stream, we were clearly foreigners, we were very close to the Delta, and explaining that we didn't work in the oil sector did not seem like a particularly convincing defense.

A shade whiter than usual, I returned to the table and instructed everyone to avoid any mention of Holland under all circumstances. We were at the edge of one of the main kidnapping venues on earth, we had zero security, and kidnapping was apparently the area's second-most-practiced profession after email scams.

I sat down next to Onyeka, and he began to ask me questions about our broader work. He wanted to travel, to see the world, and it appeared our jobs would provide him with such opportunities. However, Nigerians have certain difficulties obtaining visas to travel abroad, and thus Onyeka asked me if I could help him get a visa to leave the country.

"Look, if you get a visa to go to Europe, it is not easy to get a job, and they are really strict on illegal immigrants there. Life would be miserable. You would have to do badly paid, boring work, and you would always fear the police, and you would have no healthcare if you have a problem. It really isn't a good life."

Onyeka then told me his personal story of the last few years. His wife had died of a medical complication, and he was lonely without her and wanted a change, a fresh start. Perhaps he could do jobs similar to ours?

"There's a bunch of people watching this assignment, from Grameen Foundation in America to Oxfam Novib and Triple Jump in Holland, to all the other investors and rating agencies. If we pull this off, it will establish your name as a top IT professional in the microfinance world. You could actually use that to get legal work, where companies directly hire you to help them. There are few good IT people in African microfinance, so there's plenty of work. But do it legally—it really would be better for you."

He actually seemed to agree with me, and we discussed the situation at LAPO. It wasn't technically that difficult, but it involved extensive time in the field, and Onyeka was the only person to be able to roll this out across the sprawling LAPO network. Onyeka saw that fixing LAPO actually served his CV well, and aligning our interests with at least one talented person inside the MFI is critical for any project. We seemed to have our man.

Weng left Nigeria a couple of days later. He decided to fly rather than risk the road of death. We saw him onto the plane, it took off, and then returned for an emergency landing due to "birds." It took off again a few minutes later, and I found out a few days after that Weng had arrived safely home. Our time in Nigeria was coming to an end, and we knew the magnitude of what had to be done. We had enough evidence that a Grameen Foundation consultant had caused a few of the problems. I was confident we could get financing from them. We knew what was wrong and how to fix it, putting us ten steps ahead of Grameen Foundation, which had every interest in getting this resolved. Having already devised the plan, they would presumably rather pay us to return and fix it than attempt it themselves.

The rest of the trip was relatively uneventful. Shortly before I left LAPO, the CEO approached me beaming from ear to ear. "Thank you, very appreciated. Triple Jump agree to give money to LAPO from ASN-Novib fund for investment."

This had absolutely nothing to do with me. How anyone could invest in this institution was utterly beyond me, but I hadn't spoken to the Triple Jump CEO, only to my colleague Lukas to explain the absolute mess we had discovered. How could Triple Jump have invested while I was physically there, on-site, ideally positioned to provide some highly pertinent feedback? Surely this was a mistake.

Alas, it was not, and the stakes were about to get a lot higher. I couldn't believe that even my boss would invest in LAPO without knowing more about it, or at least waiting to speak to his own employee who was actually there. I was wrong. Welcome to the murky world of microfinance due diligence—it is a mythical beast that few have ever seen.

Our internal flight back to Lagos was canceled and we had to go on the road of death again, but we returned to Holland alive if not shaken. Upon arriving at the Triple Jump office the next day the CEO called me to the meeting room immediately to find out how the trip had gone. I explained that LAPO was probably the worst MFI I had ever seen, by a wide margin. He had little idea about microfinance in practice, so there was little point trying to explain the details, other than to say it was a totally dysfunctional, uncontrolled, unmanaged chaos run by people with limited understanding of the absolute basics of finance and charging the poor astonishingly high interest rates.

"We've lent them 750,000 euros. Will they repay it, do you think?"

"Sure. They earn a ton in interest from their clients, and they are desperate to get as many investors as possible, so they will not want a default held against them, but that's not the point. There is no way the poor can grow a business at those interest rates, and the institution is totally out of control. It's not even legal—they don't even know for sure how many branches they have."

"Yeah, that's all interesting, but you reckon they will repay? That's the main thing. And these problems, can you fix them if you go back?"

"Well, yes, but it will take months, possibly a year, and cost a serious amount of money. They'll have to at least get legal software licenses— they owe Weng about $25,000 for stolen licenses—and it will involve a big team of people."

"Cool, OK. Well, you fix it. I just wanted to make sure our investment is safe. Cheers."

The only thing that keeps a microfinance fund manager awake at night is the threat of default. Poverty eradication, client outreach, ethical treatment of clients—these are details to be discussed on the website and made up at the appropriate moment at conferences. Until recently, when reputational risk became a major concern, default was the only thing to worry about. LAPO never defaulted, but it would subsequently put reputational damage firmly on the table.

The endless patter on websites and in conferences about the amazing social impact of microfinance is almost entirely theoretical. Because people repay loans, it must be helping them out of poverty. It was only relatively recently that serious studies about the impact of microfinance on poverty reduction have been made, and the evidence to date is underwhelming. Genuine evidence supporting such claims is surprisingly scarce.

With my boss's words ringing in my ears, I called Grameen Foundation and delicately explained that the situation was a terrible mess, partially caused by their former consultant, but that we knew how to fix it. They cautiously accepted some "understanding" of the situation and were pleased with our work. We had the top microfinance IT experts in the world on our proposed team; we were personal friends of Weng, the CEO of the IT company; and Triple Jump would be willing to finance a third of the trip cost if Grameen Foundation would cover one-third and LAPO the final third; and only once LAPO had purchased M2 licenses.

Grameen Foundation agreed. It would cost them several times as much to fix the problems themselves, and it was questionable whether they had the expertise, which we clearly did. We also discussed the interest rates. This was in March 2007. In July 2007 we would go on the second, larger mission to Benin City. In October 2007 Woody Brewster of Grameen Foundation would be the first person to accurately calculate the actual interest rates at LAPO, at just over 100 percent per year.[2]

Muhammad Yunus was preaching to the world about the evils of extortionate interest rates, and under no circumstances could Grameen Foundation USA admit that it was investing in a chaotic Nigerian MFI that was charging the poor well over 100 percent interest per year.

This had to be kept quiet.

In July five of us returned to LAPO. We hired a charming vegetarian M2 expert from Malawi called Bentry Mkandawire,* one of the finest microfinance consultants I have had the pleasure to work with; Jean Pouit,* who is considered one of the veteran experts in the sector of microfinance IT; his assistant, an energetic American called Laura; and José Manuel. We would stay at the Royal Randekhi again, since it was the best hotel in the entire city—José Manuel had checked out the alternatives during the last trip. The mind boggles as to what the others were like.

We decided to pick one branch, in Benin City itself, and entirely reconstruct the database for it. The LAPO IT department would be with us every minute of the day, taking notes. Gradually they would take over the work, and the intention was that they would be able to replicate our work by the time we left. José Manuel stayed on a couple of extra weeks to guide them through a second and third branch.

Jean was disturbed at the scale of the problem. It appeared that every possible aspect of data and IT in the bank was contaminated. Most computers were infested with viruses. IT skills were minimal. No one seemed to care much. Money went out and more came back, and everything else was detail.

Clients would arrive in large groups of perhaps twenty members. They were herded like cattle into a small room and read the riot act about borrowing, how this would help them out of poverty but they had to repay the loan, guarantee all the other members, deposit a forced saving of 20 percent of the loan amount up front and then more savings each week—and that they would face stern consequences for nonrepayment.

The genius behind LAPO's financing mechanism is not its ability to persuade the likes of Citibank, Standard Chartered Bank, Oxfam Novib, Kiva, and Triple Jump to pump in money without asking questions. Rather it is LAPO's ability to force so many poor people in Nigeria to hand over their meager savings, both at the beginning of a loan and throughout its life; pay them minimal interest on these savings; make it as hard as possible for clients to withdraw their savings; and lend these savings to yet more clients, who in turn would have to deposit their meager savings with LAPO. It is a pyramid scheme of sorts. And LAPO managed to achieve this without a banking license. LAPO has suffered some of the most devastatingly critical rating reports in microfinance history; and yet aid agencies such as Oxfam Novib continue to donate money to it. Not lend—*donate*—despite LAPO being extremely profitable.

I saw no evidence of positive social impact on the poor, nor could I understand how a poor woman borrowing such a small sum for a simple business could pay these interest rates. Indeed, most can't, and the client desertion rate is high. Very few clients continued to a second loan. The ratings repeatedly mentioned terrible client retention, and yet LAPO (and Triple Jump) seemed unconcerned about this. MFIs usually strive to retain clients as long as possible, and client desertion is a serious concern. Not at LAPO.

I began to understand that LAPO was operating according to an entirely new, innovative MFI model: perhaps LAPO did not intend to retain clients. There were 150 million Nigerians and very little microfinance. For LAPO to retain clients, it would have to drastically reduce its interest rates if clients were to have a fighting chance of building their businesses—and that would jeopardize the extraordinary profitability that attracted investors. But with such abundant demand for loans from first-time borrowers, LAPO had no need to retain clients. If they wanted a second loan, fine; if not, simply lend to a new client at the same high interest rates.

This is hard to prove, but some evidence supports this premise. According to the 2007 MicroRate rating report of LAPO,[3] the average *first* loan amount at LAPO and the average loan amount across the entire organization were relatively similar: $218 versus $256. If the average balance of *all* clients is fairly similar to the average balance of *new* clients, there are only two conclusions possible: either the vast majority of LAPO's clients are new, or they never graduate to larger loans. Given LAPO's rapid growth, high interest rates, and high desertion rates, which is more likely?

It was on our second trip, when we spent most of our time in the branches away from the supervision of LAPO senior management, that we were able to uncover the true interest rates LAPO was charging. It is not as simple as one may believe to calculate an interest rate in such an organization. It is not possible, for example, to look only at loans—the impact of forced savings has to be taken into consideration. The easiest way to calculate an interest rate is to put oneself into the shoes of a client and consider every cash flow that takes place. In LAPO's case these were broadly as follows:

1. A client walks into the office and has to pay various application fees and make a forced deposit of 20 percent of the amount requested.
2. A few days later the client receives the loan amount.
3. For 31 weeks the client has to make 31 equal payments.
    a. Capital repayments—simply the total loan amount divided by 31 weeks.
    b. Interest payments—total interest is 24 percent of the original

loan amount divided into 31 equal repayments. "Flat" interest and the loan period is not actually 8 months but 31 weeks, which is closer to 7 months, to the detriment of the client and benefit of LAPO.

c.   Weekly forced savings. These are eventually returned to the client, but at each weekly payment this is a negative cash flow for the client.

4.   Once the loan is fully repaid, the client may be able to recover her savings, which have accumulated over the life of the loan, and earn a token amount of interest that will not have even covered inflation.

Using all these cash flows, it is easy to calculate the overall cost of the loan to the typical LAPO client. As the loan balance declines each week with repayments, and the savings balance grows each week with forced savings, for approximately 7 of the 31 weeks of the loan the client has a higher savings balance than loan outstanding. For nearly a quarter of the life of the loan it is LAPO who owes the client money, not vice versa, and yet the client continues paying interest every week on the original full loan amount.

Estimates of the interest rates charged by LAPO range quite widely, usually depending on who performs the calculation and what their relationship to LAPO is. Grameen Foundation USA tends to understate the rates consistently. The highest published interest rate charged to the poor by LAPO is 144 percent for a specific type of loan.[4] This was calculated by a specialist NGO dedicated to publishing the real interest rates MFIs charge. The rating agencies typically suggested that the rates were over 100 percent, but sometimes excluded certain cash flows and came up with estimates of about 80 percent. Kiva initially "estimated" the rate as 24 percent, but raised its estimate to 57 percent and eventually to 83 percent.

One might wonder why the investors in such MFIs aren't a little concerned about the interest rates charged to the poor. The problem is, to the extent that high interest rates reduce the possible impact on poverty, they boost the profitability of the MFI, and thus the MFI's ability to repay loans to the microfinance funds.

After two sweaty weeks I was able to return to Amsterdam, leaving José Manuel in charge of training the IT team, which was led by Onyeka. Onyeka was more than most aware of the problems at LAPO and answered all my questions about the interest rates. I told him these rates seemed very high, and he agreed, but shrugged his shoulders. "I just do the IT things. These topics of interest and things are not for me to decide."

The project was in safe hands. Onyeka and his team would be able to fix a branch a week, perhaps two. It would take the rest of the year, at least, and probably into 2008, to get everything resolved. Even at this point LAPO would be far from "fixed." It would simply have one tool required to resolve the underlying problems—at least it would know what was happening in the branches.

In the final presentation to LAPO senior management I graphically detailed how the various fees, interest charges, and forced savings led to an interest rate in excess of 100 percent. Onyeka and Laura were present, while Godwin, the CEO, left the room at this point for no apparent reason. The remaining managers were unable to refute the only conclusion possible—LAPO was charging eye-watering interest rates to the poor.

On my return flight there was another problem with the domestic flight, so once again I took the road of death to Lagos. At the airport a KLM representative asked to see my ticket before boarding began. "You have economy class ticket. You want to check in at business class desk? Five dollars and I give you a priority boarding pass. When they call flight, you go to business class check-in."

It seemed worth $5. The guy had a KLM uniform and the priority boarding pass voucher seemed genuine. I bought it. Twenty minutes later the flight was called. Two hundred people checked in at business class, and the economy class section was almost empty. Clearly the country was not short of innovative people.

In Amsterdam I felt relieved—the project was under way and I would hopefully never have to return to LAPO. I sent all the reports and interest rate calculations to Grameen Foundation and Triple Jump management, where they were discreetly ignored. And actually, nothing much happened for a few months, until the real deceptions started occurring. Until this point LAPO was little more than yet another exploitative, highly profitable, and ineffective MFI. I thought it was embarrassing more than anything that the company I worked for had invested in this institution, and Grameen Foundation USA seemed to be playing a dangerous game by championing LAPO so vehemently while Muhammad Yunus was lambasting precisely this kind of MFI.

What I hadn't realized at this point was the complicity of the microfinance funds in such practices. How much did these guys know about the truth of microfinance? Were they actually deceiving their own investors, or were they simply naïve? Or were they actually working with these extortionate MFIs in the hope that they might reap the huge rewards of a stock market flotation, as the shareholders of Compartamos had?

By July 2007 most of the truth about LAPO was known by Triple Jump and Grameen Foundation. We hadn't actually discovered much "new" information that hadn't been included in rating reports written years prior to our trips. We had merely added detail and supporting evidence to such discoveries. Somehow these factors had managed to evade the attention of the funds. Even when information that directly challenged the assumption of massive poverty reduction was known, this did not necessarily dissuade funds from investing in the MFIs. And if the funds were perceived as tolerating such practices, what incentive was there to prevent them?

My work at Triple Jump resumed, some of which was fascinating. In Ecuador I assisted a decent MFI that was considering converting to a full-fledged bank. In Peru I advised a successful and well-run bank on a potential acquisition, as well as on some strategic positioning as the competitive landscape intensified. An MFI essentially competes for clients on three main fronts: the quality of service, the speed of disbursing a loan, and the price, or interest rate. This MFI had drifted from its intended mix of these three factors, and as a result was not efficiently confronting the surprisingly fierce competition present in the Peruvian microfinance sector.

I did two assignments in Argentina, one of which involved working with a Grameen replica MFI, assisting it with reporting requirements to aid decision-making. I also worked with a small MFI based in Buenos Aires, which offered fairly priced loans to some of the poorest urban Argentines while pioneering solar-panel microfinance loans in rural regions. It was struggling to meet the reporting criteria to apply for a donation from Oxfam Novib, which I assisted with. In Mexico I worked with Bas Jansen, of Triple Jump Fund Management, to help a client manage its exponential growth, which was placing strains on certain aspects of their operations. José Manuel and I also designed and delivered a training program for seventeen IT managers from across South America, which was one of the first of its kind. The goal of the course was to help these guys realize the value of the data contained within their MFIs and to use it to assist in decision-making.

Many elements of the work at Triple Jump were actually very rewarding and productive. Indeed, LAPO was something of an exception. Although the travel became somewhat oppressive, much of the field work was useful. The problems were principally in the head office in Amsterdam, although I did make frequent visits to positively mediocre MFIs, many of which were not that different in their practices from LAPO.

# 7

# Something Not Quite Right in Holland

Onyeka and his trusted sidekick slogged around Nigeria fixing branches. It was tedious, repetitive work, but this was their job and they were reasonably paid for doing it. I received the occasional email from Onyeka asking specific questions, and it was reassuring to see that our work was being successfully replicated. It made little difference to the poor, who continued to pay through the nose. I rather hoped that LAPO was a closed chapter. The prospect of a return visit had minimal appeal, and as long as they could limp through another year or two and continue repaying Triple Jump, I assumed that my work with LAPO was over.

Six months after our second trip to Nigeria, on January 22, 2008, I received a final email from Nigeria. Onyeka had finished.

Onyeka and his team completed a project that many in the microfinance sector would have feared impossible, particularly one performed without armies of overpriced consultants. They had taken sixty-three branches, plus a few new ones, installed updated software in each, cleaned up the databases, trained the staff, organized the process of consolidating all this data into a centralized database, and completed this largely on their own in a mere six months. This was one of the most impressive IT implementations in microfinance, given the low starting point.

I thought it would be an opportune moment to send an email to the staff of Triple Jump explaining the assignment and some of the background, avoiding the controversial topics of mass exploitation of the poor, extortionate interest rates, and the illegal mobilization of savings. It ended with the following:

> There wasn't much excitement about the news of Onyeka besides from Hugh and José Manuel and Lukas, who had the privilege of seeing him emerge with our own eyes. Some people accept this as the finest payment possible—that wonderful feeling when you find a gem in the rough, and you polish it, and it sparkles in the light.

It was more an account of empowering an individual to pull off an impressive assignment than a detailed description of the technical work we had facilitated, which would have bored or confused most of our staff. I was proud of this aspect of the work. After an hour or so, replies starting trickling in, such as, "Thanks Hugh, that's really encouraging to hear." I even got an email from Mark van Doesburgh, the CEO: "Excellent work!" An hour wasted, but people seemed to appreciate a break in their day to read something positive. Onyeka was the hero of the day.

My colleague Lukas Wellen had also received the email and was familiar with the LAPO missions. He inadvertently brought about the catastrophe that would eventually lead to me being fired from Triple Jump, a court case, LAPO arriving on the front page of the *New York Times*, and a major scandal in the sector. It was a simple act: he forwarded the email to Oxfam Novib.[1]

In hindsight this was a reasonable action for Lukas to take. He saw a positive story of what Triple Jump was doing with its investors' money, and he forwarded it to one of the investors with whom he had a good, personable relationship. Half an hour later I was at my desk, Lukas was away from his, and the phone rang. I could see it was from Oxfam Novib. I decided not to answer it—I found Oxfam Novib annoying to speak to, so Lukas usually fielded their calls. I allowed the phone to ring, but Steven Evers, the other CEO of Triple Jump, was walking past my desk, and it looked a little awkward that I was sitting by a ringing phone, entirely capable of answering it and opting not to do so. I begrudgingly answered it.

"What on earth is this?"

"Hi Bruno.* Er, sorry, what do you mean, what is what?"

"What is this document Lukas has just sent me about LAPO?"

"Oh, did he send that to you? Well, I actually wrote that today, and sent it to the staff here. I was just filling in people on a success story from the field. Sorry, it wasn't meant for formal circulation. Did you like it, though?"

"What I would like to know is why it took two trips to Nigeria, a huge technical assistance project, and nearly a year to install basic software across this bank, when we were told a year ago that LAPO had a smoothly running, centralized IT system providing data in real time to management."

"Hmmmm, I never told you that. There's no way they could have done that a year ago, or even now. They don't even have Internet in most of the branches. The IT was a complete mess, and was even worse a year ago. Let's not exaggerate, all they have is the software installed—they're still a long way off from decent internal control. Who told you it was all OK a year ago?"

"It's in the documents presented to the ASN-Novib credit committee a year ago, when we decided to do the investment. Are you by your computer?"

"Er, yes. Listen, Bruno, that's nothing to do with me. I didn't write the credit committee document, I just went over to fix a problem. That document you saw today was for internal use. You need to speak to Mark or Steven about the original credit committee documents."

"You see your email? Has it arrived? Open it now."

I looked in my email folder, and there was an email from Bruno with an attachment. I opened it.

"I have it open in front of me. What do you want to know?"

"Read it, now. Go through it. Tell me if this is what you found in Nigeria. I'll hold."

The document was perhaps twenty pages long, so I started to read it with Bruno on the phone. I skipped around looking for areas that could well be incorrect.

"Anything else wrong with it?" asked Bruno.

"Well, this bit about the interest rates is not right. It's actually way over 100 percent a year."

"What? You're kidding!"

"No, and this bit about the IT, that's all wrong. And this bit about the oil supply of Nigeria, that's wrong, and this bit here about the social impact, that's wrong. Actually, the clients are fleeing in droves. Oh, and the external auditor is the brother of one of the board members."

"Right. Go through that document. I want you to tell me everything that is wrong with it. By tomorrow, please."

"Sure, Bruno. Sorry about this. I had no idea you were going to see that document. Listen, I never saw this original document, I promise—I never wrote those things. I wasn't even consulted in the investment decision. I don't want to cause a problem here."

"Just do it. We'll speak tomorrow. Bye."

Bruno Molijn was normally so mild-mannered that one wondered if anything could ever irritate him, but he seemed irate when he confronted me with this document. Lukas had returned to his desk and was looking at me with a puzzled expression, able to hear half the conversation, and it did not sound like a typical exchange with Bruno.

"Dude, you shouldn't have forwarded that email to Bruno. It contradicts the documents presented to them in credit committee to justify doing the deal with LAPO, and now Bruno is pissed off that he's been lied to, and I've got to point out all the areas where the document he made the investment decision on is flawed, and there are tons. I'm going to get in big trouble for this."

There was not a lot we could do now. I had to do the comparison for Bruno and would just have to see what happened. There was little point getting Mark and Steven involved now. The document had two columns: the erroneous claims made in the original document presented to ASN Bank and Oxfam Novib, and the reality that we discovered on-site, with brief explanations where suitable. It was a few pages long. I sent it off to Bruno that evening.

Bruno called the next day.

"Thanks. We have a problem here. Please ask Mark and Steven to attend our meeting next Monday in the Triple Jump offices. We'll talk about it then. Bye."

Bruno was scheduled to come in for a chat on Monday anyway. I approached Mark.

"Bruno saw the email about Onyeka fixing the computers in Nigeria and wants to know why the documents presented to him last year said everything was fine. So, anyway, he sent me the credit committee documents and asked me to go through them and point out any other inconsistencies. And now he wants to have a meeting with us all."

"Did you go through the credit committee document?"

"Yes."

"Did you find inconsistencies?"

"Yes, quite a few."

"Did you tell Bruno?"

"Yes, he asked me to write them down ... so I did ... and I sent them to him ... and now he wants the meeting."

"Great, that's just great. Thanks, Hugh. Go sit down."

It didn't take a genius to observe that Mark was less than delighted with this news. I shuffled off to my desk and sent a quick message to Lukas: "coffee machine two minutes." At the coffee machine I explained the situation to Lukas. We both thought the situation was mildly amusing: at last a little transparency may seep into the investment process. At the end of the day, if Oxfam Novib had been presented with dubious-quality information upon which to base an investment decision, that had to be corrected. Most of Oxfam Novib's money came from the Dutch government. The poor Dutch taxpayer paid enough already without getting fleeced on sketchy investment decisions. Lukas and I simply assumed that this would be a rather embarrassing incident that would soon pass.

According to a USAID-funded paper summarizing the support LAPO had received over the years,[2] by late 2005 LAPO had obtained a €400,000 loan from Oxfam Novib, prior to the formation of Triple Jump. This was subsequently topped up with donations of €54,000 in 2008,[3] and a further €52,000 in 2009.[4] These are not trivial amounts, particularly to a very profitable MFI benefiting directly from the Dutch taxpayer.

When Monday, January 28, 2008, arrived and Bruno emerged through the office doors, I would be lying to say things were entirely relaxed. This was almost exactly a year after Oxfam Novib had initially approved a loan to LAPO, based on what was quite clearly flawed information. Pleasantries were kept to a minimum. We walked past Mark on the way to the meeting room. Mark would join us in five minutes, and Steven was not in the office. Lukas, Bruno, and I had a little chat, but it was tense. Mark emerged and Bruno shifted gears.

"It is clear that LAPO is not as described in this document," he said, referring to the original credit committee document upon which Oxfam Novib and ASN Bank had lent LAPO €750,000. Hugh, is this an isolated case?"

It was unusual that he did not ask for any explanation from Mark.

"Yes, to the best of my knowledge, this is an isolated case."

"Mark, when this new information about LAPO came to light, why weren't we told?"

Mark was visibly nervous. He goes red with nerves, and was now glowing. "Yes, we should have updated you. I am sorry, we were very busy trying to fix the problem, which as you saw is now fixed, and we focused on this and somehow it escaped my attention."

It was a good answer. There was no way he could deny the charges; the claims in the original credit committee document were utterly ridiculous. To debate details would dig his grave deeper.

"How come you didn't detect this when you did your due diligence of LAPO?"

This was the key question. Triple Jump had actually sent someone to Benin City, admittedly for only twenty-four hours—a young woman named Inge, formerly of Oxfam Novib herself, and not overly interested in microfinance in general. In twenty-four hours there was no way she could have detected this, and her experience of sniffing around IT systems at a shady, sprawling MFI was nonexistent.

"Well, we did a brief due diligence, but we didn't have time to go into such detail, which is why Hugh was able to find this out. He was there for weeks with a whole team, but at the time this was the best information we had."

To this day, it is a constant amazement to see the ease with which microfinance funds pump other people's money into MFIs without really knowing very much about them. How can twenty-four hours on-site ever be considered sufficient due diligence for channeling millions of dollars into Nigeria?

Bruno continued: "Right. On the basis of this being an isolated case, we are going to ignore this—but from now on, any relevant discoveries about our investments must be reported immediately to us. Is that clear?"

"Yes. Sorry about that. Of course, we'll tell you immediately," reassured Mark.

"And from now on, anything else to do with LAPO—financing, technical assistance, whatever—I want Hugh involved from the start. He clearly knows this MFI well. Is that clear? And you might want to improve the due diligence process a little."

Damn—the last thing I wanted was another trip to Nigeria. Triple Jump was looking at an equity deal in LAPO, especially with those profit margins. Mark agreed to Bruno's terms and the meeting fizzled out. Phew, nothing too serious—a slap on the wrist. Mark won't be happy with me, I thought, but it was hardly my fault—it was Mark who had presented the final credit committee documents to Oxfam Novib, and he got caught and he got away with it. End of story?

The defense was essentially that the information presented to the ASN-Novib credit committee had been *believed to be true at the time.* This was probably true, but failed to address why information contained within publicly available reports, mainly the rating report and LAPO's own 2005 annual report, had not raised more alarm bells with them during the due diligence.

Mark and Bruno had known each other for years. Bruno was annoyed, but at the end of the day they were long-term friends and this would be allowed to pass.

I then found myself once again involved with the MFI I least wanted to visit ever again. Bas Jansen was responsible for equity investments at Triple Jump. He was a slightly eccentric guy, formerly of one of the best microfinance funds in the country, Triodos Bank. He was passionate about all things Latin American and had a Latina wife. He was a good guy in his mid-forties, at a guess, who didn't mix socially with the team much, but we had visited a potential investment in Mexico together where we got to know one another. Quite what experience he had in equity valuation I was unsure, but I did clearly know LAPO better than he did, and I had done quite a bit of equity valuation previously when working in investment banking. I would presumably be able to add something.

An equity investment in an MFI requires a lot more detail and understanding of the company than simply lending money. When a fund lends money to an MFI, all it really needs to worry about in strict financial terms is whether the MFI will have enough money to repay the loan as it falls due. This involves some modest forecasting skills and ensuring that there is enough of a buffer in case things don't go quite according to schedule. With equity it is a little more complex. The fund buys shares in the MFI, and there is no predetermined schedule for getting this money back, as there is with a loan. The fund has to work out how much the shares are actually worth, because they are private companies with no public share price. The fund has to make a judgment call on how the value of the company will grow over time, hopefully enabling them to sell the shares at a later date to someone else—most likely to another microfinance fund or a Nigerian bank. Who else would buy shares in a questionable Nigerian MFI? Equity valuation techniques in the microfinance sector were primitive in 2006, and even now can generously be described as "unsophisticated."

LAPO had been threatening to convert from an NGO to a private company for years, and this would mean that it would need external shareholders, and those funds providing the original loan capital were the obvious people to turn to, causing Triple Jump to salivate—obtaining equity in a company this profitable in a country as large as Nigeria would be a dream.

Transformation is another one of the lesser-publicized tricks of the microfinance sector. MFIs are usually started as charities, NGOs, or not-for-profits. This serves two convenient purposes. First, they can get money from institutions such as aid agencies and charities on the basis that such agencies are often not allowed to invest in private limited companies. Second, they can circumvent the requirement to pay local taxes in most jurisdictions. Any profit at the end of the year can then be reinvested in the MFI.

Staff, particularly management, still earn salaries, often quite generous ones. But they do not earn as a direct result of being owners. During this period, the MFI can grow and accumulate "wealth" in the form of assets and a large loan portfolio, but because this does not belong to anyone, this is somehow ethical. Just because an MFI is a charity without owners does not mean it is without value or that it acts ethically. By December

2010 LAPO's total assets were a little over $68 million, most of which was the loan portfolio itself. Its total debts were nearly $57 million, most of which was money it owed to clients by way of savings. The difference, some $12 million, was the equity, or the net value of the company.[5]

MFIs operate for years as charities, until they have accumulated substantial sums of equity, or net worth, and then they "transform." At this point, they issue shares and become private companies. The funds provided to the charity do not vanish at the point of transformation, they are distributed among the shareholders. Thus, although it is true to say there are no "owners" of a charity, this does not mean there will *never* be owners who directly benefit from the transformation by receiving shares. In the case of LAPO, 12 percent of the shares go directly to the CEO, our friend Godwin.[6]

The starting point for an analysis of the value of LAPO was the audited accounts. Assuming these mildly reflect reality, this is a good way to get a feel for the size, growth, and asset base of a company. In the case of LAPO this was not so clear, since the accounts were audited by the brother of one of the board members and so could hardly be considered trustworthy. We also knew that things in general were not quite as they appeared with LAPO, but profitability was one thing we could be fairly confident of.

One evening shortly after the Oxfam Novib incident, I was working late and Bas passed my desk on his way home.

"I'm having difficulty making head or tail of the LAPO accounts," he moaned.

"Don't even bother, they're audited by an insider. They're a mess and were done when they didn't even have a computer system functioning, so how could even LAPO have known what was actually going on?"

"You mean the accounts presented to ASN-Novib, right? I'm using the accounts from the Calvert deal. They're much better and more recent. Anyway, see you tomorrow—we'll talk about it then."

This was the second bombshell that led me to a Dutch employment tribunal. A few days hence I would be fired from Triple Jump. Or, rather, attempted to be bribed to disappear quietly.

Calvert was a U.S.-based microfinance fund similar to Triple Jump. Often funds work together and share each other's deals, and Calvert was keen on this. They would raise money from foundations, companies, and the U.S. general public using a platform called MicroPlace, which is a PayPal company owned by eBay and regulated by the SEC. They didn't get involved in the tedium of having to pick an MFI and perform due diligence, so this would be farmed out to chosen funds. Triple Jump was one such fund.

Had Triple Jump placed a second investment in LAPO using funds from Calvert without my knowing? Surely I would have found out, either from Inge or browsing through the files, or from LAPO directly. It would be intriguing to see what Triple Jump had presented to Calvert, and when. How could I find out? There was no one in the office. Perhaps I could have a little poke around....

My detective job turned out to be rather easy. I looked on the shared drives from my own computer, and, sure enough, there was a folder for Calvert. Within sixty seconds I had identified the LAPO proposal to Calvert. Copy to a USB drive, print out a copy, shut down the computer, and get out of the building as quickly as possible?

I picked up the printout and couldn't resist just having a quick glance through it.

It was dated October 8, 2007, eight months *after* Triple Jump had so prudently invested Oxfam Novib's and ASN Bank's funds in LAPO; three months *after* we had returned from LAPO on the second mission armed with all the incriminating evidence of LAPO's operations. Would this "new information," which was irrefutably known at the point of the presentation to Calvert, appear in this new document? I couldn't go home now.

The Calvert document was largely copied and pasted from the ASN-Novib document. The same myths about the smoothly operating IT system, the same low interest rates, even large chunks of text explaining the political environment of Nigeria were simply lifted from ASN-Novib's document into the Calvert proposal—even though they were known, without doubt, to be false. The author was even thoughtful enough to copy some spelling mistakes. In the discussion of interest rates the word "flat" had been removed, obscuring this questionable practice from Calvert, although it had been mentioned in the original document presented to ASN-Novib. In another bizarre twist, at one point the document referred to LAPO as "PRIDE," which was another MFI that Triple Jump had lent to in Africa that also charged high interest rates to the poor, and in which Calvert had also coincidentally invested. A copy-and-paste error, I suspect, albeit one that no one had detected.

The author of the document was none other than Inge, the same girl who prepared the ASN-Novib document and who had recently left on maternity leave. She and I had discussed LAPO at length, including the high interest rates charged to the poor. She was entirely aware of the reality at LAPO—we had explicitly discussed the second mission to Nigeria. How could she have written this proposal, knowing that it misrepresented LAPO's operations? Inge's relative lack of interest in microfinance certainly did not suggest to me that she would deliberately fabricate evidence—she had nothing to gain, and given the controversy surrounding LAPO, such inconsistencies would surely be detected.

I drew up a third column in the sheet that I had prepared for Oxfam Novib and filled in the information presented to Calvert. In most cases the same fabrications, or errors, that had been presented to ASN-Novib were also presented to Calvert. This was potentially serious, and there was no defense of *this was the best information we had available at the time*, as there had been with ASN-Novib.

The next day I mentioned nothing. I still lacked some evidence. I approached the secretary: "I'm looking for some documents. I need to review the disbursement document for the LAPO deal for the ASN-Novib deal, please."

She knew that I had worked on this deal and was fairly close with Oxfam Novib, and that there had been some issues with the deal, so it was a reasonable request.

"Thanks. Oh, by the way, I just want to check the Calvert document, just to see something."

She showed me the Calvert documents. They had been signed by Mark and Steven and were presented in October 2007 to Calvert Foundation and approved a few days later. I now had the evidence I required.

"Lukas, coffee machine, five minutes."

I laid out my cards to Lukas. He was fairly surprised but hardly shocked.

"Lukas, this is terrible. Look, they were just naïve when they did the

ASN-Novib deal. They did no due diligence—not great for the investors, but lazy at worst. This is a different ballgame."

"Sure, but what are you going to do about it?"

"I'm going to confront them. This is willful, deliberate deception of an investment fund. This is wrong. You can't do that. Calvert, or rather MicroPlace, is regulated by the SEC—it's taking money from the U.S. people—this is serious."

"They'll fire you."

"How? On what grounds? You can't be fired for discovering something true, can you? In Holland? This isn't Nigeria, there are laws. They tried to fire you, remember, and couldn't. The poor are getting screwed by this—we have to do something."

"I don't know, but you're seriously accusing them here. They're going to be furious with you. Just think about it."

I had been working at Triple Jump for nearly two years. The work was becoming repetitive and increasingly involved picking up the pieces of other people's reckless decisions to make investments that should never have been made in the first place. Jessica and I had just bought a house and had a mortgage, so losing my job wouldn't be ideal. We had some savings, and work was abundant, but I couldn't think how this could lead to being fired.

I had seen frauds at MFIs in the past and some suspicious activities with some funds, but I had never had the evidence so firmly in my hand to be able to do something about the situation. Maybe this was some sort of opportunity, or a test? How would I feel if I let it go by? Maybe I could keep my comfortable job and ever accumulating airmiles with Triple Jump, but would I be proud of that in fifty years' time? Would I be able to challenge others for exploiting the poor if I ignored this case? My salary was paid by this same beast that was exploiting the poor—I was part of the scam, and I had been for some time.

I discussed the situation with my wife. She had a job, we had some modest savings, and there were endless consulting opportunities. Finding a microfinance job in 2008 was not hard. Jessica knew I didn't like working with the Triple Jump CEOs. But above all, she knew I despised exploitation. The poor have a tough enough time already without people offering them a false hope that a loan is going to miraculously solve their plight, and then taking what little spare money they have to line the pockets of a few. We decided that I should confront Mark and Steven and risk the consequences.

The next day, Tuesday, February 5, 2008, I sent Mark an email asking for an urgent meeting to discuss some new developments in the LAPO case. He agreed to meet me, together with Steven, on Thursday. I was so nervous I got little done the rest of that day or the next. I would rather have just got the entire thing over and done with. The approaching weekend was a long weekend—we were going to London straight from work on Thursday. The meeting was arranged. I could always dilute it if I panicked. Lukas was aware of the situation, and feared the worst, with prophetic accuracy.

On Wednesday I thought it prudent to send an update to Bruno, whom I still considered an ally. I wanted him to know what was going on *before* the meeting, so that if anything nasty did happen, at least one of the shareholders would know the context. I explained that the isolated case of the ASN-Novib document errors was not as isolated as we had thought:

> Unfortunately an almost identical document, containing the same material "inaccuracies," was presented to Calvert Foundation for a loan to LAPO some nine months later (October 8th, to be precise). By this point full information about LAPO was known by all involved, and yet this information was entirely absent from the appraisal sent to Calvert, making many of the same claims, indeed, copied and pasted from the original Oxfam Novib/ANF document which you sent me. Given that this was done with full knowledge of the real situation at LAPO, indeed, after the biggest and most expensive intervention ever under taken by TJAS to resolve these matters, the document presented an undeniably inaccurate picture of the company. This is a much more serious situation than the original document, as I am sure you appreciate. We can no longer claim "negligence," or "inadequate information at the time."

I went to the meeting room on Thursday before the allotted time and laid out all the papers on the desk, some of which were clearly visible from where Mark and Steve would sit. Others I kept in a small pile to bring out when required. If I dared.

They arrived, clearly nervous. Mark had adopted the complexion of a tomato, and Steven was edgier than usual. Steven began. "We would like to discuss your contract, as it is coming up to two years. We feel it would be better if you moved to a consulting contract. You are clearly not so interested in working here, by moving to a four-and-a-half-day week and now suggesting a four-day week. Perhaps a consulting contract would suit you better."

"Let me think about it. I'm happy with the current arrangement, but the purpose of this meeting was not to discuss this. My contract isn't up for renewal for a few months, so that's not as urgent."

"Well, we would like to discuss it now. What do you think of our proposal?"

"I would like to think about it and not answer that question now, please."

"We would like you to answer the question. Would you like to leave and become a consultant to Triple Jump?"

Their game plan was clear. They knew that I knew what was going on, but they also knew that I was familiar with Dutch employment law, and that they would have a tough job getting rid of me unless I volunteered to leave. As a consultant I could be fired easily. I insisted on not answering the question.

"I have a more pressing issue to discuss. I think there has been a fraud within Triple Jump that I would like to draw to your attention, as the CEOs of the company."

Mark piped up. I had a reasonable relationship with Mark. It was he who originally hired me and we had gone out for drinks on a couple of occasions. Steven was co-CEO, but in practice he had the final say. Mark seemed to consult Steven before making a decision, while Steven simply made decisions and informed Mark. Most of the staff preferred Mark. Some took their holidays at the same time as Mark, since working at Triple Jump with only Steven in charge was frustrating. It was always strange when Mark left; the office seemed empty.

"Who do you think committed this fraud, if there was one?" asked Mark.

"Well, it's hard to say, because it relates to LAPO and this was Inge's deal, and she's away on maternity leave, so I haven't been able to speak to her about it."

Immediately Mark and Steven seemed to calm down a bit. The mention of Inge's name could possibly be an escape clause for them. They knew Inge was away, although some were surprised she hadn't quit Triple Jump altogether. In fact, when she returned from maternity leave she resigned almost immediately. Perhaps this whole case could be blamed on the relative inexperience of Inge, on a sloppy and overly brief due diligence. They knew that Inge and I got on quite well and had friends in common outside the office, so I was unlikely to be too critical of her.

I continued, "We're aware of the LAPO case with ASN-Novib. Basically, a brief due diligence that did not uncover the real situation; we forgot to update Oxfam Novib and ASN Bank; we got a slap on the wrist; and we solved the underlying problem in the end anyway."

"Exactly, that's over—forget it," said one of them, I forget which.

"The ultimate defense was that the information presented to Oxfam Novib and ASN Bank, although subsequently shown to be false, was the *best information known at the time*. Sure, we could tighten our due diligence procedures, but that was it, really."

"Exactly, so why bring it up again?"

"Well, some nine months *after* the original ASN-Novib deal, Triple Jump did a deal with Calvert Foundation to invest in LAPO and presented largely the same document to Calvert. Here, as you can see, is the Calvert document," as I pushed it towards them. "You may remember I had to do a document for Oxfam Novib highlighting all the discrepancies between the real situation and what they were told, which is this document." I shoved a second document across the table toward them. "But now you will see there is a third column, which is the information presented to Calvert. You will see it is largely the same as the Oxfam Novib information, with one key difference."

Silence. They were both looking at this document. I reached over the table and pointed with my finger.

"In this column is the information presented to ASN Bank and Oxfam Novib in February 2007. This was the best information *we believed to be true at the time*, which was probably true. But in this column, this is the same information presented to Calvert in October 2007 when *we knew this information to be false*, as we admitted to Oxfam Novib a couple of weeks ago."

"Who exactly are you accusing?" asked Mark.

"Well, it is tempting to note that the author of both documents was Inge ...," a slight sense of relief prevailed. "But the key document to look at is the document formally presenting LAPO to the Calvert Foundation credit committee in October, which is signed here ... and here."

I pointed to two signatures: those of Mark and Steven. Inge had nothing to do with this.

"Thus, whoever wrote the document, those legally responsible are these two, you two, and you both knew the real situation at LAPO, because we discussed it at length and exchanged endless emails on the subject—and yet you still sent this document to Calvert. We were in Nigeria in February and July, so how could all that information fail to have made it to a document presented in October? We need to correct this, no?"

Another pause. Mark was shocked, bright red in fact, but he managed to squeeze out a sentence: "I think you must become a consultant of Triple Jump right now."

I waited. The ball was in their court. My cards were on the table, and Steven was about to speak.

"Get out of this office right now. Immediately, get out," he announced.

"Are you firing me? Under Dutch employment law? On what grounds? Have I breached a term of the contract?"

"Just get out of this office, get out now. We'll tell you what we are doing on Monday."

That was it. I stood up and walked out of the meeting room and over to my desk. "I've been fired," I told Lukas.

"Not entirely surprising," he replied. It seemed unnecessary to convene by the coffee machine—I would have plenty of time to grab a beer with Lukas over the coming days. In fact, it looked like I would have quite a bit of free time in general.

I realized I had all the LAPO documents, but not the emails. I plugged in my phone, and for five minutes copied my entire email directory to my phone, with Mark and Steven only twenty meters away while I pretended to be cleaning up my desk.

Just before I left I sent my final email to Bruno at Oxfam Novib, at 14:39 on Thursday, February 7, 2008: "Bruno, I have just confronted Mark and Steven with the Calvert application, which they have refused to discuss, and I have been asked to leave Triple Jump until Monday, when I will receive a letter. You have my cellphone, Hugh."

Five minutes later, armed with a plastic bag full of my few personal possessions, I left the Triple Jump office for the last time. It was the afternoon, so I rang Jessica on the way and told her the news, then began packing for a weekend in London.

I rang a friend who I thought might know an employment lawyer. He knew precisely the person, and sent us an introductory email. Later that day I wrote to her with some additional background. In London I received two emails. One was from the lawyer, Edith, confirming a meeting for Tuesday at 8 a.m. The second was from Triple Jump—a signed scanned letter confirming the details of my new consulting agreement with Triple Jump. It contained a pay raise and would be tax-free. I forwarded it to Edith. What was strange was the frankness with which they wrote.

The letter,[7] only two sides of an A4 sheet, began with a strange sentence: "This letter is to confirm the offer that was made to you during our meeting of yesterday 7th of February 2008, to fix the termination of your employment contract and to agree on an earlier starting date of your subsequent consulting contract."

I had absolutely no recollection of ever having confirmed anything of the sort.

Despite my getting the top score in the company for actual microfinance work in the most recent bonus appraisal, they asserted that "our decision is based on the fact that, over a long period of time and despite our efforts to make a change, you have shown unprofessional behavior towards your colleagues and to management." Questionable behavior toward management was fair enough—accusing them directly of willful deception is after all not part of the typical working day of most staff—but the reference to questionable behavior toward colleagues was unexplained. I suppose they needed some justification to terminate a contract.

However, the terms of the consulting contract offered a near doubling of salary, which seemed generous for such a terrible employee. Some revealing new clauses were added:

> You shall return all documents and company property made available to you before the termination date.... you shall abide by the duty of secrecy contained in the employment agreement between parties.... Both parties will observe strict confidentiality towards third parties with respect to the contents of this agreement ... the parties agree that they will not make any negative statements about one another towards third parties to the extent that their mutually legitimate interests may be harmed by such statements.... parties shall not without the consent of the other party disclose the terms of this agreement to any other party.

It seemed that confidentiality and keeping quiet about certain events occupied a disproportionate space in such a short document.

The final paragraph was chilling: "The proposal will lapse if it is not fully accepted ultimately on the said date [February 14, six days hence]. In that case, Triple Jump shall consider the next steps to be taken with regard to your employment. Possibly, we will ask our lawyer to enter into a petition before the Dutch court in order to terminate your employment as soon as possible. In that case, no consultancy contract will be offered to you after the termination date."

It appeared they were firing me, offering me a job, threatening to take me to court, acting very nervous about confidentiality, and issuing me an ultimatum, all in a single letter.

I wondered what my new employment lawyer would make of it.

# 8

# In Front of the Judge

Going to court in a foreign country accused of professional misconduct, in a language you don't understand, while counterclaiming deliberate deception on the part of the former employer, is not a relaxing exercise. Your fate is debated in front of you by people in suits and strange outfits, and you don't understand a word of what is going on.

I awoke the following week with trepidation.

To my delight, Edith was extremely cool. She was mysteriously attractive in a manner almost unbefitting a lawyer. The offices were sufficiently formal and intimidating. She appeared too sweet to be a lawyer—somehow I couldn't picture her fighting my case in court. She had reviewed the core documents and believed the case was comparatively simple: "In Holland you cannot simply ask someone to leave your office, accuse them of misconduct, offer them a new contract, oblige them to sign it without stating any genuine reason, and threaten them with a court case. This is a fairly open-and-closed case of a breach of Dutch employment law—we will have to go into detail about the reasons and context, but essentially your case is very good. In terms of obeying protocol, they messed this up, and that is your trump card."

Although I was confident, the next few months were fairly disturbing. Triple Jump would dig up all the dirt they could to discredit me. I had perhaps spent a little more time playing table tennis than strictly necessary to fulfill my duties, but nothing warranting dismissal, and they stood accused of deceiving an investor and breaching Dutch employment law. Although the aspect of "taking on the beast" was stimulating, it was also deeply stressful. Companies have deeper pockets for legal advice than most individuals. I could be in trouble for having told Oxfam Novib what was going on—communicating with interested third parties or some such legal minutiae. I had no idea of the legalistic wrangling required, and over the next few months I had to produce endless documents for Edith.

The initial deadline, Valentine's Day 2008 (hardly a romantic start to the day), came and went and we deliberately failed to respond to Triple Jump. A few days later they tried to contact me, but I asked them to direct all correspondence to Edith henceforth. Shortly afterwards, Edith called me. "They've improved the offer. You can walk away from this with some decent money if you want."

They were presumably nervous. Edith could not believe that they had written and signed the termination letter and speculated that they regretted not having obtained legal advice before sending it, only a day after the meeting had taken place. It was not written in standard legal parlance, and there was some correction fluid at one spot on the page, hardly the handiwork of a top employment lawyer. Rather than proceeding directly to court as they had threatened, they had revised the offer, so I suspected we had the upper hand. There was, of course, no mention of actually resolving the underlying problem raised by the Calvert proposal.

"If we continue, what happens?"

Edith explained that having threatened to take me to court unless we came to an agreement in the meantime, they would eventually have to do precisely that, for fear of us taking them to court, at which point they would also stand accused of making idle threats.

"Let's continue. Please reject the offer."

I began gathering the documents required for a court case. We had to ensure that we had obeyed all the protocols according to Dutch law, and one such requirement was to present the case to the board of directors of Triple Jump.

The chairman of the board of directors was none other than a former ASN Bank director and friend of Mark and Steven, a gentleman by the name of Ab Engelsman.* I addressed a detailed letter to him, not in any reasonable expectation of him accepting it and agreeing with me, but rather to comply with Dutch law. A few days letter he replied,[1] entirely refuting everything I had said and warning me to back off: "As I have already made clear to you in my previous letter after having studied your previous memo and the underlying LAPO memo, I do not see the relevance of discussing LAPO or any of the other issues you might want to bring to the table.... Please refrain from pursuing this issue any further as you are endangering the good reputation of Triple Jump." He possibly regrets writing that now.

Then a revised offer arrived from their lawyer. Edith again called me, asking what to do. "You can still walk away from this, save legal fees, and make some money. And also, their lawyer raised a potentially dangerous point. Apparently you knew about the Calvert deal with LAPO from the outset, you discussed this with Inge at the time. Hugh, if this is true, our case is somewhat undermined. Are you sure you didn't know about Calvert prior to *rediscovering* the case some months later?"

I knew that had I ever heard anything about Calvert at the time I would have been shocked. It was not the sort of thing I could ever have shrugged off or forgotten about. But Edith was correct—it would undermine our case. Why would I wait nine months to complain? I was sure this was a bluff. Could I really have forgotten something so critical? If it had been a small, insignificant client, perhaps. But not with LAPO. And would Inge risk lying in a court to protect Mark and Steven? I suspected not.

"Edith, they're lying. I never knew about Calvert until Bas mentioned it—they're grasping at straws. It sounds like a scare tactic."

"OK, I just have to advise you of the risks. What shall I do about the revised offer?"

"Reject it and tell their lawyer that I look forward to seeing them in court."

This was no moment to back down. We had Triple Jump on the run. Dutch employment law is fairly socialist and favors the employee in the majority of cases. We had a good case and they were clearly nervous. But I began to see this in a broader light. This was not simply "Hugh versus Triple Jump." This was a direct attack on those wishing to exploit the poor, whether they be unscrupulous MFIs, greedy investors or funds, or simply those turning a convenient blind eye when such activities took place. This had ramifications far beyond my trivial case.

Microfinance had grown into a huge, multibillion-dollar business. It was on CNN and the *Oprah Winfrey Show*. Celebrities supported it—usually with limited understanding of what was really going on. It had even made it to an episode of *The Simpsons*. In 2008 the Nicaraguan microfinance crisis was just getting started. The reams of academic articles challenging the core premise of microfinance were yet to emerge. No overtly negative books or documentaries had been released yet. Women in India had not yet started committing suicide en masse to avoid debt repayments. For all practical purposes, microfinance was still the miracle cure to poverty. Those of us with deep concerns about what was really happening were isolated. We did not know if other people shared these concerns. We had little tangible evidence other than our own observations and common sense. It was taboo to challenge the status quo. And there was serious money at stake. Meanwhile the insiders, the banks, the media, the large aid agencies—everyone who had ever heard of microfinance—continued to sing the praises of the magical properties of a $100 loan to eradicate poverty. Who were we to dispute this new developmental religion?

In 2006 I had attended the quadrennial Global Microcredit Summit, held that year in Halifax, Nova Scotia. This is a massive gathering of insiders who applaud one another and pat each other on the back while engaging in endless, repetitive conversations with the same old people as in other conferences, but on a grander scale than usual. A disturbing moment occurred toward the end of the summit during a fancy dinner, interrupted by speeches from sponsors and chosen insiders who enjoyed the sound of their own voices. The conference leader, Sam Daley-Harris, was about to reach the climax of the entire spectacle, when he would reveal the number of people who had been "reached" by microfinance. This was essentially the barometer of "success," although it didn't actually imply directly that these people were being helped, or were less poor, but simply that they had *access to credit*. Obviously there was no discussion of the interest rates these poor people had to pay—that would be an unnecessary detail. So, to much fanfare and prolonged drumrolls, the number was revealed on a massive screen. It was something like 100 million people. I shuddered: 100 million poor and desperate people, paying ridiculous interest rates to poorly run banks making healthy profits for the owners and the funds, many of whom were sitting in this hall. This was disturbing. But it got worse.

People were nearly in tears of joy. *We*, the people in this room, had performed a miracle. *We* were saviors. *We* had done what many said was impossible. We were no longer a fringe activity, we had 100 million clients. We were superheroes, apparently, and the microfinance sector even had a Nobel Peace Prize under its belt. People were clapping profusely, but for what? For whom? Sam clarified. "I would like to propose a round of applause for us, those in this room, who have worked so hard to bring this about. It is thanks to *you* that this has been possible, and I think *you* deserve a round of applause."

It was narcissism in its purest form. We were explicitly applauding ourselves. We had made decent money, we were all flying around like carrier pigeons saving the world, and we were the heroes. Muhammad Yunus would shortly make a speech about how, thanks to our astonishing work, poverty itself would soon be relegated to museums. We were all mini-deities.

And yet, at no point did anyone actually demonstrate that the poor were any better off. I wasn't suggesting that *none* benefit, and perhaps it *was* the claimed miracle; but where was the evidence?

This left me feeling very uncomfortable. Something was wrong. It would be half a decade before the evidence started to emerge, and it largely contradicted the self-congratulation witnessed that day.

My court case appeared so trivial in light of this new religion of microfinance. How dare anyone challenge the miracle cure of poverty eradication? And yet I was embarking on a minuscule battle that was doing precisely that. It was a solitary, lonely battle.

The case seemed now at the point of no return. Triple Jump was in a corner. They now had to follow through with their threat to take me to court, or else we could take them to court and have an even stronger hand. Edith suggested that we allow them to take us to court, as the "poor injured party."

The court case was exciting and deeply stressful. For the first time I was face to face with Mark and Steven again. I was quietly confident, but much depended on the questions asked by the judges. We had presented all the documents, with essentially two accusations: deception of investors and breach of employment law. Triple Jump presented reams of accusations against me, ranging from dereliction of duty to projection of negative energy upon management, mostly without any supporting evidence. The few valid accusations were trivial, and entirely admitted in our own defense. I was not claiming to be an angel. I did my job well, and I knew microfinance possibly better than anyone at Triple Jump. I irritated a few people in the process, but I was ultimately paid to shine a light into the dark places of MFIs, and that light continued to shine when I was in the Triple Jump office.

I had missed a meeting with a client due to taking an early-morning sauna *without* my telephone (surprisingly) during a conference in El Salvador, for which I had received an official warning from Triple Jump, which I considered unfair and had not been given the chance to refute. Much was made of this in their critique of my abilities. I had then offered to introduce them to an ideal candidate for a director position at Triple Jump if they formally withdrew my warning—which was construed as blackmail. I considered it a case of "you scrub my back, I'll scrub yours." They hadn't taken the bait; I arranged for the candidate to come for an interview nonetheless, but he had not taken the job, and I got a slap on the wrist for this from the judge. Fair enough. Like I said, I'm no angel; but I don't lie to investors, and I don't exploit the poor.

In court Edith's petite stature and mild demeanor was dwarfed by Triple Jump's arrogant and boisterous lawyer in an ostentatious suit. There were three judges. They had clearly read the defense in detail, but on at least one occasion they had to ask Edith to speak up. I was asked a couple of questions, with the aid of a translator, but I didn't feel content that I had had the ideal opportunity to discuss the real heart of the case. In fact, I didn't understand most of the proceedings. I had to rely entirely on my wife and her sister, both Dutch, to explain how it went afterwards. As we left, Mark and Steven seemed happy. That was a pity! And Jessica and her sister looked nervous.

"They didn't ask the right questions, and Edith was too timid. She didn't force the case in your direction, and their lawyer was overpowering."

This was a serious blow. If I lost this case, I would be in big trouble. I had a mounting legal bill, and possibly also the humiliation of defeat. Was Ab

Engelsman, the Triple Jump board director, correct? Was I in fact insane? Had I dreamt this entire thing up and somehow managed to convince a lawyer to defend my fantasy? This could be really embarrassing.

Triple Jump failed to repeat the claim that I had discussed the Calvert investment in LAPO with Inge in their documents or in their verbal defense, so I was at least vindicated on that point. It had been a bluff after all, or surely they would have used it.

That fortnight was tense. I hardly slept. Should I never have embarked on this battle in the first place? A 99 percent chance of success is also a 1 percent chance of failure. Taking on the beast is a noble idea, but had David missed Goliath with that fateful catapult shot, the story would probably not have made it into the Bible. Professionally the situation could also be quite unpleasant. How would I explain this to a future employer? What would Triple Jump managers tell the sector in general, off-record, at conferences? If they had a court ruling in their favor, they were immune from criticism. More than any compensation settlement, I needed vindication from the Dutch court, a document that proved that I was correct, innocent, that the beast had veered from the straight and narrow, and that justice was done.

That document arrived a few days later.[2]

It seems to the magistrate that Triple Jump, by not engaging in debate with Hugh and not providing him with disclosure of affairs about the Calvert document, fuelled the situation whereby Hugh started questioning the integrity of Triple Jump, thus permitting an unworkable situation to arise. Possibly Triple Jump refers to its point of view that the Calvert document concerned a matter of Triple Jump Fund Management which was of no business to Hugh. If this were to be true then this approach seems untenable because Hugh, in his professional role in the company, was involved in the LAPO credit request, and Triple Jump Fund Management and Hugh clearly belong to the same organization. The magistrate thus deems that the terms are there to assign Hugh a compensation for termination.[3]

Discussing the quality of the work I actually did for Triple Jump, the ruling stated:

In his function as senior consultant it was Hugh's job to examine MFIs and where necessary to advise with regards the reliability of their organization and operations. Both parties agree that Hugh in this sense was doing an excellent job.... Hugh had received a good appraisal and there was no indication that he would not complete the term of his contract.[4]

Finally, the judge alluded to the factual accuracy of the discoveries at LAPO:

With regards to the Calvert document: in principle Triple Jump does not dispute that Hugh's negative findings with regards LAPO's operations were not included in [the document]. Hugh brought this fact to the attention of management and subsequently to the board of directors. Without discussing it with Hugh, both parties informed Hugh that they saw no reason to act or make changes to the Calvert document. For Hugh apparently the case was not closed, at least he could apparently not find it in his heart to resign himself to the situation. With all this Hugh apparently started questioning the integrity of Triple Jump's management and possibly even the board of directors. This of course yielded an unworkable situation.[5]

So, it appeared that my concerns about LAPO were valid, that they had been excluded from the Calvert document, and that Triple Jump did not actually deny these claims—the central argument of my entire case. Ab Engelsman's previous comment urging me to "refrain from pursuing this issue any further as you are endangering the good reputation of Triple Jump" appeared misplaced. He failed to see LAPO as relevant for discussion—and a Dutch judge apparently disagreed.

I received a decent lump sum. Jessica was even paid for her translation work, and my legal costs were covered. In fact, under Dutch law an award for legal expenses is calculated according to fixed tables, which did not cover 100 percent of my actual legal fees, but Edith's boss was so pleased with the victory that he waived the remaining balance. The result was as good as we had dared hope for. I was explicitly criticized by the judge on one minor count: my attempt to introduce the director candidate in exchange for the removal of my written warning was described as "misguided" and "not elegant" (*misplaatst, niet elegant*), but basically we had won. Edith had done a superb job.

Who paid my lump sum? Was it Triple Jump? Or their shareholders, the good folk at ASN Bank and Oxfam Novib (that is, pensioners and the Dutch government)? Or was this paid by the MFIs who so diligently pay Triple Jump interest on their loans? Or was this money ultimately stumped up by the poor? Was this blood money?

I had found a variety of new projects to work on, including an assignment to assist a Brazilian MFI struggling with a poorly performing loan portfolio. Critically, I now had a publicly available document signed by a Dutch judge, albeit in Dutch, that I could refer to if there was any doubt as to the appropriateness of my actions. I had nothing to hide and an independent document that was hard to refute. But now I had something even more powerful—evidence of some unusual "activities" at a microfinance fund.

Of course Calvert had no idea that they had been deceived. Bruno Molijn, at Oxfam Novib, had remained suspiciously quiet during this entire process, although he had seen the entire situation emerge. What about the other investors in LAPO? Deutsche Bank might find this result interesting, as could Citibank and Standard Chartered. Muhammad Yunus was lecturing the world about the evils of extortionate interest rates, and yet Grameen Foundation was one of the largest investors and guarantors of LAPO. How could they square interest rates of 126 percent at LAPO with his usual speeches?[6]

Why had ASN Bank and Oxfam Novib subcontracted their microfinance activities to a private third party that appeared to be jeopardizing their own reputations? ASN Bank promotes itself as a leading "ethical bank," and yet here it was investing in a highly questionable MFI. The Dutch government, charities, pensioners, and individuals trust such organizations to invest their money wisely, and they were willfully investing it recklessly—what did ASN Bank and Oxfam Novib stand to gain by such practices, and was it worth the risk to their reputations?

# 9

# Rustling Dutch Feathers

With my newfound freedom I began working on a number of exciting projects, including a large assignment for the peer-to-peer microfinance investment platform MyC4, based in Denmark. The U.S. equivalent, Kiva, was growing at phenomenal rates, and learning the model in detail through my work with MyC4 provided experience useful for revealing some unusual activities at Kiva a couple of years later (Kiva had coincidentally recently teamed up with LAPO).

Still, something had shifted within me. At this point began what may best be described as my "whistle-blowing stage." I was detested by Triple Jump and its partners. By the end of this period I would be detested by much of the community of microfinance investment funds. I focused initially with getting information on microfinance failures into the public domain. My "office spat" with Triple Jump over LAPO would eventually culminate in my providing key details about LAPO for a story in the *New York Times*, which shed disturbing light on how the microfinance sector actually works from the highest levels down. My attention—and that of the *New York Times*—would begin to turn to more familiar names in microfinance like Calvert Foundation, Deutsche Bank, and Kiva.

Had my experiences of some of the more sordid sides of microfinance clouded my opinions? Perhaps I had been simply unlucky in my choice of assignments and employers. Were there any other voices sounding similar

alarm bells? This is a good place to pause to discuss some unsung—
and essentially uncompromised—heroes of the microfinance world: the
rating agencies. Few may be surprised to learn that powerful financial
institutions didn't give my warnings or criticisms much consideration. It
is a different story when objective, thoroughly referenced formal ratings
are cast aside.

Rating agencies are not currently the flavor of the month. Before the
global financial crisis they were treated with mild skepticism, but the
crisis has led to a new wave of criticism, which broadly falls into two
categories:

1. "Why didn't you warn us about these guys before they collapsed?"
   (Lehman Brothers, AIG, Greece, etc.)
2. "How dare you downgrade us? You're just making the problem
   worse and spreading fear." (USA, Italy, etc.)

In their defense, rating agencies have a tough line to walk. If they present
too gloomy an outlook, and one that fails to subsequently transpire, they
are discredited. If they keep quiet and something bad does occur, they are
also discredited. Volcanologists must face a similarly fine line—too many
warnings of a pending eruption and people stop trusting the advice.
One warning too few, and that volcanologist will be out of work for a
while. Despite the informality and immaturity of the microfinance sector
compared to other financial sectors, the specialized microfinance rating
agencies are surprisingly good. There are four main companies:

- MicroRate, a private, independent institution and the first specialized
  rating agency for microfinance
- M-Cril, which also offers consulting services
- Planet Rating, part of the large PlaNet Finance Group empire, which
  has its fingers in most pies
- Microfinanza Rating

I have had more experience with Planet Rating and MicroRate than the
other two, largely because of the regions in which I have worked.

What is the general purpose of a rating? For investors or donors, many of whom are pretty unsophisticated and inexperienced in microfinance field operations, and who spend little time on-site doing actual due diligence, a rating may form a significant part of their "analysis" of an MFI and its ongoing monitoring. This partially explains the herd instinct among investors to invest in the same MFIs—they all read the same ratings and little else. For individual MFIs, a rating is an external seal of approval that can help them attract financing from investors and donors and assist them in improving their operations.

The ratings follow subtly different methodologies, but in general they consist of one or two experienced people visiting the MFI, asking a series of penetrating questions, combining on-site analysis and spot checks with some desk research from their head offices, and slotting this information into a standardized template for management to review. An overall score, similar to the regular ratings (AAA, BB+, and so on) is then assigned. Ratings are written in a particular language, and reading between the lines is required. An agency cannot use terms like "fraud," "illegal," or "idiot," and thus uses phrases such as "lack of transparency," "incompatible with local regulation," and "challenges in the management board." Ratings are comparatively cheap, and the sector is surprisingly competitive. When one considers the typical salaries paid to ratings staff, their expertise is extremely good value for money.

The critical difference between a microfinance rating and a mainstream rating of a large company such as Microsoft is that there are thousands, perhaps millions, of people studying Microsoft, and publicly available information abounds. It is comparatively hard for a mainstream rating agency to discover and add genuinely new information or analysis to its ratings. With microfinance, the case is reversed. A rating could well represent the single most valuable source of information about an MFI available. Given that most funds spend only a matter of days on-site, barely time to visit even a subset of the branches, and have no idea about the subtleties of the IT system (where problems are often discovered) or the field operations, they rely on the ratings and are one of the biggest collective purchasers and readers of them.

The case of LAPO is not only an excellent example of what can go wrong with microfinance funds, but also how the ratings play a powerful role in the revelations. LAPO was rated four times, twice by well-qualified people at MicroRate and twice by well-qualified people at Planet Rating. The key questions to assess the integrity of the rating agencies in this case are simply "How accurately did they assess the real, underlying situation at LAPO?" and "How predictive were they?"

The benchmark rating is the publicly available 2006 MicroRate report,[1] which does not mince its words. The front page mentions large-scale, unregulated financial intermediation, high client desertion rates, governance issues, and very good profitability. LAPO's funding at this point was predominantly from Holland and Belgium (the microfinance funds Incofin and Oxfam Novib, with Cordaid and ASN Bank shortly after).[2] Nothing in this rating was ever subsequently discovered to be false, and MicroRate was invited back a year later to repeat the process, so presumably LAPO was content with its findings.

Things hotten up in MicroRate's 2007 rating.[3] There were thirteen references to the amazing profitability of LAPO,[4] despite its oft-mentioned poor operating efficiency. Where could this profitability have come from? "Highly profitable ... excellent operating margin ... very high operating margins ... [operating margins] remain extraordinarily high." The constant reference to operating margins is a direct suggestion that interest rates are high—the interest rate is by far the main driver of operating margins in an MFI. MicroRate discusses the interest rate explicitly, stating that it is "between 70 percent and 80 percent," although closer examination reveals this to be an underestimate, since the role of forced savings was excluded.

This was perhaps defensible in 2007, before the practice of quoting MFI interest rates according to internationally accepted standards became best practice. My only minor criticism of the two MicroRate ratings is the failure to notice the conflicts of interest within management. No rating is perfect, and both these ratings are sobering reads.

There are five references to client desertion rates, summarized concisely as "retaining their clients remains however a big challenge."[5] Of all the social statistics one could gather about an MFI, the simple fact that clients were leaving LAPO in droves should have rung alarm bells. It is hard to think of any company offering any product or service where the phrase "very few of our clients ever return" can be considered positively. The average loan size at LAPO is suspiciously close to the average first loan a client takes, since most clients do not progress far beyond the first loan. Of course they don't if they are paying those rates of interest.

MicroRate went on to discuss the practice of capturing savings: "Client savings intermediation without a license.... Approximately one third of funding is provided by client deposits even though as an NGO, LAPO is not licensed to mobilize savings.... In MicroRate's opinion, this policy bears a serious risk.... LAPO is neither authorized nor adequately equipped to mobilize savings from the public.... LAPO's present policy of using savings deposits to fund its operations—besides being *illegal*[6]— exposes its clients to risks of which they are unaware ... intermediating savings on a large scale without the proper authorization must be considered *unacceptable*" (emphasis added). A fund manager who failed to get the hint here should possibly not be managing a fund.

A number of lesser critiques appear in the reports, but there was little doubt that two consistent reports written by a reputable rating agency had highlighted extremely dangerous, inappropriate behavior. And yet such factors, written clearly in publicly available documents read by most microfinance funds, had not deterred the investors, who were also listed in the report.[7] These now included Triple Jump and ASN-Novib, Deutsche Bank, Citibank, Calvert Foundation (invested via Triple Jump), Kiva, and Grameen Foundation USA, somewhat in contradiction to Muhammad Yunus's usual stance on high interest rates.

For any of these funds to deny knowledge of LAPO's true nature was a double-edged sword—had their analysis not extended to reading a rating report? This would suggest unimpressive due diligence, one of the few functions of a passive fund manager. But to admit knowledge of these issues was akin to condoning it. "We knew about these issues and invested regardless" is an even more alarming response. The best course of action was to say nothing, which is precisely what the funds collectively did. If asked, drab comments such as "we are aware of the issues and are working with LAPO to resolve them blah blah" would suffice.

The rating agency had done its job. Yes, it missed a few minor things, some of which Planet Rating discovered later, but the ratings were accurate. It was the funds that either failed to read them or didn't care about the contents. Given the information that subsequently came to light, MicroRate's warnings were timely.

The microfinance rating agencies are, for the most part, bastions of transparency and worthy of respect. They contain some of the brightest practitioners in the sector outside of the actual field operations of microfinance, and are largely innocent of the accusations levied against the likes of S&P, Moody's, and Fitch. Rating agencies warned about overindebtedness in India, about multiple lending in Nicaragua, about exploitative practices in individual MFIs such as LAPO—but the people who should act on this information, the microfinance funds, have a different set of incentives—very different.

In January 2009 I was doing an assignment for an Irish company that designs software for MFIs. I had previously advised them on the acquisition of the company that made M2. The CEO, a witty and rotund gentleman by the name of Callum, had sponsored a two-day conference in an effort to promote his company. Just why he chose to sponsor a conference on this specific topic I never gathered, but he asked me to attend. The conference appeared targeted at investors in microfinance rather than practitioners themselves, but a friend of mine, Antonio, who had also worked for this Irish outfit, was going, so we could have fun in New York together. He was nervous about addressing such an unsuitable audience and asked if I would do the entire presentation.

"Dude, that's not on. I'll help, but we do it together."

"But I have no idea what to say. These guys are the wrong audience. They're not interested in a company making software for MFIs—we'll make fools of ourselves."

"So it's OK if I address them?"

The debate continued until we arrived in New York. We were on in the afternoon, and that morning Antonio pleaded with me: "Listen, how about you do the presentation? I'll help with any questions."

"No way, you're not landing me in this entirely. If we go down, we go down together."

"Would a box of Partagas D4s change your mind?"

Antonio was referring to an awesome Cuban cigar, the Partagas Series D Number 4—a legend in cigar circles and a luxury at the best of times. A box of them would cost well over $300. For a thirty-minute talk, of which I had committed to do fifteen minutes already—this seemed like a deal.

"You're serious. A whole box of real D4s? No fakes? If you're serious, I'll do it, but on one condition. I can talk about whatever I want. No negotiation. Do we have a deal?"

"We have a deal."

I had a couple of hours to prepare a presentation of relevance to a group of suit-wearing microfinance investors with little idea about microfinance other than that it could earn a quick, tax-free buck and looked good on websites. Where was the link with a technology company?

"Using technology to assist in fraud detection as part of a due diligence" was the link.

I delivered this speech initially to glazed eyes, but within minutes people had perked up. I chose a case study: "We were visiting a very large MFI that some in this room may have invested in, and thanks to a relatively simple analysis of the database, we discovered frauds within this institution relating to interest rates on loans and savings that have caused quite some headaches for the MFI and investors alike, not all of whom are aware of the situation, and most of whom did sloppy due diligences that ignored looking through any of the actual data."

Their attention was now hawklike as I described the LAPO case in all but name. One person appeared particularly interested in the case: Mark van Doesburgh, the CEO of Triple Jump. I had caught his eye early on. Perhaps understandably, he was now as red as a radish, but I never mentioned LAPO, Nigeria, or the fact that only one of LAPO's investors knew this case all too well—Triple Jump.

I bumped into Mark the following day.

"Hi, Mark. Hey, were you glad I didn't reveal the name of the MFI, or Triple Jump, in yesterday's little talk?"

"Yes, I was, actually," and to give Mark his due, he laughed, made a polite excuse, and shuffled off.

Two other important meetings occurred during that conference in New York. The first was a chance encounter with the new CEO of the largest microfinance fund on earth, Jean-Pierre de Klumpp* of Switzerland-based BlueOrchard. We had a long chat while sharing a taxi to JFK, but the relationship was not to last. The second was an inspirational woman from Women's World Bank who cornered me at some point and asked if I would speak at another conference. "We do this conference each year with JP Morgan, and your talk was great. It was clear you knew what you were talking about, and I liked the mention of gender-based lending. Would you come to our conference in a couple of months to speak about the gender aspects of microfinance lending?"

I had described how technical analysis could be used for other goals, such as scrutinizing who was benefiting (and suffering) from loans, and had mentioned that this had big implications for gender-based lending, which microfinance often claimed to do but rarely demonstrated in much detail in practice. Sure: another trip to the Big Apple—why not?

Shortly afterward, on April 17, ASN Bank held its annual general meeting (AGM). As a token investor in this *ethical* bank, I was invited. Investing in such companies is useful, if only to get an invitation to the AGM, where shareholders may ask questions, awkward or otherwise. Also, investing in such a company gives the investor certain protections under local financial-sector regulations, two facts we were to exploit fully. Guess who the guest speaker was at that year's AGM? None other than Godwin Ehigiamusoe, CEO of LAPO. This was too tempting to resist. Edith advised me not to ask anything myself, so I had to plant a question. Easily done.

I arrived at the old Amsterdam Stock Exchange, where security was so poor I was able to smuggle my mystery questioner through the front door (via the tea and biscuit stand). The usual backslapping took place for an hour or so, and then Godwin stood up and delivered his speech about the almost miraculous poverty-reducing attributes of LAPO. He touched all the right, heart-warming buttons, with stories of impoverished women buying cows and being Lifted Above Poverty by the thousand. Thanks to all the investors in the room, without the generosity of your money the world would still be such a brutal place, blah blah. Then the curveball question from a mysterious Dutch woman altered the mood abruptly:[8]

The essential battle is to the lift the poor out of poverty, and I think everyone in this room trusts their money with the ASN-Novib fund in a good cause. Now if you look at the actual cost that LAPO is charging poor Nigerian women you will see that this is approximately 110 percent per year when you consider all the costs, and you can calculate it through the Deutsche Bank interest calculator. Now this number has been confirmed by numerous independent people like other microfinance funds and independent consultants, so LAPO is basically one of the most expensive MFIs that there is, and one of the most profitable. So my question to all of you is "Is poverty alleviation really happening at these interest rates?" Thank you.

There was little left to say. The audience was stunned. The panel members, consisting of Mark (red as the setting sun), Steven, and the ASN Bank board, were furious. Godwin attempted a feeble denial, until the chairman announced a premature coffee break. The truth was out. The question of LAPO's interest rates was now part of the public record and no longer confined to private correspondence and rating reports.

I rushed home with the recording and wrote to Grameen Foundation, Deutsche Bank, and the usual suspects with the simple comment: "LAPO's interest rates are now publicly available information." Deutsche Bank at least had the balls to reply, asking to have a chat. Sarita Mehra of Grameen Foundation wrote back to say that she so hoped LAPO would reduce its interest rates. She was promptly taken off the LAPO case, since this was getting a little hot for Grameen Foundation's liking (its senior managers would take over from this point on).

We had them on the run.

In July that year I received a letter from the head of corporate communications at ASN Bank,[9] suggesting they would look into the case in greater detail, thanking me for the information, and confirming that they and Triple Jump "agreed that this particular microfinance institution will be reassessed in the near future." And yet in the very same month, shortly after the rather embarrassing question raised in their AGM, ASN Bank published a reassuring article in its newsletter. To pacify its more diligent investors who may have taken issue with the extortionate interest rates charged by LAPO, ASN reproduced an interview with Mark van Doesburgh, CEO of Triple Jump, on page 10 of its *Spaarmotief* July newsletter:

Interviewer: "How much interest do borrowers pay?"
Mark van Doesburgh: "It is quite high, on average about 25 to 30 percent."[10]

This did seem at odds with the ratings on LAPO, and did indeed appear to be a deliberate attempt to placate their own investors following the AGM. Even while ASN Bank was supposedly investigating the claims of extortionate interest rates at LAPO, an investment the bank would subsequently withdraw from, ASN was content to reassure its investors with claims of interest rates of barely a quarter of those charged in practice. Is that transparency? Is that how an *ethical* fund ought to report to its investors?

Aware of the potential power of involving a regulator, I wrote to the Dutch equivalent of the SEC, called KIFID, making a formal complaint as an investor. We exchanged a few letters, whereby I was able to fully alert the regulator of this and ASN was obliged to respond. But I had made one fatal mistake. The funds I had actually invested in were not the funds that had invested in LAPO—I had ticked the wrong boxes when I did the initial investment. Did KIFID initiate any action? Take a guess.

I also wrote to my old friend Bruno at Oxfam Novib to remind him of the concerns at LAPO, which he was obviously aware of. He had been furious when he discovered that Triple Jump had been a little short of the truth but had calmed down in the interim. Obviously, he could not officially agree with me, and I sent the letter partly in jest. Oxfam Novib, ASN Bank, and Triple Jump would all be discussing this together and working out a clever way to minimize the fallout. Their leaders were friends of many years, and there was no way they would let one of the gang suffer, even though inappropriate behavior was beyond dispute and confirmed in a court ruling and some public ratings. There may have been some internal warnings, but they would protect one another. Where the interests of the poor ranked in such discussions, I can only speculate.

I did actually get a somewhat comical reply from Bruno some months later.[11] In it he stated that they believed LAPO's practices of collecting and onlending savings was "not an illegal activity in Nigeria," and claimed this was confirmed by an official Central Bank of Nigeria document. The document to which he referred did indeed permit microfinance *banks* to capture savings.[12]

Bruno went on to write, "As LAPO *is in the process of becoming* a microfinance bank ... it will *soon* be under the supervision of the Central

Bank of Nigeria" (emphasis added). So, it appeared that he was suggesting that *soon* LAPO might in fact be legally allowed to intermediate savings, but wasn't currently, nor had been for the five preceding years during which Oxfam Novib had turned a blind eye to such activities and pumped Dutch taxpayer funds into an MFI (not a *microfinance bank*) of questionable legality. Nor did he explain why a reputable rating agency had suggested that LAPO's operations were not legal, an accusation repeated some months later by another rating agency. Well done, Oxfam Novib, but why admit this in writing?

We had bigger fish to fry now than to worry about how the Dutch government distributes its aid budget and how their *ethical* banks invest their funds. The information was out there, and ASN Novib did eventually pull out of LAPO.

I returned to New York in April to speak at the Women's World Bank Capital Markets Conference, as arranged during my previous trip stateside. I delivered a summary of some results we had detected in Eastern Europe and Latin America on gender discrepancies among microfinance clients, largely demonstrating just how clearly and seriously repayment rates diverged between the sexes. The fact that female loan repayment rates are higher than male is fairly well established. We had additional evidence suggesting that men, when they defaulted, were more likely to give up altogether, while women had a far greater tendency to subsequently resume repayments when possible.

A chance encounter in the lobby afterward proved explosive. I was talking with some random punters about the ease with which one can trick a microfinance fund into believing almost anything on account of their never actually seeking verification of the claims made. I was asked to provide an example. I replied, "Calvert subcontracted their entire due diligence of their investment in LAPO to a third-party microfinance fund, a fund that had already made an investment in LAPO and had subsequently discovered all manner of unpleasant truths about LAPO, many of which are now widely known. And yet they managed to hide this from Calvert, and even earned a commission in the process."

Much information about LAPO was now in the public domain, but one of the women called me aside. "That's fascinating. I'm good friends with Eliza Erikson* at Calvert, and I'm sure she'd be very interested to discuss this further, off the record, if you'd be willing. Can I pass on your details?"

A direct encounter with Calvert. This was too good to miss. I agreed and handed her a business card. That same day, Friday, May 1, 2009, I received an email:

> Mr. Sinclair, I was referred to you by xxxxx who said that you two spoke this morning at the Women's World Banking Capital Markets Conference. Xxxxx said that you had some information you would like to share on LAPO, an MFI in Nigeria. Could you give me a call at your earliest convenience—I am about to leave the office so the easiest way to reach me would be on my cell phone at xxxxxx. Sincerely, M. Erikson, Portfolio Manager, Microfinance, Calvert Foundation

Bingo! I could have contacted Calvert directly, but that would have looked aggressive. Now I had them asking me for information. I called Eliza immediately, and we had a long chat. She asked a number of questions and requested additional information, and we remained in contact over the next few weeks. She wanted to speak to Grameen Foundation, and I suggested she meet with Sarita Mehra and introduced them by email. Two months later, in July 2009, I received an email from Eliza requesting that I not contact her again.

The LAPO cover-up had officially started.

Calvert presumably realized that it had been duped, but the implications of taking action would be unpleasant, not only for Calvert, but for Grameen Foundation USA, for Triple Jump, and for everyone remotely involved with LAPO (Deutsche Bank, Citibank, and Standard Chartered Bank, to name but three more, and also Kiva—the public face of microfinance). No, this had to be hushed up. The money was invested, and would probably be repaid given the high interest rates LAPO was charging, so there was no reason to rock the boat. Sure, Calvert was SEC-regulated and ought to have taken better care of other people's money, but bringing this out in the open would probably not help their case. However, it would damage the reputation of the sector, and that would serve no one. We can only speculate where the interests of poor Nigerian women rated in this decision.

Citi Microfinance (part of the Citibank empire) had invested in LAPO under a guarantee from Grameen Foundation USA,[13] and it was probably unaware of what was happening on the ground in Nigeria. I wrote to Citi in July to the email address of the microfinance department, explaining our concerns about LAPO's operations, and in particular that it was operating illegally according to the rating reports. In August 2009, Robert Annibale,* global director of Citi Microfinance, wrote to me.[14]

He began by complimenting me on my work and experience in the sector and claimed that we had met. I doubted it. "As you mentioned, we have worked together with Grameen Foundation in Nigeria and with LAPO. I have followed up on some of the issues you raised with Grameen and others, as well as with our local office in Lagos."

No concrete action was mentioned, but he had raised an important issue regarding Grameen Foundation: As with Calvert and Triple Jump, if it transpired that things were not quite as they appeared at LAPO, would this be the responsibility of Citibank or of Grameen Foundation? Obviously Citibank would be somewhat irritated to be publicly exposed for lending to a money-lending operation in Nigeria of questionable legal status, but it would have a natural defense if it could demonstrate that Grameen Foundation USA had managed the deal. As with Triple Jump's investment in LAPO for Calvert, one would need to see the documentation Grameen Foundation had presented to Citi, which I have not seen so cannot comment on, but the double-edged sword exists nonetheless. Which is worse—to invest in such an MFI with full knowledge, or to admit to investing without bothering to obtain full knowledge? Best left unanswered.

During this period I received a call from the head of a large microfinance network regarding its MFI in Mongolia, which was experiencing some challenges and needed on-site support. It offered both my wife and me short-term jobs in Ulaanbaatar. We had always wanted to go on the Trans-Siberian Express to Mongolia, so we decided to seize the opportunity.

We went to Italy first to visit my godmother and met an activist friend of hers called Terence Ward. Over dinner one evening Terry suggested that the LAPO case had some mileage remaining. Triple Jump had essentially paid a fine but got away without any long-term negative repercussions. For all we knew, such practices were continuing daily, and my work had done little to stop them. Why didn't we start publicizing this case? Calvert is regulated by the U.S. Securities Exchange Commission, so perhaps it would be appropriate to refer the case to the SEC. Kiva had directed $5 million, raised mainly from the U.S. general public, to LAPO. Perhaps this should be publicized. Was the Dutch government aware that funds directed to alleviating poverty in Africa via microfinance were in fact being lent at over 100 percent to an MFI with chronic client desertion and questionable legal status? Terence was a U.S. citizen and therefore able to launch complaints in the USA. His proposal to me was simple: Let's work together to get this case the publicity it deserves and actually hold the various people accountable.

In fact, his proposal was grander still: Let's shake up this entire sector.

I had now been fired twice for confronting those responsible for exploiting the poor, and despite losing my job on both occasions, no one had suggested that the evidence presented was in any way flawed. No one was disputing the facts, but alerting the funds to the actual practices at LAPO seemed of little interest to them. We had to raise the temperature.

Terence had a fascinating and unorthodox background. As a close friend of the Indian activist Vandana Shiva and the late Teddy Goldsmith, he certainly had the skills required to unmask the microfinance sector, and he had worked in a bewildering array of countries. He had served on missions with George Soros's Open Society in Burma and the United Nations in East Timor, and he collaborated with Global Witness in resource-rich countries in Africa and Central Asia sniffing out corruption. He had written an amazing book about Iran and made a documentary in Congo-Brazzaville.[15] He was the perfect guy to work with. I was already out of my depth, this being my first-ever activist endeavor, and I needed all the help I could get. He peppered me with questions about the structure and motivations of the sector, not just about the minutiae of LAPO, and reckoned that we were on to a winner. He was familiar with the Niger Delta region of Nigeria, had pretty good knowledge of microfinance, and could see how the whole thing fit together. This was a lucky break.

Terry's basic premise was that none of the financial institutions would take corrective action unless they faced reputational damage, and that the best way to achieve that was to publicize the truth to all concerned.

"Let's have some fun."

# 10

# Blowing the Whistle from Mongolia

We took the Trans-Siberian train to Mongolia. What a delightful way to travel to work.

Much of the actual whistle-blowing concerning the more nefarious activities of the microfinance sector, LAPO, and its investors took place from Mongolia, of all places. This was ironic, since the country demonstrates one of the best examples of effective microfinance I have seen. Anyone feeling disillusioned with microfinance ought to visit Mongolia.

Mongolia is a vast country with one of the lowest population densities on earth, beaten only by Greenland and the Falkland Islands. Travel ranges from hard to impossible most of the year. Many Mongolians are nomadic, so even the notion of a fixed address can be nebulous. Temperatures are way below minus 30 Celsius for a number of months of the year, and we routinely enjoyed minus 45. The microfinance sector is well regulated and competitive. Annual interest rates do not exceed 30 percent thanks to effective regulatory oversight. Operating costs in Mongolia are genuinely high, and yet the MFIs make reasonable profits. They are obliged to be efficient because their revenue is ultimately limited by the maximum interest rates they are allowed to charge. If an MFI cannot reach a scale to cover at least operating costs, it will rely on investors to provide a subsidy or it will collapse. That the sector works at all sheds some doubt on the claims of, for example, the endless Mexican MFIs that claim they have to charge rates of over 100 percent per year to cover costs. Is it really so much more expensive to operate in Mexico than Mongolia? I saw no evidence of this, and I have lived and worked in both countries for extended periods.

My work involved organizational restructuring of an MFI; loan product development; assisting the marketing department to form a plan; and developing financial projections with the charming chief financial officer. I was not doing a formal social impact study, but I did manage to visit a number of clients, most of whom were shining examples of the very best microfinance can be: genuine entrepreneurs using loans to buy fixed assets to scale their businesses. Although our whistle-blowing focused on the sordid side of the sector, seeing the model have a positive impact was tonic for the soul.

We visited one client in particular who aptly illustrated how effective microfinance can be. She was in her late forties and lived in a hut cobbled together over several decades in a squalid suburb of a small Mongolian town. As we dodged her guard dogs and entered the house, I was confronted with an overpowering smell. Piles of unidentifiable objects loosely covered with paper filled one of the two rooms that made up her home. Goat heads lay on a table. On the window ledge was what I assumed was a stomach. She lifted the pieces of paper and revealed a veritable morgue of assorted body parts. Our translator explained: "These are various bits of animals that she buys from local farmers and herdsmen. Some is turned into dog food, but also some is used to make hamburgers. Her main specialty is processing the heads, which are otherwise often discarded."

I had eaten some unidentifiable piece of meat that day for lunch. I pushed the thought aside.

She had taken a loan to buy an electric grinder. Before this, she had used a hand-operated grinder mounted on her table, which was tiring to operate and could only process a few kilograms of meat per day. She showed us the process, armed with a rustic knife and a head. The trick was to first sever the tongue at the back of the throat, not simply the visible section in the mouth—this apparently loosened all the other bits. She cut and wrenched it out, and before placing it in the grinder she removed some fragments of grass and dirt from the tongue, as these would jeopardize the flavor of the eventual dish. Valid point: I would keep my eyes open for grass next time I ordered a hamburger. She then removed the cheeks, eyes, any bits of flesh remaining on the skull, and some remaining fragments of flesh around where the rest of the goat had presumably once been attached, while explaining what her subsequent loan allowed her to do.

"With the grinder she could work more quickly, but rather than making repetitive trips to obtain the heads and organs and sell the processed food to her clients, she needed to buy a freezer, which is why she obtained a second loan."

She opened the freezer and sure enough, it was jammed to the rim with body parts—glazed-over eyes peered out at us. "With the freezer she can buy body parts in bulk at lower prices and also store the processed food and deliver it in batches, and in the summer the freezer is essential." I had forgotten that there was in fact a summer in Mongolia. She used a third loan to buy digital scales so she could accurately weigh and price her products.

Here was a genuine entrepreneur, the type that many in the microfinance community suggest is the norm. In fact they are exceptional, but they feature prominently on websites and in marketing materials. We wanted to find such a case for a documentary we were considering, so we returned with cameras to ask her more questions. It seemed that the business was fairly successful. There was limited competition, because it required some expertise and a network of contacts to buy the raw materials and sell to clients. I wondered how it was that the apparent profitability had not led to a better quality of housing. Over the last few years she had used the proceeds of the business to send two of her children through university. In a particularly poignant moment we asked her about her future plans for the business, and whether she thought it could be built up further and be a useful business for her children to take over.

"You misunderstand me. I don't do this job because I like it or want to grow it into a big business. I do it so my children will never have to do work like this."

I have never seen so many viable micro-entrepreneurs actually benefiting from microfinance at reasonable interest rates as in Mongolia.

Perhaps tight regulation isn't the evil that the microfinance community so vehemently claims it to be?

I accept that this was an exceptional woman, but over the year we lived in Mongolia we saw many such cases. There were occasional consumption loans, but they were comparatively rare. This was microfinance as it ought to be: microfinance with a soul. It does exist, but *only if the investors and regulators want it to exist.*

As we were leaving the house of our Mongolian head processor, a colleague asked a final question, which we did not capture on film. "Now that your two children have completed university and you no longer need to pay these fees, what are you planning to do with the money you make from the business?"

"Well, maybe one day I could buy a proper apartment in the town...." She paused for a moment. Her face, up to this point vibrant and joyful, became solemn, and she looked over to the bed where her third daughter sat. She tried to speak, but struggled to find the words. "If I save enough money, maybe I can afford a cure for my other daughter."

Her third daughter, perhaps eight years old, sat motionless, looking around the room, with very obvious signs of Down syndrome. Everyone, including the translator, stood in silence. I fought back tears. I was not alone. Some dreams may be out of reach even with excellent MFIs and a great business.

We were based in Ulaanbaatar. My assignment was fascinating, and by Christmas it had been completed. I began a second assignment to establish a Mongolian investment fund focused on small companies slightly larger than typical micro-enterprises, but still too small to obtain formal credit from the commercial banks. My American activist friend Terry was shuttling back and forth between Italy and the USA and we began planning the next steps.

We decided to focus on two institutions: Calvert Foundation, which already knew of the situation in some detail but had failed to take any corrective action; and Kiva, which had inadvertently pumped nearly $5 million from the (mostly) American general public into LAPO.[1]

On August 17, 2009, shortly after our arrival at the Ulaanbaatar train station, a surprise press release altered the playing field. MicroRate had discovered that LAPO had provided it with dubious information:

"MicroRate notes the integrity of the information provided to it by LAPO, as well as LAPO's financial disclosures since the ratings have come into question. As a result, MicroRate's rating of LAPO is no longer valid."[2] To the best of my knowledge this was the first time a rating agency had ever taken such a measure. MicroRate received angry calls from LAPO and its investors. The rating agency, having presented possibly the most accurate description of LAPO on earth, had discovered new information and had warned the public, as well as investors, of pertinent information that had come to light, information it would almost certainly have been unable to discover from its offices in Geneva and Amsterdam. Were the funds pleased with this discovery?

"How dare you criticize one of our investments?" was the typical reaction.

The funds, important clients of MicroRate, were none too happy that they had been publicly humiliated. This could *not* be public information. This would raise questions about how the funds had managed to miss such factors in their rigorous due diligence and monitoring exercises. This could focus attention on LAPO, and people might actually read the MicroRate rating and wonder what on earth Triple Jump, Kiva, Calvert, and Grameen Foundation USA were doing in LAPO in the first place. No, that would not do. Something had to be done.

MicroRate had stood up for transparency, and it was chastised for doing so. Standard operating procedure: Ignore the message, attack the messenger. LAPO warned MicroRate that unless the press release was immediately withdrawn it would make sure MicroRate never worked in Nigeria again. MicroRate stood its ground. The funds fumed, but there was little they could do other than embark on a cover-up. MicroRate has subsequently worked in Nigeria, but it had crossed the unwritten line: "Never criticize microfinance ... even if you're a rating agency."

MicroRate's rating withdrawal of LAPO was a key moment for us.[3] Until then, Terry and I were little more than troublemakers asking awkward questions. Now a recognized third party, respected by everyone in the microfinance sector and used extensively by most funds, had publicly declared that something was wrong at LAPO.

One of the most fundamental problems facing a whistle-blower is that merely possessing accurate information and presenting it to the relevant parties, including even the victims, is necessary but not sufficient. There has to be an *incentive* for them to act. We were naïve to believe that these funds would thank us for our hard work, demand that LAPO improve its operations or return the investments, and then tighten up their processes to prevent this happening again. No such thing happened. The lack of any corrective action meant that we had to escalate the pressure way beyond what should have been necessary.

My career was now in jeopardy. After harassing Triple Jump, Oxfam Novib, and ASN Bank, it was clear I would never work in the closed club of Dutch microfinance again. MicroRate's rating withdrawal had irritated a number of the players in the sector that had invested in LAPO, including many of the largest players worldwide, and I was somehow associated with this case. Was this professional suicide?

This is when I got the call from Asad Mahmood, managing director of Deutsche Bank. Asad is a solid, honest, hard-working guy and a long-time friend. But Asad had also made some mistakes. Deutsche Bank had a large microfinance fund and few staff, and sometimes it had had to make an investment with less than full information. The bank had done so with LAPO. Asad was aware of the situation at LAPO. We had discussed it many times, but the MicroRate rating withdrawal had presumably rattled him into action. He formed a so-called "creditor taskforce" of investors in LAPO, and they agreed to send a different rating agency, Planet Rating, to Nigeria to provide an independent rating of LAPO. The investment funds themselves were unable to perform such a task, since they were neither competent enough nor independent. The new rating would hopefully put to rest once and for all the claims made about LAPO, address the rating withdrawal, and correct the two previous flawed ratings by MicroRate. Or so they hoped.

Asad also called me and asked me to back down. "Hugh, you've made your point. We accept this bank is doing something wrong, but it's time to back off now."

"If what I'm saying is accurate, then there's no reason to be nervous about the truth getting out. Presumably that would be a good thing, especially for the poor. And if I'm wrong, tell me. Why ask me to back down?"

"If you pursue this, it's going to cause us all some damage. We admit it was a mistake—let's now just make sure not to repeat it. But please, will you back down, as a favor?"

"Why should I back down when we have a golden chance to reveal what is actually wrong in this sector, and hurting the poor? Why back down now? The evidence is there, on the table, with the biggest names in the sector involved. I didn't cause this mess, they did."

"I'm asking you, as a friend, to back down. Please."

It was at this point that I became aware of the magnitude of what I had begun.

It was too late to back down, even though I have enormous respect for Asad. Terry and I had arranged a conference call with Calvert to discuss the mounting evidence against LAPO. We had begun initial conversations with some journalists investigating the sector, and complaints to regulators and other funds were in progress. Above all, to back down now would not be in the best interests of the poor. We had these investors on the run, finally, and still had a few cards to play. So with a heavy heart, I had to tell my friend Asad that it would not end here.

My wife was vaguely aware of what was going on and asked me if what I was doing was really that wise. She knew about the injustices present in some microfinance. She works in the women's rights movement, and to the extent that women are the focus of microfinance, they are also the predominant victims when things go wrong. LAPO was almost exclusively focused on lending to women, which bothered her yet further. But we had to consider our future. Was it sensible to irritate a group of Nigerians who could potentially make substantial profit out of this MFI? How nasty could things potentially get?

In late 2009 a rather disturbing event took place. We received a death threat. We never found out who it was from, but the call originated from a Mongolian telephone and was most likely unrelated to these broader events. My project had involved firing a number of questionable employees who could well have been retaliating. The language is too vulgar to reproduce, but the call was made to an employee of my client, demanding my phone number and threatening to kill him for failure to hand it over. The call was transcribed and reported to the police and to my employer. The stakes were rising for all concerned.

I was now detested by most of the main players in the sector, we had received a death threat, and for what? None of the accusations against LAPO had been refuted. Most had not even been discovered by me, but by the rating agencies. All I had done was draw people's attention to them. The only skill one needed to reproduce these findings was the ability to read. Here I was, in Mongolia, on the microfinance "Ten Most Wanted" list, because I was actually pointing out abuses of the poor. I had been working in microfinance for a decade. I was now at odds with the powers-that-be in the sector, but what choice did I have? Back down? Join them? Sweep this under the carpet? Join the skeletons in the ever-expanding closet of our sector? These were not small players in the sector, but some of the largest funds on earth, and more were about to join the party.

A Planet Rating team flew to Nigeria at the behest of the creditor taskforce. They had presumably been warned that this was an extremely delicate case. We waited with bated breath. If Planet Rating discredited MicroRate's analysis and subsequent press release, the investors would be delighted. They would then promote Planet Rating to be their most favored agency, a highly public defeat for MicroRate, Planet Rating's main competitor.

In December that year Jessica and I opened a bottle of champagne—transparency had triumphed. Planet Rating awarded LAPO a C+,[4] one of the biggest downgrades in microfinance history (from B+; specific scores cannot strictly be compared between rating agencies, although they are highly similar). The Planet Rating report confirmed everything that MicroRate had discovered. Planet Rating had not compromised one iota in its report. Indeed, it discovered a number of new items that had evaded MicroRate (although one must consider the head start that Planet Rating had in performing this rating). It began: "Insufficient Board of Directors oversight and persistence of potential conflicts of interest."[5]

Some items were surreptitiously buried in footnotes, such as the discussion of the *external* auditors of LAPO, Ejoh Moju & Co.: "Mr. Andrew Ejoh, head of Ejoh Mojuh & Co. is the brother of Mr. Felix Ejoh, [board of director] member of LAPO."[6] This is akin to Mr. Arthur Andersen being the brother of Mr. Enron. The general manager for corporate affairs and risk management was none other than the brother of the chief executive officer.[7]

Donors included Ford Foundation, United Nations Development Programme, Grameen Foundation USA, and USAID.[8] By far the greatest source of financing was client savings, the bulk of which were forced savings. And the IT system was still not working properly.

The discussion of the interest rates in the Planet Rating report is intriguing. To much fanfare, LAPO had issued a press release announcing it was reducing its monthly interest rate, from 3 percent to 2.5 percent, but it failed to mention that the forced savings required to obtain a loan were simultaneously increased from 10 percent to 20 percent, and that the interest the clients earned on their savings was reduced from 6 percent to 4 percent (far below the rate of inflation).[9]

"The decrease in interest rates coupled with the increase in the level of cash collateral, resulted in an increase in the Effective Interest Rate (EIR) for the clients to 125.9 percent from 114.3 percent."[10] Although this may appear to contradict the MicroRate report, a footnote explains: "The EIR without the cost of cash collateral decreased to 73.5% from 85.1% before." There was now little doubt about the interest rates LAPO was actually charging the poor.

Planet Rating took the precautionary measure of sampling random branches, where they discovered "inconsistencies of up to a 6% difference in the amounts of PAR,[11] arrears and numbers of clients." This may not sound a lot, but PAR, or portfolio at risk, the proportion of a loan portfolio that is not repaying on time, is generally between 1 percent and 4 percent, so to be out by 6 percent is quite a wide margin of error. If savings mobilization, albeit illegally, was at least done well, it might be justified, but Planet Rating commented in yet another revealing footnote: "From January to September 2009 [internal audit] detected 126 cases of frauds related to unremitted savings collection."[12] The report points out the obvious advantage to LAPO of (illegally) capturing cheap savings from their clients, but warned that "the collection of voluntary savings on the field has notably contributed to increasing risks of savings misappropriation by some [credit officers] or clients."[13]

Let's not brush this over: The savings of some of the poorest women of Africa were being stolen.

MicroRate had taken the bold step of actually describing LAPO's activities as *illegal*. Planet Rating repeated this description explicitly in the rating when describing LAPO's mobilization of savings.[14] LAPO's assurances that it would legalize its operations and obtain the required licenses from the Central Bank by January 2010 were described by Planet Rating as "not realistic."[15] LAPO had yet to meet the requirements laid down by the Central Bank in 2006.

Perhaps the greatest relief to MicroRate was that Planet Rating confirmed the "insufficient data reliability" that had led MicroRate to issue its controversial press release.[16]

Almost every aspect of the operations was criticized in the Planet Rating report: management, human resources, governance, internal audit, risk management. Little was left uncriticized in the report, other than, of course, LAPO's profitability, which remained stellar. Could this possibly explain how so many microfinance funds had managed to turn a blind eye to the other problems? LAPO had been promising investors for years that at some point it would become a regulated bank and seek external shareholders, and first priority in IPOs is given to those existing lenders. LAPO was potentially the goose that might one day lay the golden egg of a Compartamos-style IPO in Africa's most populous nation, where shareholders could make returns similar to those made by the fortunate shareholders of Mexico's most notorious MFI. Remember Maria Otero's $1 million bonus as CEO of Accion? One can only speculate if that prospect featured in the minds of the CEOs queuing up for a slice of LAPO's equity.

With these ratings in the public domain, can there be any other explanation why so many of the world's supposedly most reputable funds had invested in an institution that was so obviously exploiting the poor and had only one thing going for it—profitability? Motivation is a hard thing to prove, but more evidence would soon emerge. A final blow to the creditor taskforce was mentioned in a subtle phrase toward the end of the rating: "The insufficient transparency in reporting to funders in December 2008, combined with the Nigerian economic crisis, detracted some potential investors in 2009 and contributed to a request for early repayment."[17]

Although vague, this most likely refers to a microfinance fund canceling a due diligence midway upon discovery of "anomalies," and the other funds withdrawing from LAPO as a result of the revelations emerging.

It appeared that at least someone had actually read and understood the ratings.

The taskforce was presumably a little disappointed when Planet Rating published possibly the most negative rating ever given an MFI of LAPO's size and age. LAPO appeared every bit as bad as some had feared. MicroRate's previous ratings and subsequent withdrawal were entirely vindicated. The creditor taskforce had demanded the rating, and it was now faced with irrefutable evidence that they themselves had requested. Surely, now the taskforce members would take action?

In a word, no.

I had explained the entire situation to Eliza Erikson at Calvert Foundation in detail, in telephone calls and by email, in mid 2009. I had naïvely assumed that Calvert would be interested to know not only that LAPO was engaged in some fairly unsavory practices not necessarily to the benefit of the poor or in line with Calvert's own stated goals, but also that they had most likely been deceived by Triple Jump, who had not entirely explained the full truth about LAPO to Calvert. I did not understand, at the time, why Calvert decided to ignore our warnings. I was trying to help them with information they would struggle to find themselves. We were not suggesting that Calvert had done anything wrong, but rather that they had been duped. Given that I had the documents Triple Jump presented to Calvert, had visited LAPO on-site extensively while working at Triple Jump, and my findings had been supported by various independent documents, including a Dutch court verdict, I was a credible authority on the subject. Instead, I was ignored.

Calvert raises funds from the MicroPlace website, which is owned by eBay and is regulated by the SEC, so we had an additional channel: a formal complaint to the SEC. Terry is a U.S. citizen and MicroPlace can only accept investments from U.S. citizens or companies, so in early November Terry made a whopping $25 investment in LAPO through MicroPlace and Calvert Foundation.[18]

A few days later he filed a formal complaint to the CEO of Calvert Foundation,[19] Shari Berenbach.* The complaint highlighted the full range of problems at LAPO and made explicit references to the preconditions of the Calvert investments clearly stated on its website, some of which an investment in LAPO appeared to contradict. The complaint

discussed the legality of LAPO's operations, the rating withdrawal, and
the high interest rates that seemed utterly at odds with any semblance
of fairness. Because Terry was a U.S. citizen investing through an SEC-
regulated broker-dealer, Calvert was obliged to respond. Calvert realized that we had done our homework well. Of course, none of this was
new information. The fear of SEC investigation probably helped. Terry
made specific references to aspects of the Calvert Foundation prospec-
tus that we knew were questionable, particularly regarding its "rigorous" due diligence procedures, of which we suspected it had in fact done
little. One poignant section of his complaint asked a remarkably simple
question:

> On the MicroPlace website under the Nigeria section there is a charming
> description of a [client], Martina Okhuelegbe, who is apparently in the
> business of soap production. Her photo appears under the title "Some
> of the borrowers we serve." Perhaps you could explain why this same
> photograph appeared on the NOTS Foundation website until recently
> and was featured in the monthly magazine to ASN-Novib investors in
> Holland, *Op Koers* number 23 of February 2008.[20]

The three funds had presented identical photos of an African woman in
a classic microfinance pose dressed in colorful clothing. One had cropped
the photo in an attempt to disguise that it was in fact the same woman.
Although sharing photos is not illegal, the intention was clearly to suggest
to the investors in these funds that their money had gone to this client. In
Holland this was reminiscent of a child-sponsorship scandal the country
had faced some years previously, where photos of children sent to donors
turned out to be less linked to the donor than the NGO had claimed. As
with Kiva, the goal is to link the ultimate investor or donor to some poor
African, to create some bond, however genuine this may be in reality. It
pulls in the cash. NOTS, Calvert Foundation, and ASN Bank could not
even be bothered to get three separate photos of claimed clients for their
websites.

Calvert had no idea quite how much information we had on the LAPO
case. Although the letter was well researched, at this point they had no
idea that I, a former employee of Triple Jump directly involved in their

dealings with LAPO, was working with Terry. Their reply was interesting, but the phone call was the highlight.

Shari Berenbach, in her capacity as president and CEO of Calvert Foundation, replied to Terry on November 18, 2009.[21] It was a fair letter, acknowledging that his concerns were mostly valid, promising to look into the matter, and mentioning they were part of the creditor taskforce. She made two specific comments that caught our attention: "We want to reassure you that our investment in LAPO was made following our standard operating procedures which include a comprehensive on-site due diligence evaluation that identified many of the issues you highlighted in your letter."

We knew what Calvert's due diligence had involved, since I was at Triple Jump at the time it was apparently performed, and we knew which issues had been detected on this trip: very few. But was Calvert suggesting it knew about these issues at LAPO and had invested anyway? That was almost more worrying than admitting it had simply not conducted adequate due diligence. Regarding the new rating of LAPO demanded by the creditor taskforce, due imminently, Shari had specific plans: "If the rating concludes that the required steps have not been taken and that operating weaknesses in these areas persist, we will then evaluate our options to take further corrective actions through our standard rights as a lender."

This appeared to suggest that Calvert would review its investment in LAPO if the rating was negative. When I read the letter I developed a thin veneer of respect for this woman. Sure, Calvert may have messed up, but they were not succumbing to knee-jerk reactions. They were investigating, and were apparently prepared to take action. It was a pity they had not done so six months ago when I explained the case to them, but better late than never. This bit of respect was not to last.

Shari Berenbach eventually left Calvert and become head of microfinance at USAID, and so is not a person to criticize lightly. I therefore would not like to color the facts with my own subjective perceptions, and instead simply reproduce excerpts of the conference call Terry and I had with the senior management of Calvert Foundation on January 11, 2010 (my emphasis added). I had clearly explained all problematic aspects of Calvert's investment in LAPO more than six months earlier, and we did not actually suggest that Calvert had made the investment in full knowledge of them but rather had been misled by Triple Jump. They had replied to Terry in writing two months previously, admitting that many of his points were valid and that they would take action based on the Planet Rating report. The report is dated as December 2009, but perhaps Calvert had not yet received a copy. Let's give them the benefit of the doubt. The transcript, audio recording, and written correspondence is on the book website for the interested reader to form his or her own conclusions:

Shari: We really do appreciate the level of serious diligence and efforts that you bring to this all. I want to actually hand you [to] Lisa Hall,* who is our executive vice president and chief lending officer...[22] I would like to get her to actually be the individual to help manage and respond to your questions.... We have a few of us here from the Calvert Foundation Team that are on hand just so that we can be accessible to answer and respond.

Lisa: We also wanted to be sure that you knew that because of the conference line that we are using related to the functionality of our conference call system that the **call is being recorded.** We wanted to have this call with the idea that we would put some **closure on the issue** ... We have extensively reviewed your complaint and your questions.... We admire the thoroughness of your research and the depth of your concern. I wanted to say as the person who is responsible for our portfolio, that **I am aware of the issues** that you have raised and we are working very actively to address them. We share your goal of making microfinance as effective and efficient as it can be. And **we are standing by our decision to invest in LAPO** as part of this goal. It's very important to us that our investors are comfortable with their investments and feel confident about the use of their money and we want you to be happy, we'd like to offer to **move your investment** into another Calvert Foundation offering on the MicroPlace platform or to **provide you a refund.**

Terry: I'm interested in understanding who of your Calvert Group went to Nigeria to pay a site visit to LAPO. And when did they go, and have you been back in the space of your first visit? Would it be you, Lisa? Is there another colleague that you would have used?

Lisa: So, as I think we've indicated in our written communication to you previously, Calvert Foundation works with a network of subadvisors that conduct our on-site due diligence.

Terry: So you would have used then a subadvisor to provide you with the information, to provide you with the due diligence?

Lisa: Yes, that's correct, and again, we're hoping that the purpose of this call is to **really put closure to the issues.**... You've been really great in terms of engaging on the issues and doing a lot of research here. We feel like our written response which was quite extensive has addressed any questions that you might have about due diligence, and we're here to either refund you [$25] or move your investment because it's very important to us that investors be happy with their investment and if in any way that you are unsatisfied with your investment here **we are prepared to address that.**

Terry: What I find deeply concerning is the admitted 109 percent rate that LAPO has, in a very transparent way, reflected in Chuck Waterfield's* report on his audit. Do you consider 109 percent fair return for risk? I mean does that make sense, does it fall within the place of the 18 percent and 60 percent that MicroPlace has, as their "red line," because I guess what troubles me the most is the red lines that I feel LAPO has crossed, and I don't understand why these may not be a serious concern for Calvert.

Lisa: As we addressed in our written communication and as we stated previously on the call, we are aware of the issues that you've raised and we are working actively to address them.

Terry: But you continue to invest and to work with LAPO?

Lisa: Yes, **we are standing by our decision to invest in LAPO** as part of our goal to make microfinance as effective and efficient as it can be.

Hugh: You mentioned in your letter to Mr. Ward that the goal would be to secure this banking license by the yearend 2009. Could you tell us, has that taken place?

Lisa: ... we're not in a position at this point to discuss the current ongoing due diligence. We feel like we've addressed the issues you have raised and that you are raising once again on this call in our letter, and we are actively working with LAPO to make microfinance as effective and efficient as it can be....

Hugh: What does that actually involve? What are the steps which you are taking? Because obviously it's very difficult to know if you've achieved the steps you're taking if you keep the steps discreet. What are these steps? Because I don't think that they were mentioned in the letter.

Lisa: We do think it's very important for all of our investors to be **comfortable with their investments**. If you, and here I am speaking to Mr. Ward, if you are unhappy with your investment [of $25] and would like us **to transfer it into another offering or to refund you in full we are completely prepared to do that.**

The conversation persisted for several more minutes—but that's the most we were able to extract—an offer to refund $25. The full transcript is posted on my website and repeats the assurances that Calvert would continue to work with LAPO despite all the concerns we could raise, including the troubling public record, the replicated photos of claimed clients, LAPO's questionable legality, and other items. It came as something of a surprise to Calvert to discover that I had been working at Triple Jump at the precise time they made their investment in LAPO, adding to our credibility as sources of accurate information about what had actually taken place, but this was also brushed aside.

In truth, I had discussed most of these topics with Eliza Erikson of Calvert six months previously, including introducing her to Sarita Mehra of Grameen Foundation to discuss them further. They had explicitly said they would wait for the rating to be published and review their options. It was published shortly after this call, and yet they took no action. They made four separate offers to Terry to reimburse his $25 investment, which ultimately was what held them liable under the SEC regulations. They would have bought his silence for a $25 fee very willingly at this point. They seemed positively keen to "close the issue." They appeared convinced that their processes remained unchallenged, and I forget how many times they said they "stood by" them.

They were busted, and they knew it.

They made five separate, explicit declarations that Calvert would *not* be withdrawing from LAPO. But four months later that is precisely what they did, after Calvert was named and shamed in the *New York Times*, which is what most likely prompted their actual withdrawal from LAPO.

In January 2010, a fortnight after we had our call with Calvert, the Subcommittee on International Monetary Policy and Trade of the House

Financial Services Committee summoned six microfinance sector leaders in front of a panel to answer questions on the state of the sector.[23] This was largely a missed opportunity, since only pleasant, nonpenetrative questions were asked. Speakers were allowed to get away with their standard bromides on the merits of their activities. However, some enlightening comments were made. Robert Annibale of Citibank, investors in LAPO, stated (emphasis added): "While Citi Microfinance is a specialized group that focuses on Microfinance, we have ensured that our work with the sector is reflected in our credit policies and product processes across geographies and we serve these institutions through our Citi branches locally, in local currencies, local languages, under local law and increasingly with other domestic bank and capital market partners."[24]

What? "Under local law"? Two seats away from him sat Damian von Stauffenberg,* the founder and chairman of MicroRate, the same institution that had charged, in a public report, that LAPO was operating *illegally*. The Planet Rating, hot off the press, repeated this precise word. Could Annibale not have known that LAPO was operating illegally? I had explicitly pointed this fact out to him clearly five months before, and he had personally acknowledged me. In the Q&A, asked about sectorwide risk without regulatory oversight that could lead to a crisis, Mr. von Stauffenberg commented quite explicitly:

This is indeed a concern we have, not that we are seeing that microfinance funds are crumbling, but we see the potential, because basically the microfinance funds on the whole, with some exceptions are not terribly transparent, if you go into their websites you will find beautiful pictures of what's going on in Bangladesh or in a poor country but you will not get the kind of information that you would take for granted in any fund that you invest in here in the U.S., and that's worrying, if people invest because its microfinance and microfinance is good and Muhammad Yunus is for it, that is sowing the seeds for trouble, and so I think yes, a lot more transparency is needed in the field of microfinance funds.[25]

This was a pleasant change from blaming "rogue MFIs" for all the scandals: a direct accusation of a lack of transparency at the funds requiring regulatory oversight, made by one of the leaders of the sector directly to the U.S. House of Representatives. Have a look at any website of a microfinance fund and you may be surprised at the lack of genuine information. This echoed the words of Robert Pouliot: "Reporting is generally poor. Even the more transparent [microfinance investment funds] fail to provide the disclosure expected by investors in conventional vehicles."[26]

But then came a complete curveball comment from Wagane Diouf* of Mecene Investments, whom I had never heard of before:

> I get seriously worried when these institutions [MFIs] start mobilizing funds from institutions that attract capital from individuals in the U.S. and other western countries, such as, um, **I won't mention their name,** but institutions that have web-driven mechanisms to attract investments, but the financial reporting of the institutions that are receiving these funds are **not up to standard at all,** they are **very poorly regulated,** it's a **very opaque part of the industry.**[27] (emphasis added)

I would not dare speculate as to which institution he could have been referring to, but this seemed to be an explicit concern about the peer-to-peer (P2P) organizations. The suggestion could hardly be clearer: taking money from the general public via a website and sending it to substandard, poorly regulated and opaque MFIs. These were industry experts speaking under oath, and events were about to highlight one rather clear example of just such a peer-to-peer organization raising funds from U.S. individuals and lending them in large amounts to an institution that could well be described as poorly regulated, substandard, and opaque. I was reassured by this comment from an industry leader: I was not the only one to "get seriously worried" about certain areas of the P2P sector.

Was any action taken as a result of this? Take a wild guess.

# 11

# Enter the *New York Times*

Terry and I had discussed the LAPO case with a number of journalists who were beginning to take a hard look at the microfinance sector. On April 14, 2010, Neil MacFarquhar of the *New York Times* published a front-page article entitled "Banks Making Big Profits from Tiny Loans," which criticized the microfinance sector in general, mentioned LAPO in particular, and named three investors explicitly: Kiva, Deutsche Bank, and Calvert Foundation, which was raising money for LAPO on the MicroPlace platform.

> Until recently, MicroPlace, which is part of eBay, was promoting LAPO to individual investors, even though the website says the lenders it features have interest rates between 18 and 60 percent, considerably less than what LAPO customers typically pay. As recently as February, MicroPlace also said that LAPO had a strong rating from MicroRate, yet the rating agency had suspended LAPO the previous August, six months earlier. MicroPlace then removed [LAPO] after *The New York Times* called to inquire why it was still being used and has since taken LAPO investments off the Web site.[1]

What? Calvert had withdrawn LAPO from MicroPlace? Calvert had defended its decision to invest in LAPO and the very process by which it made the investment just weeks earlier, stating five times that it would not withdraw LAPO. The pressure from the *Times* had finally prompted action. MicroPlace's description of *any* of LAPOs ratings as *strong* was bizarre—they were some of the most critical I have ever seen.

While many within the microfinance sector were extremely irritated by this article, I was delighted. Once again the activities of a rogue MFI were exposed, but this time alongside three names of their investors, in a major publication read beyond the narrow confines of the microfinance sector. The interest rates paid by some of the poorest women of Africa were displayed prominently for all to see, with the origin of such funds discussed. All this raised a valid question very publicly: Can the poor benefit at such interest rates? This was a triumph for transparency, and for once attention had focused not simply on the activities per se, but on the source of the funding.

The *Times* article went on to quote Muhammad Yunus:

"We created microcredit to fight the loan sharks; we didn't create microcredit to encourage new loan sharks," Mr. Yunus recently said at a gathering of financial officials at the United Nations. "Microcredit should be seen as an opportunity to help people get out of poverty in a business way, but not as an opportunity to make money out of poor people...." Mr. Yunus says interest rates should be 10 to 15 percent above the cost of raising the money, with anything beyond a "red zone" of loan sharking. "We need to draw a line between genuine and abuse," he said. "You will never see the situation of poor people if you look at it through the glasses of profit-making."

While I applaud Muhammad Yunus's stance against high interest rates, what the *Times* article failed to point out was that while LAPO's interest rates were clearly above those Yunus would likely approve of, one of LAPO's biggest investors was none other than Grameen Foundation USA. Another reference in the *Times* piece is also noteworthy:

Unwitting individuals, who can make loans of $20 or more through websites like Kiva or MicroPlace, may also end up participating in practices some consider exploitative. These websites admit that they cannot guarantee every interest rate they quote. Indeed, the real rate can prove to be markedly higher.... At Kiva, which promises on its website that it "will not partner with an organization that charges exorbitant interest rates," the interest rate and fees for LAPO was recently advertised as 57 percent, the average rate from 2007. After *The Times* called to inquire, Kiva changed it to 83 percent.[2]

Kiva was in an unenviable position here. It had been criticized on numerous occasions in the press,[3] and this was yet another blow. We seemed to have a rather clear case of intermediaries either being incompetent or actively seeking to deceive their own investors. The article also referenced the Planet Rating observation of LAPO's rates actually increasing from 114 percent to 126 percent through clever use of forced savings. Again: Why did Kiva, Calvert, and the rest, when fully aware of the actual reality at LAPO, delay so long in taking action? Why did it require the *New York Times* to prompt this?

A related question: Why did some pull their investments in LAPO while others did not? ASN Bank and Calvert/MicroPlace had. Kiva was about to suspend LAPO. But BlueOrchard had only recently invested, and another Swiss microfinance fund, responsAbility, and Belgian fund Incofin were about to invest in LAPO. An unnamed fund was referenced by Planet Rating as having pulled out after discovering anomalies during its due diligence visit.[4] A final question was whether Citibank and Standard Chartered, whom Grameen Foundation had guaranteed in their investments in LAPO, had known the full situation at LAPO when they invested. These remain open questions to this day.

Terry and I still had unfinished business to attend to. Calvert had begrudgingly taken action, but Kiva, America's premier peer-to-peer (P2P) microfinance lending platform, was still siphoning money from the general public to hand to LAPO to rid the world of poverty.

The P2Ps are strange creatures, mostly not quite what they appear. They apparently differ from a traditional microfinance fund by offering a direct connection between lender and borrower. There are various P2Ps out there, springing up weekly with marginally different websites craftily designed to extract money from the hapless user, but they largely do the same thing.

I'll use Kiva as an example, since it is fairly representative and bigger than the rest. It is essentially a channel whereby Mr. Smith in Oregon can supposedly lend directly to Doña Maria in El Salvador. P2Ps play on the idea of a personal relationship. The investor (or lender, or donor, or *Kivan*, depending on the terminology and methodology—the person with the money) responds to a nice-looking photo and business story and chooses to "lend" to that person. To give the P2Ps their due, the small print often explains that this is not quite the case, but the average user doesn't read the small print and is under the impression that they lent to Doña Maria. Many, in practice, actually believe this. They will often say things like, "I know where my money is actually going!"[5]

In fact, the only major differences between a traditional microfinance fund and a P2P is the deal size and the number of photos on their respective websites. On Kiva you can invest with $25; in most funds you need substantially more than this, sometimes stretching to hundreds of thousands of dollars, just to sit at the table. Although P2Ps have been successful in raising significant sums of money from people who may never have considered investing in microfinance and brought the sector into the living rooms of the masses in a tangible way, there are some pitfalls.

First, as pointed out by the *New York Times*,[6] loans may actually have already been financed. Doña Maria may have actually already received her loan some months ago, and the Kiva user is financing this loan retrospectively. There is nothing wrong with this per se, but Kiva has been criticized for not being entirely transparent. For example, if a Kiva borrower is already in default, there is no way to see this before the hapless Kivan finances her. The process is not entirely 100 percent transparent, but is perhaps defensible on logistical grounds. The alternative would be that Doña Maria would be knocking on the door of the MFI each day asking if the Kivans had raised the money yet. A pragmatic detail of no huge importance. Is it strictly P2P? It's debatable.

Can we be sure that all the borrowers on Kiva actually exist? That is a more penetrating question. Reverting to the LAPO case, there was a wonderful example of this in November 2009, when a Kivan had astutely observed two almost identical photographs, in the same hair salon, of two separate borrowers applying for loans.[7] The photos are taken from different angles, but the shampoos on the shelves, the scotch tape holding the hair dryer together, and the décor were identical. Not only this, the photographer accidentally left the time and date stamps on the pictures, leading the Kivan to comment on the unusual fact that the photos were taken only fifty-five seconds apart.

Perhaps this was one that slipped through the net. Kiva does random spot checks in the field to verify data, but another Kivan had embarked on an eventually successful campaign to get Kiva to stop financing cock-fighting loans on animal cruelty grounds,[8] a topic that had also managed to slip through the net. "Kivans Against Cock-Fighting"—this is not a joke—has a web page and eighty-nine members.[9] Matt Flannery,* founder of Kiva, commented: "Cockfighting in Peru is legal and part of a rich cultural tradition. It may not be humane or palatable from a Western perspective, but that misses the point. Kiva, the organization, should not be making those decisions. Our lenders should be the ones voting with their dollars."[10]

So, if prostitution is legal in a country (such as Holland), can Kiva finance microloans to pimps? Kiva has financed seven cock-fighting loans,[11] and it has also branched out to coca-leaf production.[12] Both activities are prohibited under California state law *within* California— but what about financing such activities abroad? Would an SEC-regulated institution such as Deutsche Bank lend to Peruvian cock-fighting rings or coca producers without questions being asked? Is there not something unusual about the U.S. government funding large-scale coca eradication programs as part of the "War on Drugs" while Kiva provides loans to those who sell the leaves?

Data is certainly flowing in copious quantities from the MFI partners to the Kiva platform. There are photos, nice stories, details of what the loan will be used for, the loan term, usually the geographic region, the family of the borrower, her employment history, details about the MFI, the amount she wants to borrow, frequency of repayment, term of loan....

Notice anything missing? No interest rates are quoted.

How can such extensive data, including photographs, make it all the way from Bayan-Ulgii in Mongolia to California, and yet the interest rate cannot? Upon closer scrutiny Kiva does state the *average* interest rate that its partner MFIs charge, but it doesn't state the *average* loan term, or the *average* amount an individual client wants, or the *average* number of female clients—these are specified. The answer to this question is more profound than it initially appears. I am not sure if anyone really knows the answer. Claiming that it is too complex for some reason is flawed, since MyC4, a Danish P2P, manages to report this information perfectly and to two decimal places. One explanation is that Kiva is *not*, in fact, a P2P, but a peer-to-MFI—that is, just another microfinance fund with a novel means to attract capital via a website.

A blog written by Dave Algoso compared Kiva and child sponsorship, where donors could "adopt" or "sponsor" a child: "The Kiva model is similar to the present child sponsorship model: create an emotional connection between the donor/lender and the child/borrower in order to bring in the money, but run the program on the beneficiary end in whatever way makes the most sense."[13] Kiva has perfected the feeling of a bond between lender and borrower, but what actually happens in the background is indeed a little more complex.

Are all the funds actually invested in microfinance activities? Kiva is continually receiving money from its users and from loan repayments (or repayments from MFIs—let's not link these too directly to individual loans). Meanwhile, it is disbursing money for new loans and giving money back to its own departing Kivans. It may also hold the money of investors who have funds not yet loaned out, so the funds are sitting idle. Thus it has to have a buffer. No P2P can have 100 percent of its capital invested 100 percent of the time. But how large should the buffer be? According to the IRS Form 990 returns for Kiva, which it is obliged to file as a nonprofit, in 2009 the balance of this buffer account was $28,469,545.[14] By 2010 it had grown to $33,684,384.[15]

That's quite some buffer. What does Kiva do with this buffer? Well, this is explained in the notes to the financial statements quite clearly: "Kiva is entitled to the interest earned on the funds held in the FBO [FBO = for benefit of Kiva user funds] accounts, pursuant to the binding terms of use with individual users at the time a user account is established."[16] Remember that form where you clicked "I accept"? And note that this buffer amount is in addition to the $8,284,818 that Kiva has on its own balance sheet in cash and cash equivalents.[17]

These numbers seem a little high to me, but I pass no judgment. I merely make the observation that this appears like a lot of money not actually used in microfinance activities: $42 million.

The questions continue. Kiva boasts 180 field partners—MFIs that raise money from the Kiva platform. However, 33 of these are pilots. Of the remaining 147 Kiva MFI partners with a track record, 95 are active; the rest are "paused" or "closed." If we exclude the new MFI partners that are still in pilot stage, over a third of Kiva's partners have been closed or paused. Why? The website states that this could be instigated by the MFI or Kiva, and could be due to violation of policies. LAPO is a "paused" client. One cannot help but wonder what triggers "closed" status.

As an innovative platform bypassing traditional microfinance funds to deliver money from the ultimate provider to the ultimate borrower, is Kiva more efficient? Well, it is certainly profitable. Total revenue in 2010 was $13.7 million with total expenses of $8.3 million, resulting in a net increase in assets of $5.3 million (a similar concept to profit in a private company).[18] But to measure whether it was efficient, we must look at the total funds lent over the period and compare this amount with a traditional microfinance fund. This is actually difficult data to obtain. Kiva reached $100 million in loans in November 2009 and by November 2011, 24 months later, it had reached $212 million, suggesting it disbursed an *average* of a little under $5 million a month over this period.[19]

If we assume that Kiva disbursed $60 million in 2010, total operating costs were $8.3 million according to the accounts available on Kiva's website, which is actually not efficient at all. Operations cost Kiva $0.14 for every $1 loaned. This amount doesn't include the subsidy of the 436 volunteers who worked for Kiva for free in 2010, as reported on its IRS Form 990.

A microfinance fund may earn a 2 percent annual management fee, so to lend $60 million, a typical fund would charge $1.2 million, from which all operating costs would be met. Such a fund would charge $0.02 to lend $1, a seventh of the operations costs incurred by Kiva. Kiva, on the other hand, earned $13.7 million in 2010, predominantly from online donations from users and corporate donations. It appears that people are willing to pay a huge premium for the feel-good factor of Kiva. In fact, they are paying 11 times more than they would have through a typical microfinance fund. That might be justified if Kiva were in fact a P2P.[20]

Compare this to Triple Jump, which has a current microfinance portfolio of €240 million ($300 million).[21] Its net equity increased by a mere €654,211 in 2010 ($840,000).[22] Triple Jump managed a fund five times larger than Kiva's but did so for a fraction of the cost and earned a fraction of the "profit" of Kiva (Kiva is an NGO, so we cannot use the word "profit" but instead the annual increase in the value of the net assets). Using the overall increase in the net value of the companies in 2010, Kiva earned over six times more than Triple Jump on a mere fifth of the loan volume.[23]

And if the 2010 loans were on the order of $60 million, doesn't $42 million in idle cash still seem a little high? This is mostly money that does not belong to Kiva, as Kiva clearly states, but it is money that generates a tidy interest income for Kiva.

So the next question is whether the borrowers actually get a reasonably priced loan on the back of this elaborate exercise. The answer to this question is that no one really knows. The problem is that Kiva doesn't declare, or know, or both, the actual interest rates on the loans. It quotes the average interest rate of the MFI only. If we take this statement at face value and assume therefore that Kiva end-borrowers pay the same as any other borrower from the MFI, then the answer is no. The end-borrower would pay the same interest rate whether the funds came from Kiva or a regular fund. Presumably, were Kiva loans cheaper than the average loans, Kiva would be proud to mention this fact. But Kiva doesn't. And what are these rates? Well, they vary enormously, but the maximum I have found recently is 88 percent at BRAC in South Sudan (4,000 borrowers), with Credituyo and CrediComun offering loans to a further 10,000 borrowers at 88 and 74 percent, respectively,[24] so it doesn't seem that Kiva is partnering with particularly low-cost MFIs either. Whatever happened to "affordable credit"?

Some Kiva loans are surprisingly cheap for the end-borrower. However, these are not necessarily where one might expect. There is one country where *average* interest rates (actual interest rates are unknown, of course) are consistently under 20 percent, and the cheapest I have found so far on Kiva charges a positively reasonable 8.3 percent.[25] Which country?

The USA. Yes, the credit risk of Americans is so incredibly low, and the operating costs in America are so much lower than those in Mexico, that these institutions manage to offer very reasonable rates while poor Mexicans just south of the border may pay ten times more for a loan. Would an MFI charging impoverished Americans 86 percent interest generate much positive publicity for the microfinance sector in the USA?

Kivans themselves earn no return. Kiva earns substantial revenue but not from the MFIs but rather from donations and interest. The MFIs receive interest-free capital from Kiva, which they lend at their regular interest rates to the poor, who receive no beneficial pricing terms despite the money originating from Kiva. It is no surprise that MFIs are delighted to accept Kiva money—it's free and earns them the same margin as any other source of capital. Admittedly, it is a hassle having to email photos and little stories to Kiva in California.

Who donated to Kiva in 2007? It's a long list: Microsoft ($65,729), Ashoka ($25,000), Craigslist ($25,000), Dermalogia ($250,000), Google ($58,303), Intel ($64,733), Intuit ($57,109), JP Morgan Chase ($25,000), Keen ($240,328), Omidyar ($1,662,488), the California Governor's Conference for Women and Families ($75,000), Visa ($1,000,000), Walmart ($1,000,000), and that ever-faithful supporter "anonymous" ($180,929), among others.[26] But by far the largest source was the Kivans, who donated $4,850,507 in 2010.[27]

Thus a final question: What are Kiva's repayment rates? Here is a real mystery. MiCredito in Nicaragua is an example. According to Kiva, MiCredito enjoys a 0.57 percent delinquency rate and a 0 percent default rate—nearly perfect scores.[28] According to the most recent data from MIX Market, however, 9 percent of MiCredito's portfolio is delinquent for more than thirty days, and it wrote off 11 percent of its portfolio last year,[29] and yet not a single default on Kiva. Amazing.

If I put myself in the shoes of an MFI: By absorbing the occasional default from clients, which I would have to do with money from a microfinance fund, I can keep the P2P happy and get interest-free capital. If the portfolio gets so bad that this is no longer worth it, I can shift the defaults to the users of the P2P and walk away.

It doesn't cost much to hire some local staff to snap photos, write little stories, and send them off to the U.S., so why not? The P2P is happy with its 99 percent repayment rate, I'm happy (I get free capital), the clients of the P2P are happy (they're saving the world), and the poor guy gets the same loan as usual and is oblivious to these shenanigans, beyond having his photo taken occasionally.

Kiva currently reports a repayment rate of 98.89 percent.[30] Only 1.11 percent of loans default in what may hardly be considered an easy period for microfinance. I do not doubt that 98.89 percent of the capital loaned was returned to Kiva, but I wonder if this necessarily implies that 98.89 percent of the MFI clients repaid their loans.

This speculation is not without basis. Even the Kiva Wikipedia page raises this question: "Whether defaults are extremely low has been questioned on the ground that a field partner may pay Kiva for loans defaulted to the field partner in order to maintain the field partner's good credit with Kiva."[31]

These P2Ps have raised immense amounts of money. For Mr. Smith in Oregon, this is quite likely the only experience he has of microfinance. He is utterly convinced that he is helping a poor person, and who am I to disagree? In a roundabout kind of way, he is. Perhaps such companies are not P2Ps at all, but organizations selling a dream, a feeling. Mr. Smith feels better about himself for having personally, directly helped a poor person whose photo he can see online. Surely that is a service, if not to the poor, then to Mr. Smith. Kiva itself summarizes this succinctly: It allows Mr. Smith in Oregon to become a "mini-Bill Gates."[32] Who else offers this service?

I would advise users of P2Ps to consider them all with extreme caution. Look into the details, particularly the reporting of interest rates and the alignment of interests between the donor/investor, the P2P, the MFI, and the poor. There are some good ones out there, but you need to know precisely what you are doing. In the USA at least, such institutions are obliged to file certain reports on their websites, so there is some transparency, but I wonder how many users wade through an IRS Form 990 report or the financial statements. But bear this simple fact in mind. The transactions executed on Kiva are unregulated—you have almost no protection other than those afforded to you under the Constitution. Personally, I find it astonishing that such companies are permitted to operate beyond the reaches of the regulators, but then again I found the activities and subsequent collapse of AIG fairly unusual, and Kiva is small fry compared to this.

As Wagane Diouf stated to the House of Representatives, "It's a very opaque part of the industry," so investor beware; you have been warned. And do not worry, this digression on Kiva is not superfluous—its number one partner was LAPO.

I met Jessica Jackson,* cofounder of Kiva, at a conference in Spain and warned her about LAPO. She seemed to appreciate the potential gravity of the situation, but nothing happened. I had discussed my concerns with DOEN, the Dutch Postcode Lottery fund that invests in various developmental projects and had provided seed capital to Kiva. DOEN introduced me to Matthew Flannery,* the CEO of Kiva, by email in February 2009, urging him to listen to some valid concerns I had about one of its partners. We exchanged a number of emails and had various conversations on the topic.[33] Kiva was naturally hesitant to stop providing money to LAPO, which was fast absorbing huge sums from the lending platform, and it decided not to act.

Terry and I had been investigating Kiva for some time. Our general concern was that there were ethical questions regarding taking money from Kivans, lending this interest-free to LAPO, which would then lend it at extortionate rates to the poor while failing to reveal the actual interest rates that these loans were made at. Kiva disagreed and ignored the issue. The discussions took place in 2009 at the highest levels of Kiva, with the CEO and Premal Shah,* who subsequently became CEO.

Initially Kiva reported that LAPO's interest rate was a mere 24 percent per annum. Kiva would cite this figure on numerous occasions over the coming year. Not even LAPO had ever claimed rates quite this low. Using the loan repayment schedules of actual Kiva clients at LAPO, we demonstrated an interest rate approaching 100 percent (slightly lower than for non-Kiva clients at LAPO), far closer to what has subsequently been proved to be the actual rates charged to the poor. Matthew Flannery replied: "Thanks for your note. My guess is that the way that LAPO reports the interest rate to us on our website is different than the way you calculated it. Most likely, LAPO reports it to us in a way that is generalized over their entire loan portfolio and thus more forgiving to them. Most likely, the way that you are calculating it is more accurate."[34]

He never actually denied the interest rates charged to the poor, even in early 2009. A few percentage points here and there is one thing, but we were talking of a slightly larger "error."

In early 2009 Kiva clearly knew, as indicated in email correspondence and in conversations, what was going on at LAPO, but took no action and happily channeled millions of dollars from its users to Nigeria. It eventually took action a year later, when the *New York Times* named and shamed them. Why did it take so long? And what was Kiva's reaction to the *Times* article, which seemed to confirm claims that its management was well aware of?

CEO Premal Shah issued a feeble defense on the Kiva website the day after the *Times* article was published:

> Considering LAPO's social mission of serving Nigeria's poor and unbanked, **we've grown comfortable over time with their approach.** One update we're watching closely: they are currently in the process of getting approval to **legally** offer microsavings to their borrowers, which will require them to convert to become a microfinance bank. Like all of our MFI partners, we will continue to review the performance to ensure they remain consistent with Kiva's social mission.[35] (emphasis added)

This was unusual. Kiva defended the right of MFIs to charge high interest rates by referring to their "social mission" and did not suggest it would take any action against LAPO, to whom it had lent a total of $5 million of Kiva users' funds. There was nothing new in the article that they didn't already know, and yet Kiva explicitly stated that it was *comfortable* with LAPO. Kiva also suggested that LAPO's current practice of capturing savings is not legal. Why did Kiva go out of its way to draw attention to this additional problem at LAPO, even though it had now been confirmed by three ratings?

A few days later Terry and I had a call with Kiva. I asked if they had read the December 2009 Planet Rating report on LAPO, assuming naïvely that they would at least read ratings as part of the most primitive due diligence process before continuing to pump millions of dollars into a Nigerian MFI. Wrong. I suggested they contact Planet Rating, get a subscription, and read it. They did precisely this. We then discussed LAPO in some detail.

On April 29, fifteen days after the *Times* article was released, fourteen days after their public defense of LAPO, Kiva finally announced: "Kiva is suspending fundraising for loans from the Nigerian microfinance institution LAPO and refunding LAPO loans on the site that have yet to be fully funded."[36]

Kiva also added an unusual additional justification in the announcement: "Other factors like population density in the countryside and local inflation rates can also greatly increase costs of offering loans in the Developing World." It is true that MFIs in sparsely populated countries incur higher operating costs, which can feed through to higher interest rates. (Mongolia proved that even this obstacle can be overcome with efficiency and regulation.) High inflation rates also demand higher interest rates. Agreed.

But Nigeria is one of the most densely populated countries on earth and does not suffer from particularly high inflation (ranging from 5 percent to 14 percent since 2006). There are 155 million Nigerians (a fifth of all Africans) in an area slightly larger than Texas. A flawed argument from the CEO of Kiva as part of its defense of why they had pumped $5 million of funds from the general public into LAPO: Welcome to the world of Kiva.

We made two suggestions that could help prevent such cases happening again: Find out and publish the actual interest rates on Kiva loans, so that Kivans can judge for themselves what they deem reasonable; and clearly define a cap at which point Kiva would deem an interest rate charged by an MFI as extortionate. These seemed quite modest and practical suggestions, and Kiva followed neither. To this day Kiva does not reveal the interest rates on individual loans and simply quotes the average rate (or "portfolio yield") of the MFI.

But the more fundamental question, particular to the Kivans, is simply this: "You lend your money for 0 percent. How do you feel about BRAC lending this money to poor women in South Sudan and pocketing 88 percent interest while you assume the risk of the client not repaying the loan? Do you actually think the woman is going to leapfrog out of poverty at such rates?" If they are happy with this propsect, and many appear to be, fine. But to call this transparent is not a step I would personally take.

Because Kiva was *comfortable* with LAPO, I am personally *uncomfortable* with Kiva.

In May 2010, after the *New York Times* article was published and after the various funds had withdrawn from LAPO, another curious announcement appeared. The Schwab Foundation, the charity arm of the well-known World Economic Forum group that sponsors the Davos conferences, issued its social entrepreneur awards for Africa. I read with utter incredulity that LAPO had won,[37] and I then contacted Schwab. It transpired that the foundation had never actually visited LAPO, nor had its due diligence extended to reading the front page of the *New York Times*. Schwab was clearly embarrassed about this award after having reviewed the information I presented them, and we had an amiable and open conversation. However, Schwab refused to answer one simple question: How, of all the thousands of MFIs in Africa, did Schwab select LAPO? I repeated the question in an email some weeks later but received no answer.

If you look at the Board of Directors of the Schwab Foundation,[38] it contains one obvious microfinance expert with good knowledge of the sector and a clear stance regarding exploitative interest rates. He also holds a Nobel Peace Prize.

Muhammad Yunus.

Was it a coincidence that Grameen Foundation USA was a major investor in LAPO, was about the only voice in the market still actively defending LAPO, and that Yunus also sits on their board?[39] Even if Yunus was not directly involved, as a board member of Schwab, surely he would have frowned on giving LAPO such an award if only on the basis of the interest rates it charges.

Not wanting to be left out, Grameen Foundation USA jumped into the debate surrounding the article in the *Times* that had dared to challenge their noble Nigerian partner. Grameen refuted most of the article,[40] naturally, but failed to state the interest rate charged by LAPO (or defend having family members on the board, or the legality of capturing savings, or the savings frauds, or the dodgy data presented to the rating agency). Grameen simply said that LAPO had reduced its interest rate by "one sixth of its previous rate"—technically true (from 3 percent per month to 2.5 percent).[41] But Grameen forgot to translate this into an actual APR rate, or to consider that at the same time LAPO had doubled the forced savings it obliged clients to deposit, or to consider fees charged to the client. A genuine oversight I am sure, as was this comment in its 2007 newsletter: "Grameen Foundation's partner LAPO who does not ask for collateral and offers drastically lower interest rates [than moneylenders]."[42] No collateral? What about the forced savings?

In October 2010, Camilla Nestor,* one of the senior managers of Grameen Foundation USA, defended LAPO's interest rates on the Givewell blog, stating that "[LAPO] has retained the services of consulting firm MicroFinance Transparency (headed by noted expert Chuck Waterfield) to review its interest rates and related policies."[43] Despite this apparent effort to increase transparency, neither LAPO or Grameen Foundation published the results of the interest rate analysis until they appeared in the February 2011 Planet Rating report.[44] Perhaps the reason Nestor failed to subsequently explain the findings of the investigation of LAPOs interest rates is contained within the report?

LAPO had its pricing certified by Microfinance Transparency as of December 2010 for its Regular Loan. The average price for a first-time loan with insurance was estimated at 80 percent, expressed as a nominal APR. Since then, the average APR for Regular Loan decreased to around 76 percent. However, Microfinance Transparency also noted that as the client remains with LAPO, the APR can reach between 99 percent and 144 percent by the third year (depending on the loan amount and increase at each cycle) due to the cost of accumulating weekly savings that cannot be withdrawn.[45]

Grameen Foundation's attempt at transparent interest rate disclosure at LAPO had backfired. How could Grameen square an interest rate of 144 percent with its stated principle of fair interest rates? Only a few months later Grameen was insisting that the rate charged was a mere 57 percent. What would their board member Muhammad Yunus think? Simply denying the finding was perhaps Grameen's only option. But what else was in this report?

Having written what some would consider to be one of the most devastating rating reports in microfinance history, LAPO invited Planet Rating back for a second rating, as it had done with MicroRate previously. Planet Rating then rewarded LAPO with the most trivial of upgrades, from C+ to C++, performed by the head of Planet Rating Africa.[46] Profitability continued unabated and some problems were being addressed, but little else had improved. LAPO did eventually get a banking license, presumably persuading the Central Bank of Nigeria to overlook the legality of its operations over the preceding half-decade. LAPO had also hired an external auditor from Deloitte who was presumably not related to the senior management. The former auditor was promoted to the Board of Directors. But three noteworthy points jump out from this 2011 report:

- LAPO was converting from an NGO to a registered, shareholding bank, and the CEO was awarded 12 percent of the shares.[47]
- Two Swiss funds, responsAbility and BlueOrchard, had joined the roll call of proud investors, while others had dropped out. Grameen Foundation and Standard Chartered remained, of course.[48]
- Interest rates ranged from 76 to 80 percent per year (excluding forced savings), but some of the less fortunate clients were paying rates of up to 144 percent.[49] What would Muhammad Yunus say about this?

This is basically the Compartamos model applied in Africa. At last there would be a chance to cash out all the wealth accumulated during the NGO years for the benefit of the CEO and whichever investors were allowed to take a slice of equity.

Thus, after four highly critical ratings consistently exposing some serious breaches in any semblance of integrity, BlueOrchard, responsAbility, and Grameen Foundation USA remain invested in LAPO, despite the endless claims on their websites of high ethical standards. LAPO even signed the SMART Campaign, an initiative set up to protect the interests of the poor, despite SMART's full knowledge of LAPO's activities. Such funds know that their own investors are unlikely to ever visit Nigeria or read a rating, so they act with complete impunity.

Transparency is great, when it suits them. The *appearance* of transparency is even better.

In 2010 Danish filmmaker Tom Heinemann* released a scathing documentary about the microfinance sector,[50] discussed later, but a relevant exchange with Grameen Foundation is noteworthy. In the film he directly challenged Alex Counts,* the CEO of Grameen Foundation USA, about the rates of interest charged by LAPO:

Tom Heinemann: "One of Grameen Foundation's partners is the microloan bank, LAPO in Nigeria. According to the *New York Times* the annual interest rate charged by LAPO is more than 100 percent. A bargain, claims their partner."

Alex Counts: "In Nigeria, for example, an organization that we work with—LAPO has been criticized—Well, as it happens, many Nigerian banks that operate in the rural areas charge twice as much as LAPO— so LAPO is a bargain for them even though it seems high for people seeing it from the outside." [51]

At the UK premiere of the documentary *Caught in MicroDebt*, Counts appeared with Heinemann on a panel and faced the following question about LAPO.

Questioner: "[A]t one point you justified an interest rate of 100 percent on the basis that it was 50 percent lower than the local loan sharks. If that was happening, say in this country [the UK], and we were justifying loans to the poor on the basis that they were 50 percent lower than a loan shark, they would just have no credibility whatsoever in their work. Surely it should be lower than the local bank rate, not lower than the loan shark rate, if you actually want to help people out of poverty?"

Alex Counts: "On the issue of LAPO, first of all the *New York Times* got the interest rate of LAPO wrong. They quoted someone who is actually a disgruntled employee of LAPO who was trying to stir up trouble for it. The actual interest rate at LAPO is 57 percent."

So to summarize: The *New York Times* was wrong; MicroRate was wrong (twice); Planet Rating was wrong (twice). Grameen Foundation themselves asked Microfinance Transparency, an organization that does nothing else apart from calculating microfinance interest rates, to confirm the interest rates, and Microfinance Transparency calculated rates ranging from 76 percent to 144 percent; so they too were wrong. Kiva was presumably wrong also, since they had suggested that interest rates were 83 percent prior to withdrawing from LAPO. David Roodman of the Center for Global Development was wrong. Givewell was wrong.[52]

Grameen Foundation was right, and everyone else was wrong.

As unfathomable as it may seem, shortly after MicroRate had withdrawn its rating of LAPO, BlueOrchard invested $2 million in LAPO in November 2009. This was the largest and debatably the most reputable fund in the sector. That some startup fund with a few idealistic students running the show could be duped by LAPO was perhaps comprehensible, but not BlueOrchard. BlueOrchard had either invested in full knowledge of the situation, or it was guilty of particularly poor due diligence. Better to say nothing, which is precisely what they did, initially.

In response to the *New York Times* article some months later, by which point Planet Rating's 2009 report had also been published, and various investors had withdrawn from LAPO, BlueOrchard released a formal response. It was gibberish.[53]

BlueOrchard's defense seemed deliberately evasive and designed to appease an uninformed investor. Were such spin unique to just one or two funds, they could be considered isolated cases, but what was now emerging was evidence of *systematic* behavior across the entire microfinance investing community. Note how these guys all operate so *similarly*, using the *same* arguments?

In October 2010 I was in Montevideo attending some drab conference. The same people doing the same deals each year, endless talks on banal topics of limited interest to anyone other than the speakers themselves, and generally an excuse for an all-expenses-paid party. Jean-Pierre de Klumpp, the CEO of BlueOrchard whom I had met previously in New York and corresponded with sporadically, was speaking in a panel on "amazing social impact indicators" or some such spin. I thought it would be interesting to confront him publicly with his LAPO investment.

| BlueOrchard's Defense of LAPO | Reality |
| --- | --- |
| "Lift Above Poverty Organization (LAPO) is a good MFI that merits BlueOrchard's financial support." | LAPO suffered the first rating withdrawal ever, and was downgraded from B+ to C+, among other critiques. |
| "LAPO demonstrates a strong social commitment, healthy growth and proven international support.... Deep social mission and vision." | Chronic client desertion is hard to square with strong social commitment; growth and profit were certainly contributing factors, and many international supporters have subsequently withdrawn from LAPO. |
| "Ambiguous legal status" | Both MicroRate and Planet Rating defined various activities as *illegal*, and promises to transform LAPO into a legal bank entity had been made since 2006. |
| "Strong loan portfolio quality" | Both MicroRate and Planet Rating pointed out serious problems of data integrity, particularly with regard to portfolio quality. |
| "High profitability allows for continued growth and healthy margins are reinvested fully in the institution (no dividends have been paid so far)." | No mention of the extortionate interest rates. Where did this profitability come from? Nice reference to no dividends *so far*. |
| "'Compulsory savings' or 'forced savings' as mentioned in the article are common practice in microfinance." | They may be somewhat common, but they are usually regulated, are of questionable benefit to the client, and impose substantial additional costs on the client. Onlending of these savings is illegal, but is practiced by LAPO, as explicitly described in the ratings.. |
| "Nominal interest rates range from 2–3 percent flat per month, which brings the effective interest of their main product to a range of 70 percent to 80 percent." | BlueOrchard forgot to include the impact of other fees and savings, which add about 40 percentage points and result in an effective interest rate of 125.9 percent, a full 50 percentage points above BlueOrchard's "estimate." |
| "LAPO's interest rates are to cover its high operational costs." | Operating costs are not so high as to prevent massive net profit. Interest rates could fall dramatically and still cover costs. And defending high interest rates by citing poor productivity is questionable. |
| "Requests for LAPO to lower its interest rates by 0.5 percent per month in October 2009 were met with approval by the management and board and quickly implemented." | The 2009 Planet Rating report noted that this reduction in rates coincided with an increase in forced savings, leading to an overall net *increase* in client interest rates from 114.3 percent to 125.9 percent. |

I sat through the entire panel, and Jean-Pierre stood up and lectured us about how BlueOrchard could measure social impact and took this very seriously and would transform the world and rid it of poverty and make a profit in the process: the standard patter.

Question time arrived. I shot up my hand, but someone beat me to it. Next question—up went my hand. Damn, missed it again; but then one of the staff handed me a microphone. I would be next. I had the question clearly in my mind:

> Mr. de Klumpp, you managed to invest $2 million in one of the most discredited, illegal MFIs on the planet. This MFI, LAPO in Nigeria, has featured on the front page of the *New York Times*, suffered the first-ever rating withdrawal followed by a major downgrade. A number of investors, including people in this room, pulled out of LAPO, and its social impact has been challenged substantially, if on no other grounds than chronic client desertion, as well as the legality of LAPO raising $30 million in savings without a banking license and charging the poor interest rates of up to 144 percent per year. Could you explain how your social performance indicators assessed this MFI?

The guy in front of me had embarked on a ten-minute red-herring question of trivial significance. I was about to ask a question that would be the talk of the entire conference and create a huge, public embarrassment for one of the biggest players in the sector.

The panel ended. I never got to ask my question publicly. I'd ask him privately instead.

"Jean-Pierre, you remember me, Hugh Sinclair. We've spoken a few times. Including about going to Antarctica...."

I thought this was a suitable ice-breaker—when he discovered I had been to Antarctica in a previous conversation he had expressed great interest in going and asked me to send him some information. The ice did not break. He starred coldly at me.

"What do you want?"

"I want to ask you about your talk on social performance at BlueOrchard with specific reference to your investment in LAPO."

Wow, he was furious.

"How dare you speak to me like that. I have nothing to discuss with you."

"Jean-Pierre, I had that microphone in my hand. I was the next in line for a question. Had that guy not banged on for ten minutes about the importance of livestock statistics or whatever trivia, you would have faced this question in front of an audience. You are lucky to face it privately."

"I don't need to answer your questions; it's none of your business what we do at BlueOrchard."

He probably should have walked away at this point, but instead his eyes narrowed, his voice lowered, and he stayed close to me, uncomfortably close, staring at me.

"Wrong. It is my business. You invested funds that do not belong to you in an MFI that anyone capable of reading would have realized was a scam, and people trust you to invest their money with at least some integrity and care. I know people who invest in your fund."

"Who we invest in or not, is up to us," he snorted.

"Yes, and we now know the actual level of due diligence you do, and I assure you, I will be advising people to steer well clear of your so-called microfinance fund in future."

I was actually surprised that I had rustled up the courage to address him in such terms. He knew exactly what I was saying, he knew he had screwed up and that maybe no one else on earth knew this quite as well as I did. He knew that I did in fact know people who had invested in his fund. There was no valid way he could defend an investment in LAPO other than as pure profiteering at the expense of the poor. Or by admitting utter incompetence.

For a second I thought he might hit me. I had been attacked in a conference once previously for daring to publicly question the miraculous properties of microfinance, but this would certainly draw attention to my unorthodox methods and the case at hand. But common sense, albeit in scarce supply at such events, prevailed.

"I have nothing more to say to you," he said, and walked off.

I had certainly pressed the right button, and I wouldn't be applying for a job at BlueOrchard any time soon. No ground had been won, but none had been lost. The information we had about BlueOrchard could be used at any time, so there was nothing to fear. I was sweating, adrenaline rushing, thirsty. I went to the main room and got a juice or two. I just stood there, alone, on some weird high.

A young woman I had met at previous conferences and who worked at another microfinance fund called responsAbility (spelling theirs) came up to me.

"Hugh, you okay? You look a bit strange."

"Hi Louise. Yeah, sure, I'm fine.... Er, I just had a bit of a run-in with someone, just now, bit jazzed about it, all a bit weird."

At that moment, facing Louise, I saw Jean-Pierre approaching us quickly.

He brushed Louise aside in an ungentlemanly manner and addressed me: "I would like to go back in time ten minutes and forget our previous conversation and speak to you in a civil manner about how we can resolve this situation."

Let's face it, aggression doesn't suit the Swiss. Respect for the veiled apology though.

"Cool, we can do that. What do you propose?" I asked.

"Well, I think there may have been some problems with LAPO, that is possible, and I think it would be helpful if you explain in detail, maybe in an email, what you know, and we will look at it and take it seriously. Would you do that?"

This would simply return me to the endless feeble iterations of "we are looking into the claims and will investigate the case according to our rigorous standards of due diligence excellence blah blah." That would be pointless; been there before; standard operating procedure.

"No, Jean-Pierre. What I will do is the following. I will write down everything I know, point out to you all the painfully obvious sources your bullshit due diligence failed to consider, and you'll have one week to think about your investment in LAPO, at which point, if you fail to take action, we'll consult the Swiss financial sector regulator and make a formal complaint about BlueOrchard, as I did with the Dutch regulator, which led eventually to ASN Bank pulling out of LAPO; as we nearly did with the SEC regarding Calvert and MicroPlace in the U.S., until they had the sense to pull out of LAPO. They can decide. You will hear from me in a few days. Good afternoon."

And I walked off.

I wrote him the email with all the information. He never replied. I was too tired of LAPO to file another complaint with the regulator. Our daughter had been born a month before, and I had better things to do with my life. Someone else will probably do this some day, and as soon as anyone genuinely investigates BlueOrchard they will find the information readily available. BlueOrchard is not doing well now; its returns are low. They issue occasional reports about their astonishing social impact, but I don't bother reading them anymore. Frankly, with Dexia Bank facing imminent collapse, I doubt that any regulator is going to pay much attention to a $2 million loan that will almost certainly be repaid even if its poverty impact is negligible, managed by some fund manager in Switzerland. The European regulators have much bigger fish to fry right now.

The final irony in this entire incident is that almost exactly a year later LAPO gained a new investor—responsAbility, where Louise works.[54] Honestly, you couldn't make this stuff up. Is it acceptable for responsAbility to invest in LAPO? My opinion is no, but frankly, that is up to their own investors to decide now—I've done my bit.

So investors beware: These funds are the masters of spin. They are unregulated in practice, raising the question of where lies the ultimate responsibility. If an MFI exploits the poor, even though doing so may be legal in its own jurisdiction, with funds provided by an investor who either fails to do a due diligence or turns a blind eye to such activities, and then assures its own investors of some miraculous social impact, is this not ultimately the fault of the regulator of the fund? If one accepts that the regulators were asleep at the wheel, is there much hope referring such cases to these same people? If the U.S. and European regulatory authorities are prepared to allow such practices, clearly in violation of the best interests not only of the poor but also of their own citizens, who am I to disagree? I don't live in the U.S. or Europe and would never invest a dollar in one of these funds. If investors in these funds are sufficiently convinced by a glossy brochure with some pictures of poor people sitting at sewing machines to hand over their money without further analysis, I'm afraid I must say "the more fool them."

This story does not represent all funds, or all MFIs. Thankfully. LAPO may be a rare (but not unique) case. Unfortunately, the funds involved with LAPO do collectively represent a large proportion of the entire microfinance funding sector, though each of them has also invested in good, genuine MFIs. For them also, this is, I hope, an outlier. It's hard to know for sure, given the extremely low levels of disclosure and transparency.

But what message does this send to other MFIs? They observe that even behavior such as LAPO's does not preclude investment from the microfinance funds—indeed, such profitability might actually help secure it. Even Oxfam Novib continued donating funds to LAPO, an extremely profitable MFI, until 2009. Not investing, but *donating*, Dutch taxpayer funds.

The weakness and lack of sophistication of such defenses indicates the contempt with which these funds regard the ultimate investors. Do the funds and MFIs really care about what is actually happening to the poor in these countries—or do they simply care about maintaining the façade to their own investors to keep the funds rolling in? Are they seeking to provide *fairly* priced loans to the poor, or make decent returns for themselves? By *high returns* I do not refer solely to financial profit. Do not underestimate the benefits of prestige, of running a large fund where employees believe the CEO to be some sort of visionary; of speaking engagements at conferences and pats on the back from celebrities and world leaders. Of medals and awards, board seats, interviews with journalists, respect at dinner parties for saving the world from poverty. Greed is not purely financial. I would have greater respect for them if their actions were *better* disguised, if they at least covered their tracks, if their logic was better honed. They don't even use spell-check in their proposals. Triple Jump got the name of LAPO wrong in its proposal to Calvert, and no one even noticed. In any other niche in the financial services sector they would be considered amateurs. Microfinance is *their* niche, perhaps the only corner of the entire financial sector where such people can operate.

The microfinance sector essentially consists of three parts: the ultimate *capital providers* (governments, pensioners, individuals, savers, Kiva users, and others); the *intermediaries* who channel the funds (the microfinance funds in developed countries and the MFIs in developing countries); and the *poor* who receive the loans in developing countries.

The problems arise in one section—the intermediaries. It's no more complex than the relationships shown in Figure 1:

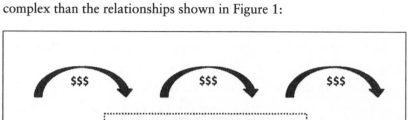

Figure 1  Possible Conflicts of Interest in Microfinance

The ultimate investors are not in practice protected by any meaningful regulation, have a limited idea what their funds are being used for, and rely entirely on the fund or P2P to reassure them. The MFI charges whatever interest rate to the poor it can get away with, in unregulated markets with minimal client protection. Profit accumulates in two segments: the MFIs (from the interest paid by the poor) and the funds (from interest or equity from the MFI). The MFI sends reassuring photos to the fund, which uses them to keep the funds rolling in. The funds have immense power over the MFIs, since this inner club not only controls a large portion of the capital available, but multilateral institutions are increasingly also channeling funds to the microfinance sector through these same players. They are the only practical means for the average investor to invest in microfinance, and they control the flow of information to these same investors. It's a club. Or a cult.

Such power does not *necessitate* fraud and deception, and there are genuinely ethical funds, but they must compete in the same opaque market to attract investors. When investors struggle to accurately distinguish between genuine intentions and window-dressing, how do they know how to invest wisely? There is so little actual transparency in the sector, to an untrained eye it is extremely hard to see through the well-honed façade. Ethical, beneficial MFIs may find it hard to attract financing from the funds, since they are generally less profitable than the sharks.

This is why one can genuinely suggest that the sector has been hijacked. MFIs are mostly unregulated in practice, and they may or may not choose to exploit the poor. But the microfinance funds are also largely unregulated in practice. Does the Swiss regulator check through BlueOrchard's microfinance portfolio? When I spoke to the BlueOrchard CEO, he admitted that they didn't even go to Nigeria because it was dangerous, so I doubt that the Swiss regulator paid a visit. And yet they were willing to send millions of dollars of their investors' capital to LAPO. The poor suffer and abandon the MFI; the capital providers (ASN Bank pensioners, Kiva users, and others) are none the wiser; and current and future profitability accrues to LAPO and its investors, the unregulated intermediaries. At the appropriate moment, they transform the entity into a private company and convert the accumulated wealth to shares and cash out. It's as simple as that.

Compartamos set the standard. Accion was the first major winner.

To keep everyone reassured that all was well with microfinance, the sector set up the SMART Campaign to establish fair and decent client protection principles. That sounds laudable. Who's behind SMART? That's right, Accion.[55] It's a closed circle.

Here ends the LAPO story. It is a sordid story that encompassed the worst of microfinance. But it is a story that needs to be told, as a warning. When Yunus said we had become the sharks we were supposed to replace, he was right, and "we" does not refer only to the MFIs. "We" are also in charge of the financing.

I began to wonder if these events were unique to my experience, the countries or MFIs I happened to have worked in, the funds I happened to have encountered—was I just unlucky, or was something even more sinister lurking under the surface? Events in Nicaragua, India, and Bangladesh, as well as common sense alone, would shed light on this question.

# 12

# Collapse, Suicide, and
# Muhammad Yunus

Picture the scene. A kite-maker in Nicaragua had managed to obtain loans from all nineteen MFIs that formed the Nicaraguan Microfinance Association.[1] With weekly repayments this would involve an average of four daily repayments. There could, conceivably, be queues of loan officers outside her kite shop. As she paid off one loan officer with the proceeds from another, the actual loan officers probably got to know one another in the process. Maybe she had to visit the MFIs rather than the loan officers visiting her premises? How much time does it take to visit four MFIs a day, queuing up, making the payment, and then shuffling off to the next? How many kites could she possibly make in the meantime? Sound like a farce? Welcome to Nicaraguan microfinance.

Nicaraguan microfinance should have served as a wakeup call for the entire sector, since its lending reached such absurd levels. Of course, it did not. The biggest single private investor by the end of 2008, that bastion of due diligence and conservative lending in the interests of investors and the poor alike, BlueOrchard, had managed to pump in a whopping $46 million alone.[2] It is quite possible that the capital provided to our highly leveraged kite-maker actually originated in Geneva.

Nicaragua was recipient of one of the greatest-ever influxes of capital in the checkered history of microfinance for the size of the country. Almost every fund piled in with such reckless abandon that the dot-com collapse looked like an act of positive prudence. At its peak, total lending by MFIs was estimated at $420 million in 2008,[3] in a country of about 5.5 million, not all of whom were poor (and MFIs generally don't lend to children). Officially interest rates were capped, but MFIs could earn as much again with a not particularly sophisticated use of fees and "other charges." The government turned a blind eye to such obvious workarounds of the law designed specifically to prevent usury. In a massive exercise of musical chairs, MFIs were encouraged by funds to take yet more money, to lend to yet more "entrepreneurs," and earn a fat margin in the process. Details, such as having nineteen simultaneous loans, were ignored as long as the music continued to play. The microfinance funds proudly announced their social impact by catapulting people out of poverty in Nicaragua, that war-torn country many had heard of but few could identify on a map, and they naturally earned their fair share of the profits. The musical Ponzi scheme continued unabated until one rather awkward moment that everyone had assumed would never occur: the music stopped.

If there was ever a country that demonstrated that the funding bodies had entirely lost all track of reality, it was Nicaragua. Many microfinance funds lost millions of dollars as MFIs defaulted—not their dollars, of course, but those of their own investors, thanks to their failure to consider the simple fact that pyramid schemes require permanent new injections of capital and limited withdrawals. But, as Bernie Madoff so elegantly demonstrated, the music can continue for a long time.

I worked in Nicaragua frequently, mainly with Triple Jump. I later spent months based in Panama shuttling back and forth to Nicaragua, and I knew many of the MFIs there. The profit potential was excellent. Every fund was desperate to invest there, and every MFI had offers from funds crawling over each other to lend them money. As long as an MFI had a senior manager who could read and write and knew a decent restaurant to take potential investors to, it had a good chance of securing capital. Poor clients would form queues in front of MFI branches waiting to repay a loan or request a new one, or perhaps both. Meanwhile microfinance funds formed queues at the head offices with checkbooks in hand. MFIs littered the entire country—every street corner had become an ATM where, with a signature and some form of ID, cash would be dispensed with few questions asked. The interest rates were extortionate, as usual, but no one really cared—the MFIs could boast of their 99 percent repayment rates (even though loans were repaid from the proceeds of a new loan from a different MFI, perhaps only 100 yards away); the funds would be delighted and provide yet more capital; and the MFI would issue yet more loans and send their investors a few random pictures of Nicaraguan entrepreneurs (ideally women) posing with spades or in a shop. This would ensure the money continued sloshing in to the funds from investors enthralled by this magical cure for poverty. MFIs would benefit, funds would benefit, and the clients didn't seem to care.

Then one day a small village in the north of Nicaragua pulled the plug. An MFI was getting unpleasant about some delinquent clients. The clients complained of high interest rates and loans that did not consider their underlying businesses—predominantly agriculture. The MFI complained of simply not being paid according to the terms of the loan contracts. Working with the police, the MFIs arranged for thirty clients to be jailed,[4] sparking a revolt. In traditional Latino style, the clients blocked a 10-km stretch of the Pan-American Highway and took to the streets. Other clients decided not to bother repaying their loans. Alas, for this MFI there were enough of these clients that it would be hard to confiscate that many fridges or TVs, and doing so would incite civil unrest. In fact, it *did* incite civil unrest, and Omar González Vílchez, the mayor of Jalapa, stepped in, siding with the clients (and ensuring votes in the process). There was little the MFI could do.

One particularly ambitious client in Jalapa had managed to rack up $600,000 in *micro*-loans.[5] Smell a rat yet?

News traveled fast, and within weeks the movement had spread across the country. Politicians faced a tough choice. Option 1 was to side with the poor and risk collapsing the MFIs, whose extensive debts were to idiotic foreigners in Geneva, Amsterdam, and Washington, while securing reelection in the process. Option 2 was to side with the MFIs, protect the Swiss, Dutch, and beloved gringos, enslave voters with unsustainable debts, escalate the civil unrest, and lose votes. To the surprise of the funds, the politicians sided with their voters. Democracy is a curious thing.

I found the entire incident rather inspiring:

The poor: 1   Microfinance funds/MFIs: 0

The employees of the microfinance funds, in their suits and air-conditioned offices in New York and Geneva, were in shock. As easy as it had been to write checks on someone else's account (their investors'), they had no plan B. As the movement spread nationwide, it became known as "*no pago*," or "I won't pay." The poor, who had been duped into endless loans at obviously usurious interest rates, now had a chance to turn the tables on the MFIs and gain total loan forgiveness—Christmas does come early some years. The MFIs panicked, and the funds were powerless. They had all lent to the same MFIs, so few were spared in the bloodbath. They returned to their investors, tails tucked firmly between their legs, and started making up excuses about the "ever-present risks of lending in developing countries." Their investors just sighed, figuring this was part of lending to "the poor," without much understanding of the idiocy that had actually taken place. The regulators of the funds in Switzerland, Holland, Germany, and the U.S. naturally did nothing, despite tens of millions of dollars of their citizens' investments being wiped out.

What the funds could never bear to admit was not that they had lost such substantial sums of money despite ample warnings, but that this was a grassroots movement. Their beloved clients, whom they so generously served in providing with loans (albeit at 60 percent interest per year), had turned on them. Politicians turning on them was understandable, and regulators turning on them would be irritating (though nothing a few strategic "visits" couldn't resolve), but they had an awkward phenomenon to explain. It was the poor, their *beneficiaries*, who had rebelled. The same people who featured so prominently on their own websites and marketing materials. *Et tu, Brute?*

Of course, the immediate reaction was to lament the destructive impact of the crisis upon the poor. If the microfinance sector vanished from Nicaragua, this would mean they would be denied their human right of access to capital—delicately ignoring the fact that this was instigated by the poor.

But whose fault was "*no pago*"? This was not as clear as it may initially appear.

The poor had taken the loans. No one had forced them to take them, although if everyone else in the village is leveraging their businesses through the ceiling and buying a new TV in the process, the temptation to join in may have been great. Although the actual interest rates were undeniably high, and often above the limits established by the regulator, the poor signed contracts agreeing to repay the loans. They could have realized they were becoming overindebted. Conversely, the combination of aggressive selling and lax terms handed easy money to them on a plate, and once they entered the downward spiral of paying one loan off with another, it was a hard drug to quit. But the poor were fundamentally breaching a contract, albeit a contract of questionable legality under the strict letter of Nicaraguan law. Kidnapping staff from the MFI Fundenuse on July 24, 2008, and attempting to burn down their offices in Ocotal were perhaps not among their wisest acts—the poor were not entirely innocent.[6]

The MFIs had without doubt been imprudent. They had limited controls in place; limited infrastructure and staffing to cope with such rapid growth; and it was one of their own ilk that took the bold step of having poor clients imprisoned, which was unlikely to soothe matters with the locals. They offered loans to clients without any genuine verification of their ability to repay, which is a cardinal sin in banking. However, as hard as it is to sympathize with their activities, the MFIs were being offered vast sums from the microfinance funds.

Perhaps Acme MFI had determined that a prudent growth rate was 10 percent. As the microfinance fund representatives disembarked planes in Managua and visited endless MFIs growing at 30 percent or 50 percent per year, they would naturally be less excited to lend to Acme MFI. As these rapidly growing MFIs received ever more money they had to search harder for new clients, so they would start poaching clients from Acme. This would tempt Acme to join the game—the alternative was to risk being marginalized. However, the MFIs presumably realized that these growth rates were only possible with multiple lending, and they turned a blind eye to it. One cannot take this for granted, but with $420 million lent and a relatively small population, any reasonable human being would be able to do the math. So the MFIs certainly shared in the blame.

Neither was the regulator entirely innocent. The laws dictating maximum interest rates had been violated for years. Few even hid this. ACODEP openly published its portfolio yield on the MIX Market, which reached 50 percent in 2007. How could this be possible with an interest rate cap under 20 percent (it fluctuated, but rarely exceeded 20 percent)? The regulator sided with the MFIs initially, permitting clients to be imprisoned despite their valid complaints of exploitative interest rates, and then it switched sides and defended the poor. It was hardly a stellar example of effective regulation.

The poor blamed the MFIs. The MFIs blamed the poor. The regulator probably blamed the MFIs—who knows? But no one openly blamed the fourth player in the equation.

The microfinance funds had pumped in much of this money, apparently on the basis of thorough due diligence reports and a deep understanding of the business of microfinance and the political landscape. Without their funding the explosion could not have taken place—they provided the fuel, with a fiduciary responsibility to their own investors in Europe and the U.S. to act with prudence. Could they fail to have realized that the margins were on the high side for a country with official interest rate caps? It would certainly be in their interest to turn a blind eye to this detail. Had they failed to understand that such massive inflows could not be lent rapidly enough unless there was extensive overindebtedness, multiple lending, or a lethal concoction of both? If they knew this was happening, why had they invested? If they didn't know this was happening, what did their due diligence actually consist of? But one rarely hears the microfinance funds either being blamed or assuming responsibility themselves. What was their reaction in response to the collapse? In many cases, to withdraw funding entirely. By early 2011 funding had fallen to a "mere" $170 million.[7] When the funds withdrew their capital from the MFIs, the same MFIs had to withdraw their loans to the clients, further precipitating the collapse. The classic reaction of the fair-weather banker: lend an umbrella on a sunny day, take it back when it rains.

Whose fault was it? None were innocent. The poor certainly suffered. The total amount in interest paid by the poor over this period, money extracted from their wallets, is unknown. Some ended up in prison, others saw their businesses collapse. The MFIs certainly lost, and some collapsed entirely. Staff were fired. The microfinance funds lost undisclosed amounts of their own investors' money, but they suffered very few consequences as a result. They could simply shift the blame onto the "Nicaraguan crisis" and describe it simply as a "peasant uprising instrumentalized by corrupt politicians"—part of doing business in risky countries like Nicaragua. Investors will believe that.

When the government attempted to enact new regulations, who were the most vocal critics? That's right, the microfinance funds, followed by the MFIs, who could smell a decline in margins looming. Enforced interest rate caps and actual regulation would limit profitability and would subvert the free market and therefore be evil. On September 22, 2009, the main microfinance funds had the audacity to publish an open letter in the Nicaraguan press.[8] To paraphrase a lengthy text, it said that "the investors (public and private) in the Nicaraguan microfinance sector are concerned with the *no pago* movement, which seeks to use force to dishonor their financial commitments to the MFIs that otherwise benefit more than 1 million Nicaraguans. We urge the government to safeguard respect for the law, provide security etc. We reiterate our commitment to support economic development in Nicaragua, and ask the state to ensure legal certainty in order not to jeopardize the flow of funding for this industry for the benefit of the needy citizens...." The letter was signed by all the usual suspects: BlueOrchard, responsAbility, Triple Jump, Deutsche Bank, Calvert Foundation, and even Kiva. As usual, their statement referenced fulfilling their social mission of helping the poor.

This ongoing commitment was particularly visible with Belgian microfinance fund Incofin, which had also signed the letter. Shortly afterward it announced that it would be making no new investments in Nicaragua and would not be renewing existing loans.[9] Is that not the textbook definition of a fair-weather banker? Where did Incofin invest instead some time later? You guessed it: LAPO.[10]

In yet another ironic twist, in late 2009 one of the leading microfinance publications interviewed some of the top dogs in the sector about lessons learned from Nicaragua. David MacDougal,* risk manager of BlueOrchard, suggested: "Microfinance institutions can be affected by a broad range of risks. BlueOrchard manages these risks by performing extensive due diligence on the MFIs it lends to. This includes an evaluation of the MFI's position in the market and its ability to survive unanticipated events. We also review the economic condition of countries in which the MFIs are located."[11]

Really?

This was from the head of risk management of possibly the single fund to have lost the most in Nicaragua, which had waded into LAPO *after* the *New York Times* article had appeared and almost everyone in the sector was deeply concerned about the MFI. If it weren't for people's pensions being squandered, it would be comical.

With the generous sponsorship of Morgan Stanley, the International Association of Microfinance Investors (IAMFI) published a report dissecting the mounting crisis and defaults among investors. It provided all manner of suggestions of how investors could strengthen their grip on the MFIs in which they invested, tighten the terms of contracts, and verify the enforceability of contracts locally. In a particularly charming section the authors ask the open question "How should the social impact motive upon which microfinance was founded affect a workout procedure, *if at all*?"[12] (emphasis added).

It was kind to raise the possibility that perhaps any social impact motive should be entirely eradicated from discussions on how to recover the maximum amount of money for investors in the case of a crisis at an MFI. Their explanations for crises included frauds at the MFIs; poor governance and sloppy audits; excessive portfolio growth; poor underwriting; natural disasters; local macroeconomic and political conditions; and inappropriate regulation. Their specific explanations for the Nicaragua collapse included reduced remittances from the USA (from poor Nicaraguan dishwashers who were fired when the recession hit), antagonistic sociopolitical circumstances, unsustainable growth at the MFIs, and even a decline in the price of beef.

There was little suggestion that the microfinance funds pumping hundreds of millions of dollars into Nicaragua with almost zero due diligence, fueling a bubble of gargantuan scale by local standards, may have had something to do with the collapse. The blame lay entirely with the corrupt government, questionable MFIs, and those irritating peasants who dared to complain. And who are these IAMFI folk anyway? BlueOrchard, Calvert Foundation, Triple Jump, and much of the rest of the posse. Was it just me, or was there a pattern forming here?

For the interested reader concerned about the outcome of our leveraged Nicaraguan kite-maker, the last known comment was simply: "And with that she disappeared off the map. We don't know if she left the country or is hiding out somewhere."[13] Villain or heroine? I'll buy a kite next time I'm in Central America.

Finally, to deviate momentarily into the world of economic statistics, there is a rather disturbing analysis possible with the Nicaraguan crisis. Essentially we have a closed time period: microfinance hit the country like a tsunami, then collapsed. This is a neat case study. Over this period the Gini coefficient of Nicaragua hardly changed. This statistic measures the inequality of income and wealth in a society. The poor got neither better off nor worse off compared to the rest of the country.

The Human Development Index is the UN's overall measure of well-being. When I first entered microfinance, in 2001, Nicaragua was the 106th poorest country in the world as measured by this index. Microfinance was almost unheard of in Nicaragua at this point, and there were no large microfinance funds throwing money around. By 2009, when the full Nicaraguan microfinance meltdown occurred, Nicaragua had slipped to 124th place. Thus, eight years of microfinance had done little to redistribute resources or improve the quality of life of most people within the country, which had in fact fallen 18 places compared to all other countries. This is an oversimplified example and certainly not a comprehensive analysis. But it does shed some doubt on the miraculous claims of microfinance.

Over the same period Bangladesh, the epicenter of microfinance, slipped a similar amount—14 places, from the 132nd worst-off country on earth to 146th by the same index.

Ha-Joon Chang and Milford Bateman, two well-known academics in the development arena, went even further: "All told, there is actually surprisingly little real evidence to suggest that the microfinance model in Bangladesh has succeeded in establishing a sustainable and generalizable exit mechanism out of poverty. It is striking that compared to its neighboring South and East Asian countries, Bangladesh is one of the least successful in sustainably reducing poverty and promoting 'bottom-up' productive enterprise development."[14]

Of course, the microfinance devotees can respond, "Ah, but imagine if there had been no microfinance. Maybe these countries would be *even worse off*." Such are their typical defenses when presented with actual data. They have few other defenses to offer.

One might assume that certain lessons were learned by this rather awkward experience. One would be wrong. Fortunately for the microfinance funds, the news about what actually happened in Nicaragua barely reached the mass media in the countries where their investors were based. The funds had learned from previous experiences in Bosnia, Bolivia, and Morocco, among others, that even when massive embarrassments such as the Nicaraguan *"no pago"* crisis struck, they would still receive huge influxes of capital from new investors who had been inspired by microfinance by having seen Kiva on the *Oprah Winfrey Show* or Muhammad Yunus on *The Simpsons*. The only real question was simply: Where next?

The answer was India. A billion people, most of whom didn't have a credit card yet. Some even spoke English, which was all the better. Let the game recommence.

Complicity with the microfinance funds, sleazy MFIs, abuse of the poor, cover-ups ... this is all mildly exciting stuff, but the activities described thus far pale into insignificance when one looks at the state of the Indian microfinance sector. I've never been to India, but I've watched with horror from the other side of the planet as the mess emerged. These problems appeared to be systematic across much of the microfinance sector but were not obvious to those outside the inner circle. Similar patterns of exploitation of clients, complicity of the investors, generous sums earned by a few, deliberate neglect of clear warnings—these are not outlying observations but how much of the sector routinely works. But India takes the cake.

To concisely summarize the mass of debate surrounding perhaps the sector's most embarrassing single collapse so far is hard, but I'll give it a go: India = millions of poor people densely packed together = ideal breeding ground for microfinance.

Although India has a culture of credit stretching back decades, regulation was lax in practice. The country was unprepared for the microfinance tidal wave. It had been relatively ignored by microfinance outfits, despite being right next to their darling Bangladesh, until early this century, precisely when microfinance was becoming sexy. An abundance of cheap and qualified labor; microfinance funds sitting on oodles of money they could hardly distribute quickly enough; and the caste system—all these combined to form a petri dish for a microfinance experiment of Frankensteinian proportions.

The subtle twist here, which was a novel development on the previous crises in Bosnia, Bolivia, Nicaragua, and even, debatably, Nigeria, was that in India the practices actually led to scores of suicides, occasional abductions, and some forced prostitution thrown in for good measure, to add a final veneer of respectability to the sector once and for all.

India's microfinance sector had grown from $30 million in 2002 to $460 million only three years later, according to MIX Market, and this does not necessarily include all microfinance activity. One report estimates that the Indian microfinance sector will reach $30 billion (note the "b") by 2014.[15]

Microfinance practitioners suggest that the crisis in India was a terrible shame, led by a few rogue lenders—the standard argument. In fact, there had been previous crises in India providing serious warning signs, but they were insufficiently publicized and did not stimulate any meaningful regulation or to deter investors: Krishna, Nizamabad, Kolar, and Idukki, to name but four districts in the south of this vast country. Many had warned of a crisis, even M-Cril, a microfinance rating agency, but they were of course ignored.

One journalist from the *Wall Street Journal*, Ketaki Gokhale, wrote a critical article in August 2009 (just as MicroRate was withdrawing its rating from LAPO). She suggested that moneylenders were thriving in Andhra Pradesh,[16] borrowers were under immense pressure leading in some cases to suicide, and that a lending bubble was forming.[17] What was the reaction of the microfinance community? Did such warnings in the *Wall Street Journal* attract any attention? Enter Vikram Akula,* one of the most divisive people in all of microfinance.

Vikram was CEO of SKS, the largest MFI in India. In response to the *Wall Street Journal* articles criticizing his sector, he criticized Ketaki Gokhale for her "poor and irresponsible piece of journalism" and suggested that "the esteemed journalistic standards normally found in your newspaper have been trampled upon with this story."[18] Vikram was not going to allow facts to get in the way of protecting his baby, since SKS was preparing for a huge stock market flotation. The fact that the

*Wall Street Journal* article proved to be prophetic rather than speculative was a detail. The MIX Market had ranked SKS as the number one MFI in India and the number two MFI in the world in its annual beauty parade in 2008 based on outreach, transparency, and efficiency.[19] So this must be a great institution catapulting the poor out of poverty. Ring any bells?

SKS claims to be a microfinance institution of sorts, making small loans to poor people, and yet it managed to make a rare exception to its normal maximum loan size and lend Vikram $350,000 interest-free with which to buy shares in ... SKS.[20] To add to his good fortune, he was allowed to buy these shares for approximately 1 percent of the price at which the shares were launched on the stock exchange some months later.

Just before the shares were floated, Seattle-based microfinance fund Unitus announced, to the surprise of the entire sector, that it was giving up altogether on microfinance, firing its staff, and selling its shares in SKS for something in the region of $75 million. The remaining SKS investors included some interesting characters. The Quantum Hedge Fund (led by George Soros) bought shares shortly before the stock market listing at only two-thirds of their value, another bargain. Sequoia Capital had a tidy 21.8 percent, two other funds held an additional 20 percent, and a billionaire named Vinod Khosla had a mere 6.6 percent. Our friend Vikram cashed in $13 million of his shares during the year,[21] making him the highest-paid banker in India, while still holding shares worth approximately $55 million at the price the shares were sold in the stock market flotation. And still no one wondered if this was all a bit fishy. The share price has since plummeted by over 90 percent, so poor Vikram is not as wealthy as he could have been.

When the flotation finally took place in March 2010, it was thirteen times oversubscribed and managed to beat the alluring valuation of even Compartamos in Mexico. A new standard had been set. Muhammad Yunus was none too pleased about this and likened SKS to the loan sharks that microfinance was supposed to replace. It is worth noting that Grameen Foundation USA was *not* an investor in SKS, but the World Economic Forum *did* hand Vikram Akula the Young Global Leaders Award in 2008. The interest rates SKS charged to the poor were actually comparatively reasonable (20 to 30 percent), a bargain compared to loans from LAPO. The share price rose about 50 percent, until scandal reared its ugly head, and has plummeted ever since. From a peak of about 1400 Indian rupees in September 2010 it had fallen below Rs 100 by January 2012.

The problem was that clients were massively overindebted. MFI A would lend to a client, who would then repay that loan with a loan from MFI B. There were more microfinance loans than poor people in Andhra Pradesh, but no one found this surprising. As long as the cycle continued to spin both A and B could report excellent repayment rates, ever growing volumes, and no defaults, all of which would attract investors. Until the music stopped, of course. As long as the cycle continued, interest on loans would accumulate, and eventually clients would find themselves in unsustainable situations—much like Greece. This would presumably be a big problem for the MFIs, but they employed increasingly aggressive practices in the field to pressure clients to repay—until clients simply started killing themselves. Numbers vary of the number of microfinance-related suicides, but the generally accepted number is fifty-four *currently*.

In October 2010 the *Times of India* reported a case of physical abduction entitled "Agents Kidnap Girl to Punish Mother for Loan Default."[22] Quoting the indebted woman, the *Times* reported: "My sister said the agents accompanied by three self-help group women came to our home and took away my daughter. They had threatened her that they would release Anushka only after I clear the dues."

A first for the microfinance sector, as far as I know.

In the spirit of continual innovation, another first was established in the sector. According to the *Indian Express*, "Collection agents are widely reported to use abusive language against defaulting borrowers. MFIs tend to appoint agents locally to make collections.... Some have been reported to ask women to take up prostitution to be able to pay their installments.... This is in contrast to what they say when they come to your doorstep to offer loans. They promise that there will be no harassment."[23]

This seemed to overstep a certain line of client protection principles. I wonder what the SMART Campaign would say about this: they don't have a specific policy about forced prostitution or child labor.

Then, when more heinous crimes were barely conceivable, some loan officer had the bright idea to combine the two. The teenage daughter of the borrower "was asked to do prostitution for repayment. She was kept in a house under lock, under wrongful confinement, and the girl committed suicide."[24]

These are surely isolated cases, and one should not succumb to the temptation of branding the entire microfinance sector as harmful. However, the suicides were well documented. The Society for the Elimination of Rural Poverty (SERP) identified 123 cases of harassment and 54 deaths,[25] reporting the loan details, MFIs involved, the name of the victim, and a brief description. To be fair, not all are suicides: one woman was killed by her husband while arguing about a loan repayment. Sometimes suicides would coincide with the confiscation of assets such as scooters and televisions; poisoning was a fairly common method; and harassment by loan officers is mentioned repeatedly in the report. The social stigma and fear of the aggressive techniques of the loan officers simply pushed some already desperate women over the edge. The MFIs involved vary widely, and SKS features regularly, although often the clients had loans at various MFIs. Some of the advocates who continue to defend the sector calmly pointed out that suicide is a fact of life in India, and that a bank has to expect a certain number of suicides as a statistical likelihood. How kind of them to take such a sympathetic view.

One SKS spokesman pointed out that although many of the suicides were of SKS clients, they also had loans with other MFIs and were not in default to SKS.[26] This seems to suggest that SKS was therefore innocent (or that it had applied the greatest pressure). SKS could have made a fair, ethical loan to the clients within their repayment abilities, unaware that the client was indebted to other MFIs. The problem is that all of the MFIs can use precisely the same argument. They are all innocent. Microfinance prevails unscathed. And are we to believe that none of the MFIs knew of the overindebtedness and multiple borrowing taking place?

Vikram Akula wrote a book called *A Fistful of Rice: My Unexpected Quest to End Poverty Through Profitability*, and then quit SKS in December 2010.

SKS is a signatory of the SMART Campaign for the protection of microfinance clients. Naturally. SMART's second principle is "prevention of over-indebtedness." SMART's fourth principle is "fair and respectful treatment of clients."

The suicides were a particularly dramatic turn of events. Something did appear to be going slightly wrong with the miracle cure. Do we believe that harassment, often leading to suicide, occurs only in this one region of India? Frankly, I fear this is more widespread than we yet know. An investigative journalist in Bangladesh recently discovered that some clients were selling their own organs in order to get money to repay loans.[27]

As tragic as such cases are, there are cases in Europe and the U.S. of people becoming overindebted and taking their own lives. The major difference is that in such countries there are genuine protection mechanisms in place: bankruptcy protection, usury laws, and protection from physical harassment by bank employees, such as following and humiliating delinquent borrowers in front of their neighbors. The only conclusion I can draw is that serious regulation is required to combat the inevitable consequences of unbridled greed and predatory lending in poor countries.

Some have attempted to shrug off these cases, but it's worth pausing a moment to simply imagine the despair, the pressure, the humiliation, the shame that is required to drive a poor Indian woman to suicide. I don't care if there is only one such case. If even one teenage girl was forced into prostitution to repay a loan, or one child kidnapped, is that acceptable? We claim to be alleviating poverty (to a nebulous extent and with scant evidence), and yet MFI staff are bordering on torture to obtain a $2 repayment from some of the poorest people on the planet. As if the entire affair could not get any worse, the *Times of India*, making references to the same SERP document that listed the suicides and "sources," made this startling claim: "A government study has found that some MFI agents themselves are encouraging the debtors to commit suicide so that their loans are repaid. This happens because the borrowers are covered by insurance."[28]

The Andhra Pradesh suicides have done little to promote belief in microfinance in general. Unfortunately, a suicide in India due to overindebtedness and harassment by an MFI is barely newsworthy anymore, so abundant are the press releases criticizing the sector. Calmeadow is one of Canada's largest NGOs involved in microfinance, and in a disturbing interview in mid 2011 its president was asked which region he thought might have a crisis approaching. "Mexico is a market I would be very watchful of. A lot of what was happening in India is happening in Mexico."[29] Do we learn from our mistakes? It appears not.

The title of an enlightening book by Milford Bateman of the Overseas Development Institute asks the question bluntly: *Why Doesn't Microfinance Work?* Inevitably the usual suspects attacked the book, with one of them admitting in the same review that he had not actually read it. Few dared to defend Bateman for fear of being branded heretics. The book raised valid concerns about the sector, but it was attacked on mainly personal grounds or by raising endless debates about minutiae that distracted from the core issue—the standard operating procedures of those in charge of the sector. I sent a copy to Deutsche Bank as a cheeky Christmas gift and did in fact receive a muted thanks. Not entirely surprisingly, Bateman left the Overseas Development Institute shortly afterwards, having irritated its top brass.[30]

The next blow came when eccentric Danish journalist Tom Heinemann released his notorious documentary, *Caught in MicroDebt* (*Fanget i mikrogjeld*), specifically targeting inappropriate behavior at Grameen Bank, and even on the part of Muhammad Yunus. Enough was enough. Criticism of microfinance will meet fierce resistance, but you may never, ever criticize the (claimed) founder of microfinance. He had won the Nobel Peace Prize and therefore had put microfinance on the map, permitting a multibillion-dollar industry to grow yet faster. Barack Obama awarded him the Presidential Medal of Freedom. Yunus is the pride of the sector. His story about lending a few dollars to some poor women in Bangladesh who then set up little businesses and were freed from the slavery imposed by the moneylenders is the stuff of legend. Its accuracy was in fact challenged in the documentary, which was still another example of heresy.

Heinemann made allegations about some suspect movements of funds provided to Grameen Bank by the Norwegian government in the 1990s, the veracity of which has been disputed. He placed supporting evidence on his website as well as the formal complaints filed by Grameen Foundation (*not* Grameen Bank) to the producer and the response to them.[31] Something unusual likely did take place, the Norwegians complained, but it had been corrected: problem solved.[32]

What I found fascinating about the documentary was not its content per se. I've never been to Bangladesh, but I have seen a lot of smoke in the sector and fires are usually not far beneath. What was most revealing was the panic that filled the sector. Heinemann's timing, as well as that of Bateman, was not convenient for the microfinance community, which was reeling from the Andhra Pradesh scandals and still a little sore over the LAPO case. In addition, the stock market flotations of SKS and Compartamos divided the sector into the free-market advocates and the development "NGO folk." Nicaragua had cost many funds a lot of money. The press was crawling all over the sector, and now the main man was in trouble.

In response to this wave of criticism, "Friends of Grameen" was hastily formed in late 2010 to rally in defense of Yunus, Grameen Bank, and the sector at large, and they went to inordinate lengths to refute Heinemann's documentary. The group attracted the usual suspects, as well as some heavy hitters. Mary Robinson, former president of Ireland and a former UN High Commissioner for Human Rights, led the movement. She wasn't the only former president—Oscar Arias of Costa Rica signed up. Jacques Chirac was roped in, undistracted at the time by his own pending charges for illegal political funding. The World Bank/IMF would not like to be left out of such a party, so James Wolfensohn and Michel Camdessus joined as well. There was a list of other founding members, with fairly predictable names, quite a few of which are from Grameen splinter companies. But the list did not end there. Yunus's highest-ranking friends joined the fray, and the United States actually suggested that diplomatic relations with Bangladesh might be in jeopardy.[33] That's friends in high places.

The debate, as usual, did not focus on the actual core content of the documentary, but on a series of red herrings and minutiae, and on personally discrediting Heinemann. Standard operating procedures once again: shoot the messenger, ignore the message.

When the Norwegians investigated the case, Grameen Bank was apparently cleared of any wrong-doing. A document circulated by Friends of Grameen as a "factsheet" claimed that "Norway promptly investigated the transaction again, and **again said there was no improper use of funds**" (emphasis in original).[34] Is that entirely accurate? The actual report clearly states that the Norwegians were not at all happy.[35] The opening page summarizes the facts behind the transaction that took place: "Norway regarded the transaction as a breach of the agreements between Norway and Bangladesh." The problem was rectified, but to refer to this as a complete vindication of Grameen Bank is not entirely valid,[36] as the report verifies.

According to the Friends of Grameen factsheet, "The documentary also claimed that Grameen Bank charged from 30 percent to 200 percent interest."[37] Grameen Bank *never* charged rates this high, but did the documentary actually suggest that it had? According to the transcript of the documentary, which Friends of Grameen posted on their website,[38] the wording is quite clear: "It is not only in Bangladesh that interest of microloans are sky high. Investigations show that in Africa 100 percent interest is not uncommon, and in Mexico it may pass 200 percent." The documentary thus never suggested that Grameen Bank charged rates of 200 percent, as Friends of Grameen suggest—and the claim that Mexican rates may reach 200 percent has been confirmed elsewhere, even by David Roodman, a critic of the documentary.[39]

I believe Muhammad Yunus is a great man, but the defense of Friends of Grameen appears to be willful obfuscation of the issues using the standard procedures of "spin": Issue vague, unattributed, unsubstantiated statements muddying the issues and shedding doubt on any criticism of microfinance.

Was the documentary successful? It won the EU Commission's Lorenzo Natali Prize 2011 Grand Jury Award, among 1,300 projects considered. It also won the Special TV Prize awarded by the same jury. The Chinese awarded it the Golden Panda Award as the best long documentary in the 2011 Sichuan TV Festival. It won Best Television Program, Avanca Film Festival 2011 (Portugal); and the Greeks, well aware of the problems of overindebtedness, gave the documentary a Special Award at the Patras International Film Festival 2011.

Hindering Yunus's case yet further was a lesser reported incident regarding, of all things, yogurt.[40] Over a period of nine days Muhammad was released twice on bail, first for a defamation suit filed in 2007 by a local politician, and again regarding allegations of Grameen Danone selling contaminated yoghurt to the poor.

These can't have been the most relaxing nine days for Yunus. This spate of bad luck did appear to have political origins, and Bangladesh is not considered the world's benchmark of transparency. Yunus had irritated powerful Bangladeshis over the years, including the current prime minister, and Friends of Grameen suggested that this was little more than payback. There was some doubt over whether Grameen Bank had drifted from its original, authorized modus operandi, and some questions about the precise shareholding of the Bangladeshi government in Grameen Bank. For a week or two there was a standoff between the government and the Friends of Grameen (with support from the highest levels in the U.S.). Surprisingly, the Bangladeshis stood their ground and eventually fired Yunus from Grameen Bank on the trumped-up grounds of being over the official retirement age.

It was an undignified end to the great man's career at Grameen. He had embarked on an ambitious mission: to rid the world of poverty with microloans. He was held up as the hero of the sector, and yet his advocates rarely progressed beyond paying lip service to his dream. Yunus abhors extortionate interest rates ("I never imagined that one day microcredit would give rise to its own breed of loan sharks"), and yet evidence of such practices is common across the entire sector. His dream was not proved wrong—it was never tested. He didn't fail, he was betrayed: the good shepherd who lost control of his ever-expanding flock. David Roodman, an insightful observer of the microfinance sector, described the political furor surrounding Muhammad Yunus as a consequence of *founder's syndrome*—"a pattern of behavior on the part of the founder(s) of an organization that, over time, becomes maladaptive to the successful accomplishment of the organizational mission."[41]

Muhammad Yunus even specifically criticized the interest rates charged in Nigeria. He was invited to speak in Lagos by the managing director of First Bank Nigeria, Stephen Olabisi Onasanya, who told the microfinance newspaper *microDINERO*, "It is clear from the deliberations here today that what we practice in Nigeria is not microfinancing ... [microfinance] is not about the rush to make profit, it has got to provide solutions to problems."[42]

If the microfinance sector respects Yunus as much as it claims, why doesn't it listen to his concerns? Much of the sector has replaced Yunus's original vision with simple profiteering. With so many poor people, and such potential profit on the table in an entirely unregulated sector, is this really a surprise?

Whatever the truth behind Grameen Bank and Heinemann's claims; however many suicides can be proved to have been caused by the aggressive behavior of MFIs; whatever arguments are presented to promote unregulated microfinance; whatever the proportion of those poor who actually benefit from microfinance versus those that suffer actually is, I am sure of one thing. Something has gone wrong.

Wealthy, powerful, influential people now run the sector. They have $70 billion at stake and a lot more potentially if they can oblige the next billion poor people to take a loan, and they will go to extraordinary lengths to prevent genuine regulation or scrutiny. Smokescreens are fine, actual enforcement of principles is not.

Think about that a moment: $70 billion. Let's be clear what that means. If the average *actual* cost of a loan to the poor is 45 percent, they are collectively paying $1,000 in interest each second.[43] That's enough to send five kids to school for a year in Africa. Maybe it's more, maybe less; we can argue all day about the cost of education. Maybe this capital is better deployed in offering microloans, but if so, why is there so little evidence to support this claim? Those who suggest that such evidence exists are those who have the most to gain from promoting microfinance. But there is *reasonable evidence* that it costs approximately $14 to fully vaccinate a child.[44]

If we took this $70 billion out of microfinance and shoved it into a bank account earning 2 percent per year, the return on that investment would cover 100 million child vaccinations per year. We could buy 280 million mosquito nets per year—though I suspect that would soon result in too many mosquito nets. Compromise: We could provide 75 million kids with vaccinations *and* a mosquito net per year. Would the micro-entrepreneurs be worse off? The evidence to date is, to put it generously, that not many would suffer much. "Sorry, the days of overpriced credit cards are over—but we'll vaccinate your kids and give them a mosquito net instead."

Obviously the refutation of this argument is that if we couldn't make the returns currently available from microfinance, the $70 billion wouldn't be on the table in the first place. Is that something to be proud of? Have we gone down a massive blind alley? Yunus dreamt of a day when our great-grandchildren would visit museums to learn about the awful atrocity of poverty that once plagued the planet. Is it not equally possible that our great-grandchildren will read about our foray into microfinance and ask, "What on earth were you guys thinking?" Surely the argument is not whether microfinance is a miracle cure or an evil menace, but rather whether this is the *best, wisest* way we can use $70 billion in an attempt to rid the planet of poverty. Why are so few in the microfinance cult so unwilling to address this question?

Alternatively, we could simply offer the poor microloans on fair terms, at fair interest rates, but then some of us wouldn't make quite as much money. Fewer IPOs. No $1 million bonuses. The private sector would be less inclined to fund it. Let's face it—the only reason the $70 billion is on the table is *because* of the profit.

This is not the sector I signed up to work in a decade earlier. Had I done more harm than good by playing along with the game for so many years? The sector had treated me well. I had earned millions of airmiles; traveled the world (fifty-three countries at last count); learned some new languages; and met my wife. I had even learned some useful skills. Perhaps due to the immaturity and size of the sector I had been able to see the sector from the bottom to the top. Big salaries are possible, often tax free on pleasant ex-pat packages with healthcare and free education for children and fancy cars. I could boast to my friends about how I was saving the world and still making a decent buck—excellent supplies of dinner party talk.

But you have to play by the rules of the game, and everything I saw at Triple Jump, in Nigeria, at the microfinance funds, during the cover-ups, in Nicaragua, and from the evidence emerging from India and Bangladesh began to leave a sour taste in my mouth. I had not seen the claimed fruits of our collective labor. The poor were just as poor as they had been a decade ago. Suicides may be rare, but the cases touted on websites of the miraculous lifting out of poverty on the back of a $100 loan are also rare. How many children had been removed from school, or denied the freedom to play and enjoy a carefree few years, obliged instead to work in some backbreaking job of minimal net impact on the family? And why did no one want to even address these questions? Had I facilitated such activities, even unwittingly?

I had seen some genuinely good MFIs and funds. I had seen some bad MFIs and funds. It had been a fascinating decade, and often great fun, but the actual impact we as a sector had had on the poor was disappointing. So what had I learned during the ride?

# 13

# The Good, the Bad, and the Poor

*Favelas*, or slums, litter Latin America, not just Brazil, where the word originated. They are parking lots for people. No one intends to live in a *favela* forever; they intend to use the slums as a springboard into a new life. Many migrate from the countryside to the big city in search of work, a better life, the chances that rural society no longer offers them. Half the planet now lives in cities, and *favelas* house a decent proportion of them. Quickly erected, lawless, often without the basic amenities many take for granted, *favelas* are sufficiently large to develop their own characters. Many inhabitants are never able to leave, because the new life never emerges. For me, the *favela* is a place of hope. The inhabitants are there as a stepping-stone to fulfill a dream. They look forward to something, aware that they may never achieve it; but at least they have a dream. The very existence of the ever-expanding *favela* is testimony to how many never realize their dreams in the great parking lot of life. But some do, and they keep the dream alive for the rest.

Microfinance is a *favela*.

We sell dreams. We promote the successes: the guy who turned a little business into a big company, the woman who managed to buy her own house or educate her kids. All of us dream. Perhaps the dreams of the poor are for simpler items: a home, freedom from hunger, health, maybe even a holiday one day. Microfinance touts two main dreams. The first is that you can have that thing now, today—you can go to the shop, or the doctor, or the school, and buy it now, on credit. The second is that if you work hard and grow your business, your dream will materialize from the fruits of your labor.

But is it true? You can have your dream now, but you'll pay through the nose later. You can work like a dog now, but will you actually be any better off in the end? This is not an ethical, subjective question. It is a simple, empirical question. Show me the proof that our dream shop is actually working.

We hail microfinance as an almost sacred solution to global poverty, but few are promoting *favelas*. The idea of a *favela* is to get out of it as soon as possible. The idea of microfinance is to keep people in it as long as possible.

David Roodman of the Center for Global Development in the U.S. examined the case of LAPO and verified most of my findings.[1] Phew. He interviewed Damian von Stauffenberg, the founder of MicroRate, who had visited LAPO as early as 2002 and had raised substantial concerns even then: "I could see that they were perfectly positioned to cozy up to donors, but not be financially viable. They had an efficient branch network, making lots of tiny loans, but a bloated headquarters, with a big office studying women's issues, social impacts, and so on. Those were donor concerns. It was well equipped to sing the songs the donors wanted to hear."

Roodman noted the irony that despite various investors withdrawing, two new funds, responsAbility and BlueOrchard, had pumped in an additional $3 million, and he wondered what could explain this: "The willingness to invest in an MFI despite signs of poor service suggests that pressure to invest is distorting decisions, overriding social mission. If there were less money looking for a home, perhaps there would be fewer tough calls to make. And perhaps there would be fewer LAPOs, organizations skillfully crafted to attract foreign funds."

It's a valid point, but an additional, simpler explanation is required: good, old-fashioned greed. The microfinance sector was hijacked. What began as an interesting idea soon attracted the vultures. It was too easy to make money. Investors were wooed by the message and photos, but they had no way to verify what their money was being used for. The poor dreamt of building their little shop; the unscrupulous funds dreamt of discovering the next SKS or Compartamos investment opportunity. MFIs pumped out loans. Regulatory oversight of microfinance in the developing countries, and in the developed countries where the funds operate, is mostly nonexistent in practice. The sector promised that it would effectively regulate itself, given the chance. But as the Indian professor M.S. Sriram aptly observed, even before the Andhra Pradesh suicide crisis, "Self-regulation is an oxymoron."[2] Cheap or free money flooded into the sector, which would inflate the bubble yet further, and the well-positioned few could then make huge personal fortunes when they eventually privatized the largest MFIs.

Meanwhile, advocates and funds employed sophisticated marketing techniques and PR operations that attracted naïve celebrities to the cause and built an aura around the sector that was both impenetrable and self-perpetuating: The proof that microfinance worked was simply that it was available in such vast quantities. That 200 million or so poor people had loans meant the sector had to grow bigger, to reach the rest who did not—those poor people who were cruelly denied access to capital. Some even went as far as to say this was denying them a human right—and who would dare suggest people should be denied a human right?[3] No one had an incentive to wonder whether these 200 million had become better off, let alone wonder whether credit as a human right would actually matter to those who are denied their real fundamental human rights every day—education, water, a decent life, freedom. Anyone who dared criticize the sector was attacked and branded as disloyal to the cause. A heretic.

But what did Muhammad Yunus actually say about this human right? "[Credit is] also a human right, so that people can create their self-employment with that money. If they can create income for themselves, they can take care of right to food, right to shelter much more easily than government can ever do it." If, as some have speculated, 90 percent of microfinance is directed to consumption, or loans cost 144 percent, how does this create employment or income? This is the difference between the *theory* and the *practice* of microfinance.

Perhaps Bono's original quote should be rephrased: Give a man a fish, and he'll eat for a day. Give a woman a microcredit loan to buy a fishing boat, and the CEOs of the MFI and the microfinance funds will eat for a lifetime.

There is too much at stake to allow any genuine scrutiny. When Milford Bateman's book was published and Tom Heinemann's documentary was aired, the sector went into lockdown mode: reputation had to be restored. Facts were secondary. The Friends of Grameen employed the services of a major PR company, Burson-Marsteller, to help. Burson-Marsteller had previously assisted the likes of Union Carbide, Philip Morris, Blackwater, Nicolae Ceausescu, and even Chile's dictator General Pinochet.[4] These were the same guys that Facebook hired to do a smear campaign on Google, which backfired when the story leaked into the press.[5] Were the Friends of Grameen in good company? Why would such an organization need the services of possibly the most feared PR company in the world? Rachel Maddow of MSNBC summarized the company concisely: "When Evil needs public relations, Evil has Burson-Marsteller on speed-dial." Friends of Grameen just added the number.

Surely there is something wrong in the sector when Burson-Marsteller becomes involved.

What actually is "Friends of Grameen"? It has attracted some high-level celebrities; it issues misleading statements and "factsheets" designed to stifle criticism; it has a powerful PR firm; it propagates its opinion with evangelical vigor; it nurtures powerful political connections; it protects a sector in which some lucky individuals have made substantial fortunes; it treats nonbelievers as heretics and tries to discredit them by any means possible; and it is built around a single guru. Is this not a fairly accurate description of a cult?

We lost our soul. We were asleep at the wheel, and are now trying to deny the crash. We created an industry that employs hundreds of thousands of people. Microfinance is taught at universities. It will soon be a $100 billion industry. But we forgot to regulate it. The efforts at self-regulation are embarrassing—yet more spin designed to give the impression that those boasting the SMART Campaign label actually obey a set of rules, when in fact there is precisely zero verification or monitoring, or even a mechanism to expel members. To join this illustrious list of ethical practitioners apparently adhering to the Client Protection Principles you need a first name, a surname, and an email address. With one click of the mouse you're an endorser, and they will kindly offer you a checkbox to avoid having to receive any tedious communication from them.

I discussed this farce with the senior folk at the SMART Campaign. I referred to it as "endorsement without enforcement," and they eventually agreed to add a small text in the bottom of their website stating that they "cannot vouch for the level of commitment or practices of endorsing organizations." On the weightier point of adding formal protection for child labor within their inaptly named Client Protection Principles, this proposal was flatly rejected. One can only speculate why such an obvious principle of universal concern should be omitted from the list.

To suggest that the SMART Campaign is the only ineffective transparency initiative apparently promoting fair treatment of the poor would be unfair. The lesser-known Africa Microfinance Transparency (AMT) initiative in Luxembourg is another bastion of ineffectiveness. I contacted AMT in May 2009,[6] pointing out the irony of LAPO's membership in the network,[7] listing the criticisms and evidence. This was news to AMT (first alarm bell). However, the group did engage in a healthy dialogue and did not dispute any of the evidence presented, and it eventually agreed that this was worrying. Nothing happened until December, when they wrote to LAPO demanding an explanation in a surprisingly frank letter:

> It has come to our attention through a variety of sources that there has been some scrutiny as to the reliability and integrity of the data provided to external parties by LAPO over the last year or so. Furthermore, it has been noted that LAPO is collecting savings without adequate licensing, although we are aware that steps were to be taken to remedy this by your institution. Obviously, as a forum that seeks to promote transparency of African microfinance institutions, AMT cannot ignore such rumors surrounding its members. [8]

This was prior to the Planet Rating evaluation of LAPO, which was released a month later, confirming not only every criticism of LAPO but discovering a few new ones. In light of such "rumors" what did AMT do? Absolutely nothing.

Then the *New York Times* article came out in April. We exchanged some more emails. What did AMT do? Absolutely nothing. Notice a pattern here?

As of late 2011, LAPO remains a member of AMT (and SMART). According to its website, "The purpose of AMT is to reinforce the credibility of the African microfinance sector by encouraging a larger number of MFIs to provide transparent and standardized financial information."[9]

Perhaps to redeem themselves, Luxembourg set up LuxFLAG, a seal of approval for microfinance funds that meet certain ethical and operational criteria, much like SMART or AMT: "Your [fund] is annually scrutinized by an expert panel and meets internationally recognized standards in the Microfinance sector; you are committed to going the extra mile in order to deliver confidence and a high service level to your customers; your MIV demonstrates a responsible commitment to the double bottom line."[10] BlueOrchard and responsAbility investors should be delighted— they got the flag of approval.

Most of these so-called transparency initiatives are not merely useless, they in fact give a deliberately false impression to the general public that transparency is present and membership in such initiatives actually means something. They are thus little more than PR exercises to protect the frail reputation of the sector. They are financed by insiders and managed by insiders. That no MFI chose to explicitly protect children from forced labor is merely one indication of how flawed they are. Analogies to the so-called research initiatives financed by the tobacco lobby to counter reports on the health hazards of smoking spring to mind. Indeed, the standard argument of the tobacco lobby, *If people want to smoke, who are we to stop them?*, may be one of the best arguments in favor of microfinance. Let's then at least provide a health warning on the bottom of all loan contracts: "Microloans may lead you into crippling debt, you can lose your collateral, you may be forced into prostitution or have to remove your kids from school to work in your micro-enterprise, and some people may commit suicide."

Perhaps the silver lining in the gray cloud that represents these so-called transparency initiatives, in addition to the rating agencies, is Chuck Waterfield's NGO MFTransparency.[11] His team seeks to publish the interest rates the poor are *actually paying in practice*—a novel idea, and certainly an irritant to some MFIs, but a step in the right direction. Admittedly, this depends on MFIs volunteering the information in the first place, but perhaps the real concern is the interpretation of the published results. Some may see an interest rate of 125 percent and think, "Oh, that's rather high—I may steer clear of that MFI," but others may drool at the prospect of investing in such an MFI, sharing in the profit, and maybe winning the lottery via a stock market flotation. But without doubt this is a concrete step in the direction of transparency in an otherwise opaque sector.

LAPO is one case of an MFI with questionable practices, but it is not the only case. The fanatics will claim it is an unfortunate outlier (except Grameen Foundation, which actively supports LAPO and has serious money at stake if LAPO collapses), but evidence suggests otherwise. No country on earth has shown any demonstrable, substantial reduction in poverty that can be reasonably attributed to giving millions of its poorest citizens overpriced credit cards. If the European Union could barely perform due diligence on Greece, is it any surprise that most investors in LAPO barely even bothered to visit the Niger Delta?

In the aftermath of the financial crisis perhaps we ought to have a little more humility in preaching the religion of unregulated debt so vocally. If we insist on providing the poorest billion with precisely the same tools of debt that landed us in such trouble, would it not be wise to employ competent people to do so and perhaps regulate the process? The microfinance lobbyists throw up their hands in despair at the very mention of the word *regulation*, charging that it will contaminate "the smooth functioning of the free market"—the same free market that has performed so wonderfully well in their own countries.

I began to despair in 2007. I could have walked away from the sector, as many colleagues did, but for various reasons (lethargy being one) I stuck with it. Then I began to realize that others had deep concerns about what was happening to the poor despite the so-called miracle cure for poverty. But is it too late? Do we risk throwing out the baby with the bathwater?

The problem is neither that the entire microfinance sector is evil, nor that the basic model is fatally flawed. It is that greed, lack of oversight, recklessness in investing other people's money, and ill-aligned incentives have allowed large parts of the sector to ignore the actual impact they are having on actual poverty reduction.

There are a few enlightened MFIs and funds that do actually benefit the poor. Starting in 2008 I gradually began refusing to work for certain MFIs or funds that I considered unethical. My list of potential clients became shorter by the month. Ethical funds do exist—they're just hard to find.

The model does work.

Take a (real) lesser-known South American MFI, of which I am a board member. It is neither a mega-MFI nor does it feature in the popular press. It grows at a modest pace, serving nearly 40,000 clients. This MFI recently converted to a regulated bank and is owned by a European NGO with a deep social mission. A rating agency awarded it an A–rating and described it as among the better MFIs worldwide. It offers group and individual loans, and it screens all clients for capacity to pay. Loans are tailored where possible to the needs of clients. It offers specific loans for handicapped clients, clients with HIV/AIDS, and young entrepreneurs, who receive free business coaching. It is one of the few MFIs to distinguish between microcredit loans (for productive uses) and consumption loans, the latter consisting of only 10 percent of its portfolio. It focuses on the poorer communities, with loan sizes well below the national or continentwide average, and its offices are in the rougher areas of the towns and cities in which it operates. Its total portfolio is $30 million, which qualifies it as a mid-size institution.

Because this MFI focuses on marginalized regions, it faces limited competition and benefits from good client retention compared to its peers. Prudent growth and a mature parent company have led to comparatively low leverage (external debt, typically provided by microfinance funds, is not high for the size of the MFI). To control for overindebtedness it checks all clients at the local credit bureau, and it will reject any client with more than two existing loans, even at the expense of obtaining new clients and growing yet faster.

The country in which this MFI operates benefits from (or suffers from, depending on your stance on regulation) strict regulations on interest rates. Its interest rates are comparable to the rest of the sector, ranging from 16 to 30 percent per year. Portfolio quality is excellent, particularly considering a significant downturn in the local economy in 2009 in the wake of the financial crisis, and currently less than 2 percent of its portfolio is delinquent more than thirty days. This is notably strong performance.

The MFI is not perfect, and it has struggled to standardize its operations. It is currently modifying its IT system, which is a delicate process, and the cost of transforming to a bank has placed financial pressure on the institution. It has suffered from isolated cases of fraud, which have been dealt with promptly.

It also requested a social rating from the same rating agency, which awarded it 3.5 stars out of a possible 5. Approximately two-thirds of its clients are women, and it donates 5 percent of all net profit to promote youth sport and to assist children with special needs.

Is this an inefficient, sluggish charity with limited profit potential?

Net profit in 2010 was $1.5 million, it enjoys a 6 percent operating margin (versus a Latin American average of 3.6 percent), and a return on equity marginally above the continent average. Its external capital providers include a short list of some of the usual suspects, including Kiva, BlueOrchard, and Triple Jump. The bank challenges the temptation to form generalizations about the sector in a number of ways:

1. It is possible to be efficient, profitable, and ethical while offering reasonably priced loans.
2. It is possible to serve the lower end of the socioeconomic spectrum, where competition is lower and client retention is higher, and still make a reasonable return for investors.
3. The portfolios of some microfinance funds and P2Ps may simultaneously contain some of the worst MFIs on the planet and some of the best.

If this is possible, why aren't more MFIs doing it? I have attempted to explain motivations elsewhere, but in a nutshell: greed. It is easier and more profitable, at least in the short run, to ignore any genuine social mission.

How does this MFI manage to accomplish its goals? It has a clear social mission monitored closely by the parent company, which does not have an overtly for-profit focus, combined with a decent regulatory framework that keeps all players in check. This MFI will likely never be the next Compartamos or SKS and make huge sums for its investors. Nor will its clients rise up in revolt, or worse, kill themselves. The owners are content to make a reasonable return, no more, in the knowledge that they are chipping away at poverty. This is far less ambitious than Vikram Akula, but is that a failure? Scaling up to millions of clients may be profitable, but what is the point if so few of them benefit?

Simply knowing that such MFIs exist is inadequate: there is no guarantee that an investor can identify such an MFI from the masses out there, which may appear similar and make the same claims. And there is no guarantee that a microfinance fund would find such an MFI the most attractive opportunity available, given the higher profitability of many of the less scrupulous candidates. Once again, the debate is not whether microfinance works, but how the inherent conflicts of interest can be managed.

The tragedy of this example is that to the extent the microfinance sector is tarnished by criticism of the genuinely rotten apples, good MFIs suffer in the process. Rather than discard the basket, would it not be wiser to identify and remove the rotten apples and then try to prevent the remaining apples from suffering the same fate? Investments in genuine MFIs are likely to provide real benefits to the poor (although not necessarily *miraculous* benefits, nor to *every single* client), and are possibly more compatible with the goals of the ultimate investors, who wish to use their capital to reduce poverty.

One *possible* solution may involve owner-operated networks of MFIs with strong internal governance.[12] Essentially these are large funds that own and actively manage all their MFIs. Their MFIs do not usually have external shareholders or rely on funding directly from the microfinance funds. Training and senior recruitment is often performed by the "mother company." To the extent that the owners are ethical, principled people, they have some hope of actually enforcing their vision on the ground level due to their *proactivity*. Regular microfinance funds tend to be *passive*, in that they are not involved in day-to-day decision-making or operations at the MFI. This is no guarantee of best practice, but owner-operation aligns the incentives of the investors and the operators. They are the same people. Fraud can still occur at all levels, and if the core strategy is not aimed at genuine, sustainable poverty reduction, that will not be the outcome. However, this solution *may* reduce *one* of the misaligned incentives that leads to many of the problems with microfinance.

Of course, the moment an MFI does an IPO, it will strive to maximize profit—it is often legally obliged to do so—and it is clear where this profit must come from.

Answering the question "How can we fix microfinance?" would require writing an encyclopedia.

But perhaps we could at least start by offering the poor a financial product they actually need.

Much is made of the amazing ability of microfinance to help the poor smoothe their often volatile incomes and expenses arising from work in the informal sector. In fact, there is indeed a rather simple financial product that could have a great impact here, but very few MFIs offer it to their clients: a checking account with an overdraft limit.

When the poor have some money left over at the end of the week, they can deposit it in a checking account and earn modest interest on the balance, perhaps enough to cover inflation. When they need money to cover a shortfall, they can withdraw savings from their own account instead of getting a loan. If this is insufficient, they can use their overdraft limit, which they can repay as soon as they have some spare funds, and avoid paying more interest than necessary. It's a fairly simple product, common among the billion or so richest people in the world, but rarely available to the poor.

Such a product would be far more useful in helping them through the financial ups and downs of daily life than a fixed-term loan. So why do so few MFIs offer them?

First, such an account would enable the poor to use their own savings rather than obtaining a loan, a solution that might better meet their needs but would not be as profitable for the MFI. Second, the MFI would far rather lock in a client for a larger sum to be paid back over six months or a year, often with juicy fees and interest added on, than earn modest amounts in interest only over the short term when the client actually needed the money. The few MFIs that have even considered offering such accounts have come up with an impressive array of excuses for not doing so. However, it is encouraging to see that a first few MFIs are now actually offering this product, so widely taken for granted by the nonpoor across the planet.

But perhaps I should offer some practical advice to people more broadly involved in the sector. Above all, tread with extreme care.

**For those interested in investing in microfinance:**
- Assume *a priori* that the funds or peer-to-peer organizations you consider are crooks out to serve their own ends. Be happy to be proved wrong with actual, solid evidence.
- Ensure that you know who is actually deciding which investments to make and what their due diligence and monitoring processes actually are. Ask probing questions. Treat evasive answers with suspicion.
- Find out what ground-level microfinance experience those managing the investments and making decisions on your behalf have. MBAs and fancy degrees are no substitute for field experience.
- Consider the alignment of interests: If an investment collapses, does the fund manager stand to lose financially?
- Does the monitoring process involve actually visiting individual clients, and if so, who selects which clients are visited?
- In a peer-to-peer lender (like Kiva, MicroPlace, or MyC4), make sure you can track the actual flow of money from your account to the poor person's wallet and back. Fancy photos and heartwarming stories are nice (and important marketing materials for the platforms), but look for hard data. Can the platform confirm the actual interest rate being charged, for example? If it cannot provide this one piece of critical data, demand a very good explanation. This is a *major* alarm bell.
- Read rating reports. Ask the fund if they have at least read the ratings for their MFIs if they exist. If they are investing in MFIs that do not have ratings, and the fund is unwilling to insist upon a rating, proceed with extreme caution.
- Ask specifically about the policies of controlling and reporting the actual use of funds, in particular what proportion of the loans are for consumption, productive use, and inventory finance. Make sure

the answers are compatible with your view of what actually helps the poor.

- Ask for specific policies regarding protection of clients, and be sure to focus on the actual interest rates the poor are paying, verified by someone credible, and find out whether client protection extends to the children of the micro-entrepreneurs. Do not be fooled by meaningless endorsements by self-regulated bodies. What do they actually do to check these issues in practice?

- Ask for social performance data. There is no point in knowing about a few success stories of micro-entrepreneurs if you don't know how many failures there were and how many showed no notable effect either way.

- Attend AGMs and ask annoying questions. Record the questions and the answers, if any.

- Check where your pension fund invests. Private pension funds have invested billions of dollars in microfinance, usually through investment companies like BlueOrchard, and count this as being "socially responsible." Ask for and critically check their investment criteria and processes, and complain if you suspect that your money is being invested in unsavory activities.

- Examine fund websites in detail to determine if the level of disclosure is adequate for a formal regulated investment fund. Is it a glorified marketing brochure?

**For the microfinance funds:**

Frankly, I think the only means to rein in these guys is to formally regulate them. Pensions, savings accounts, and fund managers in the "developed world" are all formally regulated, and this hasn't worked entirely smoothly to date. That a microfinance fund remains unregulated in practice is entirely ridiculous and inevitably leads to problems. However, even if a microfinance fund or lending platform is technically subject to national regulation such as Calvert by the SEC, BlueOrchard and responsAbility in Switzerland, and Triple Jump by KIFID in Holland, this means little in practice—the sector needs specific, dedicated, qualified regulators who understand the microfinance sector in particular. There are none currently.

For the few funds that do strive to honestly tackle the problem of poverty, here are some suggestions to help produce positive results:

- Demand a higher management fee—2 percent is not enough to cover genuine due diligence and will inevitably lead to cutting corners. If your investors don't appreciate the benefit of this, find new investors or close your fund. Pay peanuts, get monkeys.
- Assume *a priori* that every MFI you consider is a jazzed-up Ponzi scheme. Be happy to be proved wrong.
- Listen to what your investors actually want. If you can't actually deliver it, don't take their money.
- Do proper due diligence, on-site, including an auditor; take an IT expert to sniff around in the MFI's back office; do background checks on managers and look for conflicts of interest within the MFI. Don't subcontract due diligence to another fund, particularly one that has already invested in the same MFI.
- If you engage in debt and equity investing, actively manage the potential conflicts of interest that occur from mixing these two.[13]
- Verify the actual interest rates charged on-site by visiting actual clients and hearing from them how much they actually pay, and ensure this corresponds with the accounts, ratings, and other documents.
- Publish your investments and the interest rates the MFIs charge openly on your website. If you're embarrassed to publish either, perhaps you shouldn't have made the investment in the first place.
- Hire staff with actual microfinance field experience.
- Do random spot checks on clients. This is easy and cheap. Ask a trusted person living in the region but unrelated to the MFI, perhaps working at a local NGO, to visit clients and ask some questions, particularly about treatment at the hands of the loan officers and the rates charged. The MFI need not know you are doing this.
- Expect to make mistakes, warn your investors you will make mistakes, and, if they don't accept this, don't take their money. When you (inevitably) make a mistake, tell your investors. There is nothing wrong with making a mistake, correcting it if possible, and learning from it. There is something deeply wrong with claiming you are invincible and covering up your mistakes.

- Always read ratings, and if there are none, or they are out of date, employ a rating agency. This is a service to you, a service to the MFI, a service to your investors, and a service to the poor. This may actually save you money both in the short run (reduced due diligence expenses) and in the long run (you will know more about the investment, and be less likely to make a mistake). Don't simply read them—take note if they have words like "illegal" on the front page—these are warning signs you may wish to consider. These guys invariably know way more than you do about microfinance.
- People are watching you increasingly closely. There are whistle-blowers in most funds—I know them.

**For the management of an exploitative MFI:**
- Quit.

**For the management of an ethical MFI:**
- Pick your investors carefully—they can have a surprising influence on your operations and mission, not always for the benefit of the poor. Wolves wear sheep's clothing.
- Microfinance funds will often structure deals to personally benefit the management team, in the name of "aligning interests" or "providing tangible performance incentives." Ask yourself if this is any more than veiled bribery, and whether such actions will actually benefit the poor.
- Beware of "free" technical assistance from a microfinance fund. They are invariably trying to sniff you out or secure a deal for themselves. Exploit such offers by all means, but do not consider them "free." What assurance do you have that information will not discreetly benefit a competitor if the fund has other investments in the region? Many funds have technical assistance arms that they claim are separate, independent entities. Dream on.
- Good customer service and fair interest rates for your clients generate loyalty, which appears to be an expensive asset in good times. However, when a crisis strikes you will be better protected than your competitors.

- Review your mission statement, and rephrase it if necessary in a measurable, explicit way. Then do it.
- Beware of unintended consequences of incentive plans—you might just get what you incentivize.
- Ensure that your staff know that sometimes rejecting a loan application is the kindest thing you can do for the client. And also for the MFI.
- Take an explicit decision on the share of consumer loans in your portfolio, and publish it, along with the interest rates you actually charge the poor.
- Do not give in to pressure from your investors to endlessly grow at any expense. Slow and steady wins the race. Exponential growth often involves either taking your eye off the ball or screwing your clients. You are in charge. Grow at the speed you think suitable.
- If you have a problem, contact your investors immediately and be open with them from the outset.
- Do not accept clauses in contracts with microfinance funds that you think will place you under huge pressure if a crisis strikes.
- Spend time on your own in the field visiting clients. This reinforces the idea that management is aware of the field operations and is proactive. Chat informally with junior staff about their working conditions. Time simply sitting in a branch will provide the best sense of the actual customer experience at your MFI.
- Get ratings, ideally paid for by your investors. Sit down with the rating agency informally after the rating and ask their frank advice on what they think you might want to focus on. These guys have seen endless MFIs and you can tap this wisdom over a beer. Doing so is worth its weight in gold.
- Know who you are actually lending to. Capture more data on clients. This will help you understand which clients are likely to benefit and repay a loan, and which are not. It's a service to you, and a service to the client. The IT staff are not "geeks," they are the guardians of some of the most critical information within the entire MFI. Get to know them.
- Beware—a growing number of people are watching you, and blowing the whistle is getting easier by the day.

**To a potential regulator:**

You have a massive, miserable job ahead of you. You are going to discover endless problems and will face huge resistance. A disturbing number of the funds or MFIs you are regulating will fall way short of even modest regulatory requirements. When you ask funds detailed questions about their investments and they eventually reply "no idea," they are probably telling the truth. Consider hiring a bodyguard.

- Ensure that all MFIs have a formal complaints procedure—also for the investors in the microfinance funds themselves.
- Oblige all MFIs and their investors to publish the actual, total cost of capital charged to the poor, according to internationally agreed best practice, and considering the effects of all fees, taxes, and forced savings. Invite MFTransparency to assist—it's cheap, quick, and easy.
- Consider a prudent use of interest-rate caps to prevent usury. They should not be so low as to dissuade any MFIs from operating.
- Insist, and verify, that all forced savings are deposited in a reputable external bank, and are only used by the MFI for onlending if this is expressly permitted within the country.
- Promote the use of local credit bureaus.
- State and monitor accepted debt collection practices.
- Hold microfinance funds legally liable if they are found to be investing in illegally operating MFIs without due effort to check the legality of the MFI.
- Consider encouraging, or obliging, all potential investments to undergo a formal, external rating performed by a reputable rating agency. This may not be possible with private financing, but can be required with public financing.

**To the poor:**
- Think at least twice about obtaining a loan.
- Find out the complaints procedures within the MFI (if any).
- Understand the interest rate you are being charged, and try to do some simple calculations of how much you estimate your business will grow and if it will be sufficient not only to repay the loan com-

fortably but also to make a reasonable profit. If it isn't, don't take the loan.

- If you are thinking about getting a consumption loan, don't do it unless it is an absolute emergency. Save up first and then buy it. Doing so is way cheaper.
- The moment you have to get a loan from MFI A to repay MFI B, you already have a problem. Stop immediately—things will only get worse.
- If you are ill-treated or threatened, don't commit suicide—complain directly to the MFI, investigate if there is a local regulator, or go to the local press. Journalists love pictures of loan officers harassing poor clients. Do not hesitate to use this method of publicizing your problem as a last resort.
- If you suspect that such practices are common and can find enough other victims or sympathizers, you may collectively have enough negotiating power to simply refuse to repay your loans. Individually you are weak, but if you can gather hundreds or thousands of clients together, you will get media coverage more easily and can genuinely threaten the bank with widespread defaults and contagion to other regions.

**For microfinance whistle-blowers:**
- If you are working in an MFI and perceive injustices or are obliged to perform unsavory acts to "problem clients," go online and anonymously blog about this almost anywhere. There are enough people now aware of the problems that someone will eventually pick up the thread. Be very careful to protect your identity. Consider contacting the regulator if appropriate. If the MFI is rated, contact the rating agencies as to "areas they may wish to investigate in more detail." They will not publish anything unless they can back it up, but they may consider such advice. It's worth a try.
- If your MFI uses Kiva, go to www.Kivafriends.org. They are particularly paranoid about yet more bad publicity, so this will probably get picked up quite quickly. Again, stay anonymous.
- Local media is also possible. There are a surprising number of journalists willing to sniff out the latest microfinance scandal. If you

explain you are an insider, they will often take the case seriously. Often you need do little more than slip the phone number or address of an abused client to the journalist. The reporter will do the rest, and no one need know you were the source. Journalists usually protect the identity of their sources, but do take care.

- If you are considering a major whistle-blowing exercise on a large scandal, get a book on the subject if possible—they exist and are helpful. It is a risky undertaking, and the good guys do not always win. Do not embark on such a journey unless you have sufficient funds to weather up to a year of unemployment. If you are doing this within a "developed" country, take extra precautions, get legal advice, and consider moving assets or bank balances out of your name.

- Never reveal all your information. Keep something up your sleeve, so if the MFI or fund attempts to attack you, you still have something additional to leak. For as long as they don't know how much you know, they will tread carefully. By formally attacking you they risk full disclosure of all documents, at which point you can have a field day.

- Be bold. A simple photograph, with supporting evidence, can have a huge impact. I will personally pay $1,000 to the first person who can produce a photograph of a Compartamos client who has had to remove her child from school to work in some microbusiness in Mexico. I need the contact details of the client, the interest rate she is paying, and a photograph, and I will then do the rest. Proof that this is taking place at the behest of one of the most divisive MFIs in the sector, which generated hundreds of millions of dollars for Accion via its stock market flotation, will be explosive. Accion is, of course, the mastermind behind the SMART Campaign, and the irony of this connection will not be lost on the international media. Compartamos naturally endorsed the SMART Campaign, as did LAPO. If you prefer, expose the situation yourself. This book explains how.

Were a fund to openly state: "We do not care about the poor, we have no social mission, our sole goal is to maximize profit and the easiest way to do this is to charge the maximum interest rates possible to the poor and use whatever methods necessary to ensure they repay," as much as I would lament the existence of such a fund, I would at least applaud its transparency. No such fund exists (to the best of my knowledge) although the activity debatably does, though it is shrouded in a web of nebulous terms such as *empowerment*, *social focus*, and *triple bottom lines* to woo its own investors.

So, if not microfinance, what alternatives are there?

This is a valid question. Personally, I would never invest a single dollar in a microfinance fund nor in most of the P2Ps. I know of only a handful of trustworthy funds and one P2P platform that I personally would trust. If my goal is to relieve poverty, I can have more impact for less hassle by simply throwing money out of the window of an airplane flying over a poor area. This is the so-called "airplane theory of microfinance," first explained to me by the CEO of an IT company servicing the microfinance sector.

This theory was in turn superseded by the "advanced airplane theory of microfinance," which involves a two-stage procedure to ensure maximum impact on poverty for minimum expense:

- Take 20 percent of the money you wish to donate and throw it over the villages at 6 p.m. on a Saturday evening. The men will grab this money, by force if necessary, and get drunk.
- At 7 a.m. on Sunday, fly over the same region and dump the remaining 80 percent of the funds. The women in the village will be the only people awake, and at least you have a fighting chance of them doing something remotely useful with it.

The proportion of microfinance that is actually used for some remotely productive purpose largely results in legions of basket weavers, rickshaw drivers, trinket vendors, shoe polishers, and kids selling chewing gum and cigarettes on street corners, and yet more supply of vegetables in a market where demand remains constant. There are exceptions, which a decent MFI can detect, but the long-term impact of this sector is likely to fall short of mass poverty reduction, as the last thirty years have shown. Not all poor people are entrepreneurs. The availability of activities that they can profitably engage in while paying interest is finite. Why not look at an entirely new area of the economy to invest in?

Apple, Google, Microsoft, Ford, Coca-Cola, and their like all started as small acorns and grew into mighty oaks. When a micro-entrepreneur actually benefits from loans from an MFI, there arises a point when the MFI is no longer able to offer them more credit. Maximum loan sizes may be $1,000 or $10,000, depending on the region and the MFI. But at this point the entrepreneur has few options. They are still unable to obtain a loan in a commercial bank. There is a gap: the so-called "missing middle."

Funding such minicompanies has a host of benefits that the typical microbusiness lacks: they are often more formal, and they may even pay tax to the local government. They have a higher chance of actually creating new jobs (and not simply employing their own kids at the expense of their getting an education). Job creation leads to developing skills, reducing unemployment, and a chance for an employee to build some form of resume. The more formal the business, the more likely it is that the minicompany will actually obey some of the labor regulations of the country. Unless the acorn can bridge the gap to becoming a small tree, how can it ever become a mighty oak?

This sector is largely ignored by the investing community, but attention is gradually shifting in this direction. Unfortunately, some of the same people who messed up the microfinance sector are also sniffing around in this niche, so care will be required. Quite likely the book *Confessions of an SME Heretic: How the Same Idiots Who Broke the Bottom Rung of the Ladder Are Now Ruining the Next Rung Up* will probably be out in a few years. I hope I'm not the author.

Perhaps funds currently directed at microfinance could be successfully redeployed in savings and credit cooperatives, where the borrowers/clients are the owners. This is, after all, the UN Year of Cooperatives. Cooperatives are not immune from fraud or mismanagement, but at least the incentive to maximize profit at the expense of the clients in the hope of floating an IPO is largely removed. Co-ops seem out of favor in the microfinance community, however. Savings services for the poor are all too often the forgotten side of microfinance. Of course, such services are not so profitable for investors, and funds cannot survive by saddling them with debt, but the poor do not only need (overpriced) credit but savings as well.

The current fad is for "impact investing," which superficially appears to offer some of the same promises of microfinance—triple-bottom-line, profitable investing. The niche is relatively young, and some of the traditional microfinance investors are entering this niche also, which is perhaps cause for alarm. I sincerely urge investors and intermediaries (such as funds) to learn some of the sobering lessons from the microfinance sector and not to build hype around overly optimistic claims that will inevitably not be met. Impact investing is unlikely to be *miraculous* either. I do not believe there are panaceas for poverty reduction—it is hard work and requires a number of tools used wisely and collaboratively.

Further, a genuine cleanup would probably result in a smaller sector, fewer MFIs and funds, and greater operating costs as MFIs and funds are obliged to actually obey some regulations. Would this be a bad thing? If 20 percent genuinely benefit from a sector comprising 50 million clients, that may be far better than 2 percent genuinely benefiting from a sector comprising the current 200 million clients.

Expect resistance to such a cleanup from MFIs and microfinance funds—the two parties that stand to lose the most in the process. They will present quasi-academic research to back up their claims, distort facts, promote exceptional cases of successful microfinance as the norm rather than the exception, attack the reputations of any critics, try to evade the key questions, and maneuver to preserve their own existence. But instead of *attacking* the critics, why not *hire* them to actually address the issues? After all, oil companies hire environmentalists.

I don't know how to embark on this massive cleanup. Even when the funds and MFIs are clearly presented with hard data about the damage they are causing, they are inclined to do nothing. There is a major temptation to brush such problems under the carpet. The sector is structured to operate as it does, and only regulators can lay down rules to change this. Self-regulation is a joke, and very few are laughing.

However, regulators in Europe and the U.S. have bigger fish to fry. They are unlikely to lose too much sleep over a few stray Africans or Latinos getting screwed by some unscrupulous MFIs while their own citizens are becoming increasingly belligerent about the financial sectors in their own countries. The few decent funds in the microfinance sector, which you can count on one hand and still have a finger or two to spare, are generally moving out of the microfinance sector entirely. The signs of investor fatigue are present, and critical media reports on the sector are popping up almost daily.

Improvement will not take place until the problem is acknowledged and bright, ethical people start taking a stand. This is happening now. Some are doing so openly, others discreetly. Even some of the traditional advocates privately express concern over beers after conference sessions. Critical academic research is gaining momentum. The broad idea that financial services can sometimes have unintended consequences and be manipulated by greed is not an unbelievable concept. A growing number of insiders, activists, academics, and even some funds are beginning to take action. Yet while a few good people can make some changes in the sector from within, my experience shows that only strong pressure from the outside can hope to change the rules of the game.

Another possible glimmer of hope is the emergence of cloud-based IT systems for managing MFIs. These may offer a cheap solution to a common problem faced by most MFIs, and cost savings *could* enable reduced interest rates. More important, they could allow proactive ethical microfinance funds to keep a closer eye on what their MFIs are actually doing, and claims about not knowing the true cost the poor are paying in practice will be harder to make. Technology has already led to cost savings within the sector, such as the prevalence of mobile phone banking; loan officers use handheld devices in the field (sometimes with printers to issue receipts), which reduces time-consuming paperwork and ideally improves data quality.

Finally, the specialized microfinance rating agencies have recently made a tentative step into rating the actual microfinance investment funds, although the depth of analysis can best be described as light. However, a little more scutiny applied directly to these funds can only be a step in the right direction. Likewise, some countries are tightening the reporting requirements for their MFIs and publishing such reports for general release, so that, for example, the actual interest rates and levels of overindebtedness of the microfinance clients are now becoming publicly available for individual MFIs.[14]

I sincerely hope that this will be the dawn of a new era in microfinance, where those practicing the more sordid activities mentioned here are simply not invited to the table. Reducing poverty is not easy. The idea that we can rid the world of poverty and have a free lunch in Geneva in the process is, frankly, ridiculous. It is astonishing that so many were duped into it. Then again, with hindsight we can say the same about any fad—the Internet bubble, subprime mortgages, Dutch tulips—history is littered with such irrationality.

I may be one of the few to put my name so openly to a critique of the sector, but I am not alone. As was pointed out in a fascinating blog by a German PhD student and microfinance researcher earlier this year in light of Tom Heinemann's controversial documentary and Milford Bateman's critical book:

> [The documentary] doesn't shed a good light onto microfinance, and in return has come under fire from the microfinance community, an epistemic community which doesn't take criticism well.... The intensity of the reactions to Bateman's book is a gauge for measuring just how worried many in the development industry have become about their poster child. A systematic critique of microfinance touches highly sensitive nerves with many researchers and industry insiders, whose reaction is to challenge the person rather than the argument.[15]

Regarding my personal course of action, I am going to see what happens in 2012, lie low, and probably fend off attacks from those mentioned in this book ("attack the messenger"). I'll continue working with a handful of genuinely ethical funds and their decent MFIs, but otherwise I'll be excluded from most of the microfinance sector, having dared to break the golden rule: Never criticize microfinance.

# Appendix

## Microfinance Economics 101

Economic theories supporting microfinance abound. The broadest principle is that of the efficient allocation of resources. The argument suggests that some people have excess cash, but do not face particularly interesting investment opportunities. Meanwhile, the poor face amazing economic opportunities but cannot realize them for lack of cash. Microfinance acts as a conduit to channel capital from A to B. This belief has some validity, but digging a little deeper reveals fundamental flaws in the microfinance model.

The first flaw in economic debates about microfinance relates to the abundance of profitable economic opportunities. This is often used to justify the extortionate interest rates charged the poor. The poor can apparently buy tomatoes in one village, sell them in another, and make incredible profits in the process, so large in fact that they are more than happy to pay 100 percent annual interest for the capital to fuel this venture. What's more, these opportunities exist indefinitely and are in near-infinite supply. While it is no doubt true that isolated cases of this nature do exist, it is highly questionable that 200 million people are able to find and exploit such opportunities indefinitely. It is true that some people win national lotteries, but it is dubious to generalize this fact as a solution to poverty across a whole country.

Who is buying all these tomatoes? Microfinance fanatics can talk endlessly about the tomato vendors, but they rarely discuss who their customers are. Microfinance focuses on supply. What about demand?

I witnessed a disturbing case of this kind in rural Mozambique. An entrepreneur with a clothes stall in a medium-sized market had visited neighboring South Africa and used a microloan to buy a large box of low-priced, high-quality clothing, providing an opportunity to charge an attractive margin, in theory. He estimated the margin to be 200 or 300 percent. Sales had been very slow on these particular items, which was puzzling him. I identified the source of the problem: in this hot, poor, semi-desert region of southern Africa price was unlikely to be the determining factor in the market for ski clothing. Supply is useless without demand.

A second flaw is that the sectors in which the poor operate are thought to be immune from the laws of competition. If a bright woman discovers that tomatoes are available in Village A for $1 and can be sold for $2 in Village B, how likely is it that no one else discovers this opportunity? Presumably, the first people to worry about this influx of competitively priced tomatoes would be the existing tomato vendors in Village B. Our entrepreneur would be selling her tomatoes at lower prices than other people in Village B's markets and would therefore be poaching clients from the existing vendors.

The existing tomato vendors have their livelihoods and incomes at stake, and they are not stupid. They will react quickly to protect their businesses. They will either reduce their prices to remain competitive, in which case they will earn less, or they will try to discover how it is that this disruptive woman is able to get her tomatoes so cheaply, and do likewise. This is not rocket science. If Sony invents some incredible new product, it may take some years for competitors to understand the new product and be able to replicate it—but few micro-entrepreneurs are in businesses as complex as Sony. Typical activities include buying food to sell in the market; buying fertilizer to sell to farmers; buying inventory to stock shelves. How difficult is this to replicate? The businesses are usually very simple, and the products and prices are clearly visible to customers and competitors alike: "Tomatoes—only $1.50!"

Competitive forces play just as significant a role in developing countries as in developed countries. Indeed, in London or New York it is quite possible that the price of tomatoes varies *more* than in a developing country. Many people are not too concerned about a small variation in the price of tomatoes, or cannot be bothered to walk to the other side of town to save a dollar or two. In developing countries the poor are much more sensitive to such prices, and may walk an extra mile to buy tomatoes more cheaply, particularly when such purchases account for a large proportion of their disposable income. Seemingly small variations in price can mean the difference between a family eating three meals a day or two.

What will be the consequence of our new entrant in the tomato sector of Village B? As in any other market, the vested interests of the players in the market will combine to bring about a new status quo. First of all, our entrepreneur will begin to attract customers at the expense of her competitors. She will buy more and more tomatoes from Village A. Sooner or later someone else in Village A, perhaps even her tomato supplier, will start selling tomatoes in Village B directly. Why let her make all the profit? Perhaps, if the profit margin is really so good, her supplier will simply increase the cost of the tomatoes he sells to her. As the incumbent vendors notice their client numbers dwindling perhaps they too will sniff out the supplier in Village A and start buying tomatoes from him also. Eventually he too will start running low on tomatoes and will realize that he can justifiably increase the price accordingly.

The net result will be that the incredible economic opportunity our heroic entrepreneur discovered will soon vanish. This process could take place in a matter of days or weeks. In the longer term, however, other dynamics will take place. The tomato supplier in Village A, who is now supplying other vendors in Village B and perhaps selling in Village B directly, will become wealthy initially, but other people in Village A will start growing tomatoes, or finding out where he gets his tomatoes, and they will also enter the sector. Follow the chain long enough and eventually everything will stabilize in a new equilibrium.

The overall price will have fallen marginally in Village B, and as a result a few more people who previously couldn't afford tomatoes now may be able to. Some who previously bought five tomatoes a week may now buy six. Although the price of tomatoes has fallen, to the disadvantage of the initial vendors in Village B, their cost of buying tomatoes is likely the same, so the reduction in the final sale price will reduce their profit margin. And let's not exaggerate the benefit of the price fall to the customers now planning ever more elaborate tomato dishes—the price can only fall modestly without rendering the entire tomato business unattractive to the vendors.

In the majority of microfinance businesses, such "incredible" returns will be earned for only short periods of time by a few individuals. This doesn't mean that buying and selling tomatoes is not profitable in the long run, but rather that it is only *slightly* profitable. Huge returns eventually attract attention. When all the costs of transport, renting the stall, losing some tomatoes to thieves or spoilage, hiring a helper, repaying the loan, and so forth are considered, *perhaps* the annual return is 30 percent, or 50 percent, but it is unlikely to be 500 percent other than for very short periods. The critical problem the microfinance community collectively tries to ignore is that charging ludicrously high interest rates, however they are excused, eradicates the profit of these micro-enterprises all the more quickly. A carefully undefined proportion of the profit of micro-enterprises is simply skimmed off as profit for the benefit of MFIs and investors in the form of interest. A convenient way to disguise this is to simply claim the profit margins of such enterprises are astonishingly huge. Evidence and common sense challenge this view.

I do not doubt there are *exceptional* cases of *some* entrepreneurs earning 500 percent. Nor do I doubt *many* entrepreneurs may make 200 percent *for short periods of time*. What I challenge is that 200 million entrepreneurs are making enough to warrant paying 50 percent annual interest or more for the privilege.

At this point it is worth looking at some basic economic theory. Without progressing much beyond Economics 101, the belief that microfinance loans automatically lead to poverty reduction or economic development violates the simplest of economic principles.

In general the more expensive something is, the less people buy of it. If prices decline, people will generally buy more of a product. This is the fundamental logic behind the demand curve. Economists plot such curves on graphs with price and quantity on the axes and play with them incessantly.

Likewise, suppliers are generally happier selling their product at high prices than low prices. This applies to tomatoes, airplane tickets, and

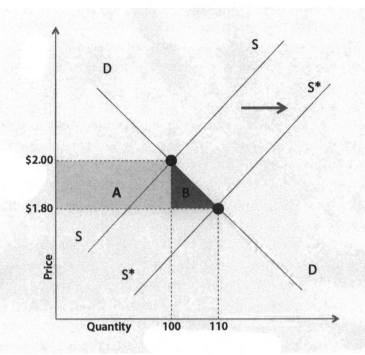

Figure A1   Microfinance: Supply and Demand Curves for Tomato Sales in Village B

even to employment. A person offers his or her labor to an employer for a price, and would usually prefer a higher price to a lower price.

In Figure A1, we observe two lines: DD is the demand curve, and SS is the supply curve. The horizontal axis is the quantity (of tomatoes, for example), and the vertical axis is the price. At lower prices customers demand more tomatoes, but suppliers are less willing to sell them. As the price increases, suppliers are increasingly willing to sell, but customers are less inclined to buy. There is a point, which economists are fascinated with and refer to as *equilibrium*, where the interests of the customers and vendors in the market coincide. In this example the price happens to be at $2 and the quantity is 100 tomatoes (per day, perhaps).

Let's continue the example of our extraordinary tomato-selling lady. She obtains a microloan to obtain tomatoes from Village A and sell them more cheaply in Village B. Perhaps she was not previously selling tomatoes—this is a new business. She sets up her stall in the marketplace with 10 ripe tomatoes proudly on display.

What happens in the diagram above? Initially at $2 the market vendors supplied 100 tomatoes. Now there are 110. Indeed, with the new tomato stall in the market, at every price level there are now 10 additional tomatoes. The supply curve has therefore shifted to the right, as seen.

Because our entrepreneur has entered the market, there are more tomatoes for sale, and the price falls, to $1.80 in this case, and the quantity increases to 110. This makes sense: when laptops cost $5,000 in 1990 few were sold. Now they cost as little as $500 and millions are sold.

The customers in the market are delighted. They previously had to pay $2 each for their tomatoes, and now tomatoes cost only $1.80. They are certainly not complaining. That's why they collectively buy 10 additional tomatoes. In the diagram above shaded area A reflects the benefit to the existing customers. They previously bought 100 tomatoes for $2 each (or $200 in total), and now the same number of tomatoes costs only $180. They are collectively $20 better off.

Triangle B represents the new people who previously did not buy tomatoes at $2, but who do so at $1.80; or they may be existing customers who decided not to simply save money on the 100 original tomatoes they bought, but to buy some extra. Or a combination of both—it doesn't really matter. The key thing to consider is that both A and B reflect the benefit to the consumers. More tomatoes at a lower price—it is a measure of their "happiness."

But what about the suppliers or vendors? Previously they had happily sold 100 tomatoes at $2 each, and now they are getting only $1.80. This must irritate them. The advantage to the clients, area A ($20), is exactly their loss. The benefit of the extra 10 tomatoes sold accrues entirely to our new entrant. We cannot focus on triangle B without considering the implications of area A.

Most microfinance is precisely of this nature: street vendors, market stalls, small shops. This is what a micro-enterprise actually consists of in most cases. If we ignore those borrowers who do not invest their money in a business at all and simply spend the loan on a new cellphone (borrowing for consumption) or use it to repay other debts (refinancing), most loans finance these sorts of activities. No one has actually calculated the exact proportion, but a quick glance at any microfinance bank's client list, or a stroll around a market, or a scan of loans offered on Kiva's website, demonstrates this clearly. The romanticized idea that the woman buys a goat or a sewing machine is mostly a myth—so-called productive assets may account for only 5 percent of the total microfinance loans made, but these are the celebrated cases touted at dinner parties and on websites. Does 5 percent sound like an exaggeration? Well, John Hatch, one of the pioneers of the microfinance sector and founder of one of the largest microfinance networks, Finca, has estimated that consumption loans account for 90 percent of all microloans.[1] If productive assets count for half the remaining 10 percent that might actually be optimistic.

The microfinance sector is remarkably quiet about the vendors who are displaced or forced to sell their wares at a reduced price (area A), but is particularly vocal about the new entrants (triangle B). Although the end clients do benefit from reduced prices, the simple, unavoidable fact about the incumbent vendors is that they earn less money and therefore their relative poverty level actually *increases*. In economics this is referred to as job displacement. Some 200 million microfinance clients have apparently benefited from small loans, but there is no mention of those who have been squeezed out of their businesses, or are forced to work additional hours to make ends meet, or take a second job, or sell their possessions, or their businesses simply collapse and they join the unemployed.

MFIs will go to extraordinary lengths to cut costs and be more productive and therefore profitable. One of the easiest ways to achieve this is to make loans in densely populated areas: a single loan officer can service many more clients. MFIs love marketplaces, where there are hundreds of vendors crowded together selling their wares. In the previous example, the incumbent vendors observe that our entrepreneur friend selling tomatoes was able to do so by borrowing money from an MFI. Why don't they do likewise? The loan officers constantly wander around the market offering loans, and it may seem like a good idea to get one. Indeed, what alternative do the incumbents face? If they do not obtain their tomatoes at a cheaper price, or start selling new products, then they will have to make do with reduced income henceforth. Perhaps getting a loan offers them a path out of poverty, as the MFIs proudly proclaim.

The MFIs establish detailed incentive plans for their loan officers to push the maximum number of loans feasibly possible. The easiest place for a loan officer to attract significant new business with minimal effort is not in sparsely populated rural regions, but in crowded markets.

Once an MFI has made a few initial loans in a marketplace, there is a tendency for it to snowball. Loan officers are aware of this, and they are rewarded accordingly. If enough early entrepreneurs are able to disrupt the market equilibrium by offering a better or cheaper product, they will achieve a degree of fame, and envy, from others. Others, facing corresponding pressure, react by doing precisely the same—they obtain a loan. The MFI is delighted, since this means that their loan officers can service large numbers of clients in a single location. After a short while the market reverts to a new equilibrium, and the early additional profits of the first pioneer entrepreneurs disappear as the other vendors in the market imitate them. The first wave of clients served the MFI's purpose in creating the initial impetus for the others to obtain loans, and now the marketplace collectively serves its purpose in paying the MFI interest.

The advantages of such lending for the MFI do not end there. If a client defaults on a loan, the MFI can easily confiscate the inventory of the client, which is usually put up as collateral for the loan, and sell it rapidly to another person in the same market.

The Japanese invented just-in-time inventory management—a principle replicated around the world ever since. Tying up large amounts of capital in inventory was unproductive—far better to have the minimum possible inventory. Microfinance promotes the precise opposite of prudent inventory management. Micro-entrepreneurs by the million obtain loans to buy inventory that sits on shelves in competitive markets gathering dust before sale but accumulating an interest expense in the meantime. Genius.

If it appears that the situation could get no worse, there is still one missing ingredient, one that the microfinance sector also conveniently ignores.

In a marketplace with a few hundred stalls, after a while the MFIs saturate the market. After a year or so the majority of stalls will boast increased levels of inventory, and will be paying collectively perhaps 50 percent or 100 percent in interest to the MFIs for the privilege. In order to cover this cost, they have to increase the prices of their products. Returning to the previous example, the net result is that the supply curve actually shifts back to the left. The money extracted from the market in the form of interest has to eventually be passed on to the end clients via price increases. The interest rates charged by MFIs are not trivial, and often exceed 60 percent annually (often much higher in Mexico, for example, where rates approaching 200 percent per year are well documented). But even this does not fully reflect the true peril of expensive microfinance to such markets.

Where are the customers?

In order for a vendor to sell something, there needs to be someone to buy it. At which point, in our fictional marketplace, did the total number of customers increase to absorb these "new" products? Where do they get the money to buy this additional stream of homogenous products?

The answer is simple: they also get a loan from the MFI—consumer credit.

The total size of the microfinance sector is estimated to be $70 billion. If a typical loan costs 50 percent per year, $35 billion in interest is being extracted from these markets. MFIs do not usually report the proportion of loans that are used purely for consumption, and microfinance funds have little incentive to find out. Equally, no one knows how much of this total debt is used to simply repay other microfinance loans. Of the proportion of loans that are used for neither consumption nor refinancing other loans, the majority is spent on inventory, gathering dust and incurring interest charges. It is hard to gather empirical data on this since the MFIs capture scant information on the actual use of funds by their customers, and neither they nor the funds have much incentive to publicize such results.

What is undeniable is that this wealth extracted from markets via interest rates is little different in practice to a tax. The overall level of widgets bought in a market depends not simply on their supply (aided by endless microfinance loans), but also on demand, and a simple analysis of supply and demand suggests that this is likely to be marginal. But the tax remains. A tax levied by the microfinance sector upon the poor, one that does not accumulate in the coffers of governments but in those of MFIs, microfinance funds, and, to a lesser extent, in the pockets of the ultimate investors. It is a tax on economic activity, and a new channel by which to siphon wealth *from* the poor.

Since MFIs lend to both the microentrepreneurs (supply) and consumers (demand) in a market, charging interest to both, economic theory quite clearly predicts the outcome. The supply curve will shift upwards, since suppliers have to charge a higher price to cover the cost of interest. The demand curve will shift down, since consumers will have less disposable income available after servicing their own loans. This is the reverse of the initial impetus. The net effect in the long run: prices don't actually change much, but the new equilibrium is at a lower quantity level—because of an effective tax that does not accrue directly to a government, but to the MFIs and their investors.

The conclusion, however, is simple: there is a dark side to micro-entrepreneurial activity that is rarely discussed by the microfinance community. It is ignored for two reasons. First, it challenges the miraculous claims of microfinance as a poverty reduction tool. Second, MFIs and investors can make substantial returns by pumping overpriced loans to the poor in the meantime. They can profit from lending to both sides of the market simultaneously—supply and demand, vendor and customer. Even insiders concede that buying a new television with a loan costing 60 percent a year is unlikely to have huge developmental impact on a family. And all agree, reluctantly, that obtaining a loan to repay another loan is not productive.

The astute reader may wonder what happens if voluntary or forced cartels are formed in the marketplaces. Perhaps incumbent vendors will pressure new entrants to not lower prices, ethically or otherwise. This would be somewhat rational, although not necessarily to the benefit of customers. As with OPEC, forming cartels is a natural tendency, and although usually illegal, there are no regulations in practice in the typical markets where micro-entrepreneurs exist, and it is *possible* that cartels form, albeit informally.

If it is feasible that the tomato vendors might agree to protect their collective interests by not reducing prices significantly, is it inconceivable that MFIs may gather together informally and agree to not compete too fiercely with one another? It would be *rational* for them to consider this strategy, and given the various national associations they all join and conferences they attend, there is plenty of opportunity to discuss such ideas. Could this explain how interest rates in countries such as Mexico, where competition is apparently fierce, seem to remain persistently high? Much is made of the "competitive pressures of MFIs to reduce interest rates"—arguments made predominantly by those who potentially benefit most from cartels. This is pure speculation, but it is surely a possibility.

In theory, competition between MFIs would drive down interest rates, and there is evidence of this occurring. In Bolivia average interest rates charged by MFIs fell from 30 percent to 21 percent from 1998 to 2005.[2] In most other countries this has not taken place, and it is an open question why not. If there are so few MFIs to provide competitive pressure, this could explain the absence of interest-rate competition. Poor regulation could contribute. But a tacit agreement among MFIs would also be a *possible* explanation.

I conclude with a practical example of these phenomena occurring in *practice*:

> In Bosnia, for example, many poor individuals signed up to receive microfinance in order to purchase a cow in order to generate a little additional income from the sale of raw milk. While this was widely seen as a very sensible and compassionate intervention by the international donor and NGO community, the development outcome was extremely problematic. The local over-supply of raw milk in many communities led to a general price decline. This undermined all 9 incumbent producers, of course, but especially other non-client "one-cow farms" who quickly saw reduced margins and incomes, and were thus more likely to fall into poverty than before. However, it also had a negative longer run effect by undercutting the day-to-day operations of potentially sustainable larger dairy farms.... Most MFIs prefer to "look away" from the almost insurmountable problems likely to face their new poor clients with limited capabilities to diversify in already "saturated" local markets.[3]

Microfinance claims to be more effective than traditional donor/bank project financing, or "aid," both of which are rife with corruption and inefficiency. Perhaps—but let's not crack open the champagne too soon. This is an empirical question, and after thirty years or so of microfinance the evidence is far from conclusive that this is the miracle cure for poverty.

# Notes

Additional information, supporting documentation, and updates can be found on the website for *Confessions of a Microfinance Heretic*:

www.microfinancetransparency.com.

### Chapter 1 Thou Shalt Not Criticize Microfinance

1. According to the 2011 Global Microcredit Summit, 205,314,500, of whom 153,306,542 are women. See http://www.microfinancegateway.org/p/site/m/template.rc/1.26.17926/.
2. As calculated in *Pricing Certification Report: Grameen Bank* (Lancaster, Penn.: MFTransparency, 2011).
3. LAPO has rates reaching as high as 144 percent, as confirmed by independent institutions and rating reports, and Grameen Foundation USA is a principal investor.
4. Duvendack et al., *What Is the Evidence of the Impact of Microfinance on the Well-Being of Poor People?* (London: EPPI Centre, University of London, 2011), p. 75.
5. One of the pioneers of commercial microfinance has coined the phrase "goat economics." See http://blog.800ceoread.com/2010/11/08/explaining-goat-economics-by-vikram-akula/.
6. David Roodman, "Does Compartamos Charge 195% Interest?" Center for Global Development, David Roodman's Microfinance Open Book blog, January 31, 2011, http://blogs.cgdev.org/open_book/2011/01/compartamos-and-the-meaning-of-interest-rates.php.
7. Jonas Blume and Julika Breyer, *Microfinance and Child Labour* (Geneva: International Labour Office, 2011). Only one microfinance fund has explicit policies regarding child labor: World Vision, which operates a number of MFIs through its subsidiary Vision Fund International.
8. Marguerite Robinson, *The Microfinance Revolution*, vol. 2, *Lessons from Indonesia* (Washington, D.C.: World Bank, 2002).
9. See http://indiamicrofinance.com/bono-quote-microfinance.html.

10. Vivienne Walt, "Does Microfinancing Really Work? A New Book Says No," *Time*, January 6, 2012.
11. See Nicholas Kristof, "The Role of Microfinance," NYTimes.com, December 28, 2009, http://kristof.blogs.nytimes.com/2009/12/28/the-role-of-microfinance/.

Chapter 3  Bob Dylan and I in Mozambique
1. World Relief FCC Review of Funding Situation, May 15, 2003, slide 3.

Chapter 4  Another Mozambican Civil War
1. See "FCC – Fundo de Crédito Comunitário, Audit Report," September 30, 2004, www.mixmarket.org/sites/default/files/medialibrary/20501.758/FCC_AFS_0304.doc.
2. Available at www.mixmarket.org/mfi/fcc/report. Set the years of interest to generate a report; I suggest 2002 onward.
3. Only the quotes are taken directly from the report. The explanations and comments are my interpretation.
4. The entire recording is on the book website. The section discussing the legality of using client savings appears between 1 hr 15 minutes and 1 hr 36 minutes.
5. See www.mixmarket.org/node/22532/report.
6. Still announced on http://worldrelief.org/financial.

Chapter 5  The "Developed" World
1. See its "business philosophy" at http://www.procredit-holding.com/front_content.php?idcat=23.
2. Although Lukas was demoted, Triple Jump Advisory Services required three directors to comply with Dutch law, so Lukas remained registered as a director at the Dutch Chamber of Commerce, unbeknownst to Lukas.
3. See www.triplejump.eu/page/Mission+/1088/.
4. See www.blueorchard.com/jahia/Jahia/.
5. Reported at www.triplejump.eu/news/Triple+Jump+with+Desjardins+in+Africa/3290/.
6. Chuck Waterfield, "Explanation of Compartamos Interest Rates," May 19, 2008, www.microfin.com/aprcalculations.htm.
7. Ira W. Lieberman, Anne Anderson, Zach Graffe, Bruce Campbell, and Daniel Kopf, *Microfinance and Capital Markets* (n.p.: Council of Microfinance Equity Funds, 2008), p. 18, www.cmef.com/document.doc?id=575.
8. Roodman, "Does Compartamos Charge 195% Interest?"
9. See, for example, www.microfin.com/compartamos.htm for a good summary of Compartamos. Some valuations are estimated, or depend on the share price at a certain point in time. What is beyond doubt, and visible on websites such as www.charitynavigator.org, is that Accion International's net assets grew from $34 million in 2006 to $332 million in 2007, an increase of $298 million in one year. This same website publishes the 2009 salary of the CEO, but not for previous years. See also *Focus Note* no. 42, p. 14, www.cgap.org/gm/document-1.9.2440/FN42.pdf, or "The Implications of Increased Commercialization of the Microfinance Industry," MFI Solutions/La Colmena Milenaria, July 2008, p. 9, www.microfinancegateway.org/gm/document-1.9.30269/51567_file_Implications_of_Increased_Commercialization.pdf, which states that the sale of 50 percent of Accion's shares in Compartamos earned it US$134,965,740 net of fees, suggesting a

total valuation of just under $270 million, and accounting for more than 90 percent of the increase in net assets that occurred over this period.

10. As announced on Accion's website, www.accion.com/.
11. "Implications of Increased Commercialization of the Microfinance Industry," p. 6.
12. Accion IRS Form 990 2008, pp. 34 and 35, available on book website, described vaguely as "investment."
13. Accion IRS Form 990 2009, p. 9, available on book website.
14. See www.youtube.com/watch?v=kUfHfbsEaWU, at minute 31.
15. IRS Form 990 2010, p. 43, http://cms.kiva.org.s3.amazonaws.com/Kiva_Form_990_-_2010.pdf.
16. Steve Beck and Tim Ogden, "Beware of Bad Microcredit," *Harvard Business Review*, September 2007; summary available at http://hbr.org/2007/09/beware-of-bad-microcredit/ar/1.
17. David Lascelles and Sam Mendelson, *Microfinance Banana Skins 2011: The CSFI Survey of Microfinance Risk* (London: Centre for the Study of Financial Innovation, 2011); available at www.cgap.org/p/site/c/template.rc/1.26.15503/.
18. Ibid., p. 5.
19. Ibid., pp. 10–11.
20. Ibid., p. 27.

## Chapter 6  Something Not Quite Right in Nigeria

1. For example, in 2001 the Cambodian government banned flat interest entirely. See www.mftransparency.org/pages/wp-content/uploads/2011/10/Case-Study_Cambodia_Regulation-Outlawing-Flat-Interest.pdf.
2. Woody and I discussed this in person in a conference in El Salvador. My initial estimate of the true cost of capital had been erroneously high, and Woody pointed out correctly that it was actually closer to 100–120 percent.
3. The report is on the book website, see pp. 6 and 10.
4. See Planet Rating report of LAPO 2011, p. 7.

## Chapter 7  Something Not Quite Right in Holland

1. Sent by Lukas Wellen to Bruno Molijn and Norbert Abachi of Oxfam Novib at 11:05 Tuesday, January 22, 2008, with the simple text "Fyi success with LAPO."
2. Farouk Kurawa, Dave Odigie, Kayode Faleti, and Elizabeth Ellis, *Partnerships That Work: Alleviating Poverty in Nigeria through Microfinance*, p. 9; available at www.gre.ac.uk/__data/assets/pdf_file/0004/451975/5_Kurawa OdigieFaletiEllis_FullPaper.pdf.
3. See p. 60 of Oxfam Novib 2008 annual report.
4. See p. 5 of the document Investeringen O-N 2009.pdf on the book's website.
5. Planet Rating report of LAPO 2011, available from www.planetrating.com.
6. See Planet Rating report of LAPO 2011, p. 4.
7. See book website. This formed a key part of the documentation subsequently presented to a Dutch judge.

## Chapter 8  In Front of the Judge

1. Email on book website, dated March 20, 2008.
2. Available on book website, or from the Amsterdam cantonal court for €2.50. Case EA 2008-533, ruling of 28 April 2008 (in Dutch).
3. Bullet points 11, 12, and 13 in court ruling.

4. Bullet points 3 and 5 in court ruling.
5. Bullet points 9 and 10 in court ruling.
6. Investors are listed in the ratings, which are publicly available. However, not all investments are publicly available, so it is hard to estimate who is, and was, the largest investor. Supporting evidence on the book website.

## Chapter 9 Rustling Dutch Feathers

1. See the summary at http://microrate.com/mfi/microrate-public-ratings. It was previously publicly available and is therefore also on the book website in full.
2. ASN-Novib invested in 2007.
3. This is available by subscription only. See www.microrate.com. However, MicroRate has kindly permitted me to upload the full report to the book website as an act of transparency, for which I am grateful.
4. See the rating report for individual references; a selection is reproduced here.
5. MicroRate 2007 LAPO rating, p. 2.
6. MicroRate 2007 LAPO rating, p. 6, also subsequent "unacceptable" reference.
7. MicroRate 2007 LAPO rating, p. 5.
8. The recording of this question is on the book website. I was unable to record the response because my phone permitted only 60 seconds of recording. A full transcript of the AGM may be available from ASN Bank.
9. Available on book website.
10. *Spaarmotief*, July 2009. Available at www.asnbank.nl/index.asp?nid=9492 (in Dutch).
11. Dated November 12, 2009. Available on book website.
12. *Regulatory and Supervisory Framework for Microfinance Banks (MFBs) in Nigeria*. Available on book website.
13. "Grameen Foundation Supports Citibank's USD 1mm Financing of Nigerian Microfinance Institution LAPO," *MicroCapital*, May 11, 2007, http://microcapitalmonitor.com/cblog/index.php?/archives/806-Grameen-Foundation-Supports-Citibanks-USD-1mm-Financing-of-Nigerian-Microfinance-Institution-LAPO.html.
14. Full email on book website.
15. Terence Ward, *Searching for Hassan: An American Family's Journey Home to Iran* (Boston: Houghton Mifflin Harcourt, 2002).

## Chapter 10 Blowing the Whistle from Mongolia

1. See www.kiva.org/partners/20.
2. Press releases section of MicroRate website, August 2009. Also reproduced on book website.
3. Or, more accurately, the "expiration" of its rating. LAPO's own rebuttal to the press release referred to it three times as a *withdrawal*, so I use LAPO's term. The LAPO response to MicroRate's press release is available on book website.
4. *Lift Above Poverty Organization (LAPO), Nigeria* (Dakar: Planet Rating, 2009). The Planet Rating LAPO report is available at www.planetrating.com/EN/girafe-ratings.html and on book website.
5. Ibid., p. 1.
6. Ibid., p. 4n7.
7. Ibid., p. 5n11.
8. Ibid., p. 5.
9. Ibid., p. 6.
10. Ibid.

11. Ibid., p. 9n22.
12. Ibid., p. 10n26.
13. Ibid., p. 12.
14. Ibid., p. 7.
15. Ibid.
16. Ibid., *passim*; see esp. p. 11.
17. Ibid., pp. 12–13.
18. Receipt of $25 investment on book website.
19. See book website for full letter.
20. All photos are on the book website, www.microfinancetransparency.com. ASN Novib's is visible online, on p. 19 of the February 2008 *Spaarmotief* magazine on the ASN website, www.asnbank.nl/blob.asp?id=13844; screenshots from the NOTS Foundation and Calvert/MicroPlace websites appear on book website; Calvert Foundation's photo can be seen on www.flickr.com/photos/7746754@N05/1640836254/.
21. Available on book website.
22. She was promoted to president and CEO in 2011.
23. Full video on http://financialserv.edgeboss.net/wmedia/financialserv/hearing 012710.wvx.
24. See the second paragraph of page 2 of his testimony, available at www.house.gov/apps/list/hearing/financialsvcs_dem/hr_012110.shtml.
25. See video at http://financialserv.edgeboss.net/wmedia/financialserv/hearing 012710.wvx (1 hr 48 minutes in).
26. Robert Pouliot, "Governance, Transparency, and Accountability in the Microfinance Investment Fund Industry," in Ingrid Matthäus-Maier and J.D. von Pischke, eds., *Microfinance Investment Funds: Leveraging Private Capital for Economic Growth and Poverty Reduction* (Berlin: Springer-Verlag, 2007), p. 150.
27. See video at http://financialserv.edgeboss.net/wmedia/financialserv/hearing 012710.wvx (1 hr 43 minutes in).

### Chaper 11 Enter the *New York Times*

1. Neil McFarquhar, "Banks Making Big Profits From Tiny Loans," *New York Times*, April 13, 2010.
2. The very first estimate on Kiva regarding LAPO's interest rates was a mere 24 percent.
3. See, for example, Stephanie Strom, "Confusion on Where Money Lent via Kiva Goes," *New York Times*, November 8, 2009.
4. See pp. 12–13 of the 2009 Planet Rating: "The insufficient transparency in reporting to funders in December 2008, combined with the Nigerian economic crisis, detracted some potential investors in 2009 and contributed to a request for early repayment."
5. See, for example, http://mubi.com/topics/kiva-change-the-world-one-loan-at-a-time.
6. Strom, "Confusion on Where Money Lent via Kiva Goes."
7. See www.kivafriends.org/index.php/topic,1028.160.html. Pictures also on book website.
8. Lauren Smiley, "Kiva's Microloans Underwriting Cockfighting in Peru," *SF Weekly*, February 27, 2008.
9. See Kiva Lending Team: Kivans Against Cockfighting Loans, www.kiva.org/team/kacl.
10. See the Skoll Foundation website, www.socialedge.org/blogs/kiva-chronicles/archive/2008/03/29/cockfighting.

11. Note the discussion at www.kivafriends.org/index.php/topic,3447.msg 77346.html msg77346.
12. See, for example, the account at www.kiva.org/lend/21967, together with a photo showing large bags of coca leaves.
13. Dave Algoso, "Truth in advertising: ChildFund, Kiva, and Bolsa Família," Find What Works blog, September 10, 2010, http://findwhatworks. wordpress.com/2010/09/25/truth-in-advertising-childfund-kiva-and-bolsa-familia/. See also "Disappointing: Kiva Is Hosting Loan-Sharks," A Division by Zer0 blog, http://dbzer0.com/blog/disappointing-kiva-is-hosting-loan-sharks.
14. See the Kiva Microfunds IRS Form 990 2009, p. 50, http://cms.kiva.org. s3.amazonaws.com/Kiva_Form_990_-_2009.pdf.
15. Ibid., p. 45.
16. *Kiva Microfunds (A Nonprofit Organization) Financial Statements for the Years Ended December 31, 2010 and 2009*, p. 16, available at http://cms. kiva.org.s3.amazonaws.com/2010%20Kiva%20Audited%20Financials. pdf.
17. Ibid., p. 4.
18. *Kiva Microfunds Financial Statements for 2010 and 2009*, pp. 5–6.
19. "Infoporn: Kiva's Microloan Map of the World," *Wired* (February 2012); see www.wired.co.uk/magazine/archive/2012/02/start/kiva. Kiva lending in 2010 was £45.5 million (not USD), suggesting that my figure is in fact conservative.
20. A typical fund would charge its investors $1.2 million to lend $60 million, whereas Kiva received $13.7 million from all sources, 13.7/1.2 = 11 (approximately).
21. Reported at www.triplejump.eu/news/Triple+Jump+with+Desjardins+in+Af rica/3290/.
22. See *Triple Jump B.V. Financial Statements 2010*, www.triplejump.eu/upload/ media/Triple_Jump_BV_Financial_Statements_2010.pdf.
23. The increases in net equity were $5.3 million for Kiva versus €650,000 for Triple Jump on respective portfolios of $60 million versus €240 million.
24. See the Kiva partner web pages at www.kiva.org/partners/107, www.kiva. org/partners/18 and www.kiva.org/partners/158, respectively.
25. See the Kiva partner web page for ASI Federal Credit Union, www.kiva.org/ partners/200.
26. Reported on Kiva Microfunds IRS Form 990 2010, pp. 18–28, http://cms. kiva.org.s3.amazonaws.com/Kiva_Form_990_-_2010.pdf.
27. *Kiva Microfunds Financial Statements for 2010 and 2009*, p. 5.
28. Report on MiCredito, Kiva.org, July 7, 2011, www.kiva.org/partners/176.
29. Available at www.mixmarket.org/node/27819/report.
30. The latest statistics are at www.kiva.org/about/stats.
31. See http://en.wikipedia.org/wiki/Kiva_%28organization%29; also see the section entitled "Full-repayment frequency uncertainty," just above the section "Bloodsports."
32. On www.facebook.com/kiva?sk=info.
33. All emails are reproduced on the book website.
34. Flannery to the author, March 9, 2009.
35. "*New York Times* Article on Microfinance Interest Rates and Profits," http:// kivanews.blogspot.com/2010/04/new-york-times-article-on-microfinance. html.
36. See www.kiva.org/partners/20.
37. Full press release on book website, or www.google.com/url?sa=t&rct=j&q =&esrc=s&source=web&cd=1&ved=0CBsQFjAA&url=https%3A%2F%2

Fmembers.weforum.org%2Fpdf%2Fschwabfound%2Fseoy%2FPressRelea
se_SEOY2010_Africa.doc&ei=4X7OTuGdHYrf0QGri-2sAw&usg=AFQjC
NFn1kq1O3kt4XwNtYFRiBG0hluOgg.

38. See the Schwab Foundation Board of Directors, www.schwabfound.org/sf/
    AboutUs/Board/index.htm.
39. See Grameen Foundation USA Board of Directors, www.grameenfoundation.
    org/who-we-are/people/board-of-directors Muhammad%20Yunus,%20
    Director,%20Emeritus.
40. Alex Counts, "What Is the True Cost of Microfinance," Grameen Foundation,
    www.grameenfoundation.org/what-true-cost-microfinance.
41. Original press release on book website, removed from LAPO website.
42. The newsletter *Connections* (Fall 2007), removed from its website; copy on
    book website, or from MIX Market: www.mixmarket.org/sites/default/files/
    medialibrary/10001.652/GrameenFoundationNewsletterFall2007.pdf.
43. "LAPO: Case Study on Due Diligence by Microfinance Funders," Givewell
    blog, http://blog.givewell.org/2010/10/13/lapo-case-study-on-due-diligence-
    by-microfinance-funders/.
44. *Lift Above Poverty Organization (LAPO), Nigeria* (Dakar: Planet Rating,
    2011). Available by subscription only: see www.planetrating.com.
45. Ibid., p. 7.
46. Ibid., p. 1.
47. Ibid., p. 4.
48. Ibid., p. 5.
49. Ibid., p. 7.
50. See http://tomheinemann.dk/; a preview of the documentary is available on
    this site.
51. Minute 28 of the documentary.
52. The video footage of this question is on the book website and was provided
    by Tom Heinemann.
53. The full response is on the book website.
54. Nisha Koul, "Microcapital Brief," MicroCapital.org, October 17, 2011,
    www.microcapital.org/microcapital-brief-responsibility-loans-local-
    currency-equivalent-of-4m-to-microfinance-institutions-pearl-microfinance-
    limited-of-uganda-lift-above-poverty-organisation-of-nigeria-sinapi-aba-
    trus/.
55. See  www.smartcampaign.org/about-the-campaign/campaign-sponsors,  as
    well as the footnote buried at the bottom of the website: "An initiative of
    The Center for Financial Inclusion at ACCION International."

## Chapter 12 Collapse, Suicide, and Muhammad Yunus

1. Elyssa Pachico, "'No Pago' Confronts Microfinance in Nicaragua," NACLA.
   org, October 28, 2009, https://nacla.org/node/6180.
2. David Roodman, "Death of a Microfinance Institution," Center for Global
   Development, David Roodman's Microfinance Open Book Blog, August 9,
   2010, http://blogs.cgdev.org/open_book/2010/08/death-of-a-microfinance-
   institution.php.
3. See "6 Microfinance Crises That the Sector Does Not Want to Remember,"
   *Microfinance Focus*, April 22, 2011, at www.microfinancefocus.com/6-
   microfinance-crises-sector-does-not-want-remember.
4. See (in Spanish) http://tertuliapolitica.bligoo.com/content/view/1134653/
   CRONOLOGIA-DEL-MOVIMIENTO-DEL-NORTE.html.
5. Elizabeth Minchew, "A Movement to Acknowledge: The Nicaraguan
   Movimiento No Pago," Microfinance Focus, September 14, 2011, www.

microfinancefocus.com/movement-acknowledge-nicaraguan-movimiento-no-pago.

6. Ibid.
7. Center for Financial Inclusion, "Nicaragua's Microfinance Crisis: Looking Back, What Did We Learn?" Microfinance Gateway, January 26, 2011, www.microfinancegateway.org/p/site/m/template.rc/1.1.9463/.
8. Scan of article on book website.
9. Iván Olivares, "Millones en Riesgo por 'Ley de No Pago,'" *Confidencial*, March 8, 2010.
10. Rohan Trivedi, "Microcapital Brief," MicroCapital.org, September 2, 2011, www.microcapital.org/microcapital-brief-incofin-lends-9m-to-microfinance-institutions-mfis-pride-tanzania-lapo-of-nigeria-sinapi-aba-trust-fasl-of-ghana/.
11. Matthew Fuchs, "Lessons Learned from Microfinance Crises: Viewpoints from Investors," at Microfinance Focus, November 4, 2009, www.smartcampaign.org/news-a-highlights/in-the-news/7-2009/76-lessons-learned-from-microfinance-crises-viewpoints-from-investors.
12. International Association of Microfinance Investors, "Charting the Course: Best Practices and Tools for Voluntary Debt Restructurings in Microfinance" (New York: IAMFI, 2009), available at www.morganstanley.com/global citizen/pdf/IAMFI.pdf.
13. Patricia Padilla, "The Micro-Financing Institutions Are Politically Very Attractive," *Envio Digital*, August 2008, www.envio.org.ni/articulo/3856.
14. Milford Bateman and Ha-Joon Chang, "The Microfinance Illusion" (March 2009), p. 12, available at www.hajoonchang.net/downloads/pdf/Microfinance.pdf.
15. Sanjay Vijay Kumar, "Microfinance Industry in India to Cross 11 Crore by 2014: Microfinance & Business India Digest," Microfinance Africa, June 14, 2010, at http://microfinanceafrica.net/microfinance-around-the-world/micro finance-industry-in-india-to-cross-11-crore-by-2014-microfinance-business-india-digest/.
16. Ketaki Gotkhale, "As Microfinance Grows in India, So Do Its Rivals," *Wall Street Journal*, December 15, 2009, http://online.wsj.com/article/SB126055117322287513.html.
17. Ketaki Gokhale, "Group Borrowing Leads to Pressure," *Wall Street Journal*, August 13, 2009, http://online.wsj.com/article/SB125008232217325553.html.
18. Vikram Akula, reprinted in Welcome to Paradox Valley blog, August 22, 2009, http://paradoxvalley.blogspot.com/2009/08/vikram-akulas-response-to-wsjs-article.html.
19. "SKS Microfinance Ranked No. 1 MFI in India by Mix Mkt," moneycontrol.com, January 2, 2009, available at www.moneycontrol.com/news/business/sks-microfinance-ranked-no-1-mfiindia-by-mix-mkt_373595.html.
20. Ramesh S. Arunachalam, *The Journey of Indian Micro-Finance: Lessons for the Future* (Chennai: Aapti Publications, 2011), pp. 93–94.
21. Shashi Tharoor, "The Crisis of Microfinance," Aljazeera, March 11, 2011, http://www.aljazeera.com/indepth/opinion/2011/03/20113911535158522.html.
22. "Agents Kidnap Girl to Punish Mother for Loan Default, *Times of India*, October 13, 2010.
23. "SKS and the Crisis of Corporate-Led Microfinance in India," Pragoti, February 2, 2010, www.pragoti.in/node/4202.
24. "54 Committed Suicide in AP Due to Microfinance Debts, Says SERP: Report," *International Business Times*, October 29, 2010, www.ibtimes.

com/articles/77043/20101029/microfinance-deaths-sks-microfinance-spandana-asmitha-share-l-t-andhra-suicides-india-microfinance-d.htm.

25. "Exclusive: 54 Microfinance-Related Suicides in AP, Says SERP Report," *Microfinance Focus*, October 25, 2010, www.microfinancefocus.com/content/exclusive-54-microfinance-related-suicides-ap-says-serp-report.

26. Erika Kinetz, "Suicides Spark Scrutiny of Indian Microfinance," *Bloomberg Businessweek*, October 19, 2010.

27. Sebastian Strangio, "Is Microfinance Pushing the World's Poorest Even Deeper Into Poverty?" *The New Republic*, December 14, 2011.

28. Jinka Nagaraju, "MFI Agents 'Forcing' Debtors to Commit Suicide: Study," *Times of India*, October 20, 2010 .

29. "Is the Mexican Microfinance Sector Approaching Crisis Point?" *Microfinance Focus*, July 17, 2011.

30. Milford Bateman, *Why Doesn't Microfinance Work?: The Destructive Rise of Local Neoliberalism* (London: Zed, 2010).

31. "Grameen Foundation Complains to NRK," Flip the Coin, February 22, 2011, www.flipthecoin.org/?p=380.

32. Ministry of Foreign Affairs: "Norad's report shows that Grameen Bank transferred a total of NOK 608.5 million to its sister company Grameen Kalyan in 1996. Norway's share of this amount is estimated to be approximately NOK 170 million. The Norwegian Embassy in Dhaka reacted immediately when it discovered the transfer in 1997. In the embassy's view, the transfer was not in accordance with the agreement. The matter was raised with Grameen Bank. Following negotiations, it was agreed in May 1998 that NOK 170 million was to be transferred back from Grameen Kalyan to Grameen Bank," www.regjeringen.no/en/dep/ud/press/news/2010/report_grameen.html?id=627366.

33. David Roodman, "U.S. Government Pressure on Behalf of Yunus," Center for Global Development, David Roodman's Microfinance Open Book Blog, February 28, 2011, http://blogs.cgdev.org/open_book/2011/02/u-s-government-pressure-on-behalf-of-yunus.php.

34. No author stated: www.friendsofgrameen.com/dl/2011/02/Friends of Grameen, Grameen-Bank-Fact-Sheet-FINAL.pdf.

35. See Norad, "Review Commissioned by the Norwegian Ministry of Foreign Affairs of Matters Relating to Grameen Bank," December 6, 2012, www.regjeringen.no/upload/UD/Vedlegg/Utvikling/Grameen_Bank_main_report_eng.pdf.

36. See also the Wikipedia entry on the subject, which states, "NORAD published an official statement clearing Yunus and Grameen Bank from any wrongdoing." This is open to interpretation on the exact meaning of the word *clearing*, but the truth appears slightly less clear-cut than the mainstream media cares to present. See the section "Disproved allegations from a Danish documentary," http://en.wikipedia.org/wiki/Muhammad_Yunus.

37. Grameen Bank Fact Sheet, third paragraph, p. 1.

38. The site, www.friendsofgrameen.com, was recently removed and then restored. Original documents available on book website.

39. Roodman, "Does Compartamos Charge 195% Interest?"

40. "Yoghurt Adulteration: Yunus Lands in Court," Rediff Business, January 28, 2011, www.rediff.com/business/report/yoghurt-adulteration-yunus-lands-in-court/20110128.htm.

41. David Roodman, "The Persecution of an Imperfect Man," Center for Global Development, David Roodman's Microfinance Open Book Blog, January 29, 2011, http://blogs.cgdev.org/open_book/2011/01/the-persecution-of-an-imperfect-man.php.

42. "Yunus Criticizes Profiteering in Nigerian Microfinance," *microDINERO*, September 7, 2011, at www.microdinero.com/nota_eng.php?subseccion= D1&notId=4030.
43. $70,000,000,000 x 45% ÷ (60 x 60 x 24 x 365) = $998.86.
44. See http://givewell.org/international/technical/programs/immunization.

## Chapter 13 The Good, the Bad, and the Poor

1. David Roodman, "Last Chapter Revised!" Center for Global Development, David Roodman's Microfinance Open Book Blog, April 29, 2011, http:// blogs.cgdev.org/open_book/2011/04/last-chapter-revised.php.
2. M.S. Sriram, "What Is Wrong with Indian Microfinance," *Forbes India*, May 5, 2010, at www.mssriram.in/sites/mssriram.in/files/Forbes%20India%20 -%20What%20is%20Wrong%20With%20Indian%20Microfinance.pdf.
3. For example, see "Q&A with Muhammad Yunus," *Enterprising Ideas: Social Entrepreneurs at Work*, www.pbs.org/now/enterprisingideas/Muhammad-Yunus.html.
4. Burson-Marsteller Watch, http://bursonmarstellerwatch.com/ (also Rachel Maddow quote).
5. Dan Lyons, "Facebook Busted in Clumsy Smear on Google," The Daily Beast, May 11, 2011, at www.thedailybeast.com/articles/2011/05/12/ facebook-busted-in-clumsy-smear-attempt-on-google.html.
6. All correspondence available on book website.
7. LAPO's profile is available on www.amt-forum.org/nc/fr/membres/ membresactuels/profilmembres.html?vdreports[page]=1&vdreports[profi le]=22.
8. Available on book website.
9. See www.amt-forum.org/en/quisommesnous.html.
10. The LuxFLAG website, www.luxflag.com/MIV_aboutLabel.htm.
11. See www.mftransparency.org.
12. An example is Pro-Credit, although Pro-Credit does not engage in microfinance any more, but now focuses on small business finance.
13. Robert Pouliot notes that "the twin capital approach can become a minefield of conflicts of interest," Pouliot, "Governance, Transparency, and Accountability,"p. 158.
14. See, for example, www.luminismicrofinance.com or www.copeme.org.pe.
15. See Phil Mader's blog "Governance Across Borders," part of the Max Planck Institute's "Institution Building Across Borders" research group, http://governancexborders.com/2011/10/08/that-evil-evil-microcredit-documentary-on-tour/.

## Appendix Microfinance Economics 101

1. Steve Beck and Tim Ogden, " Beware of Bad Microcredit," *Harvard Business Review* online (September 2007).
2. See Michael Chu's presentation to Canning House, April 24, 2006; on book website.
3. Bateman and Chang, "Microfinance Illusion," pp. 8, 14.

# Acknowledgments

The list of people I would like to thank for their support during my adventure in microfinance is extensive. Some would probably prefer not to be named here for fear of being branded co-heretics. You know who you are. That my girlfriend, now wife, put up with this is of daily astonishment to me, and she deserves special thanks for her unwavering support. Many insiders were willing to risk speaking to me privately and proofread chapters to check for accuracy, for which I am very grateful. The ongoing support from the folks at Berrett Koehler, for the work of a first-time author, has been unparalleled.

Finally, I reluctantly thank all those unscrupulous moneylenders disguised as ethical microfinance banks; the inept managers in the investing community; and those involved in building up the hype around the microfinance sector over the last decade with scant evidence of much positive impact on poverty. Without your work this book would not have been possible. Or necessary.

# Index

# About the Author

Hugh Sinclair is an economist and former investment banker. Since 2002 he has worked in the microfinance sector, living in the UK, Mexico, the Netherlands, Mozambique, Argentina, and Mongolia. He holds a BA and an MSc from the University of Durham in England; an MBA from IESE Business School in Spain; and the Guinness World Record for the fastest traverse of the Americas by motorbike. This is his first book. He lives with his wife and daughter in a remote region of South America.

**Berrett–Koehler**
BK Publishers

**Berrett-Koehler** is an independent publisher dedicated to an ambitious mission: *Creating a World That Works for All*.

We believe that to truly create a better world, action is needed at all levels—individual, organizational, and societal. At the individual level, our publications help people align their lives with their values and with their aspirations for a better world. At the organizational level, our publications promote progressive leadership and management practices, socially responsible approaches to business, and humane and effective organizations. At the societal level, our publications advance social and economic justice, shared prosperity, sustainability, and new solutions to national and global issues.

A major theme of our publications is "Opening Up New Space." Berrett-Koehler titles challenge conventional thinking, introduce new ideas, and foster positive change. Their common quest is changing the underlying beliefs, mindsets, institutions, and structures that keep generating the same cycles of problems, no matter who our leaders are or what improvement programs we adopt.

We strive to practice what we preach—to operate our publishing company in line with the ideas in our books. At the core of our approach is stewardship, which we define as a deep sense of responsibility to administer the company for the benefit of all of our "stakeholder" groups: authors, customers, employees, investors, service providers, and the communities and environment around us.

We are grateful to the thousands of readers, authors, and other friends of the company who consider themselves to be part of the "BK Community." We hope that you, too, will join us in our mission.

**A BK Currents Book**

This book is part of our BK Currents series. BK Currents books advance social and economic justice by exploring the critical intersections between business and society. Offering a unique combination of thoughtful analysis and progressive alternatives, BK Currents books promote positive change at the national and global levels. To find out more, visit **www.bkconnection.com**.

**Berrett–Koehler**
Publishers

A community dedicated to creating
a world that works for all

### Visit Our Website: www.bkconnection.com

Read book excerpts, see author videos and Internet movies, read our authors'
blogs, join discussion groups, download book apps, find out about the BK
Affiliate Network, browse subject-area libraries of books, get special discounts, and more!

### Subscribe to Our Free E-Newsletter, the *BK Communiqué*

Be the first to hear about new publications, special discount offers, exclusive articles, news about bestsellers, and more! Get on the list for our free
e-newsletter by going to **www.bkconnection.com**.

### Get Quantity Discounts

Berrett-Koehler books are available at quantity discounts for orders of ten or
more copies. Please call us toll-free at (800) 929-2929 or email us at **bkp
.orders@aidcvt.com**.

### Join the BK Community

**BKcommunity.com** is a virtual meeting place where people from around the
world can engage with kindred spirits to create a world that works for all.
**BKcommunity.com** members may create their own profiles, blog, start and
participate in forums and discussion groups, post photos and videos, answer
surveys, announce and register for upcoming events, and chat with others
online in real time. Please join the conversation!